The United States-Japan-China Triangle in the Post-Cold War Early Decades

A Case Study of Applied Political Science

Dr. JALEL Ben Haj REHAIEM

Series in Politics

VERNON PRESS

www.vernonpress.com

In the Americas:	In the rest of the world:
Vernon Press	Vernon Press
1000 N West Street, Suite 1200	C/Sancti Espiritu 17,
Wilmington, Delaware, 19801	Malaga, 29006
United States	Spain

Series in Politics

Library of Congress Control Number: 2024944717

ISBN: 979-8-8819-0217-9

Also available: 979-8-8819-0044-1 [Hardback]; 979-8-8819-0216-2 [PDF, E-Book]

Table of Contents

Acknowledgments

During the course of putting together this work about a subject as rich as U.S. foreign policy, it is hardly surprising to incur debts of deep gratitude, which should go first to His Excellency Dr. Salah Hannachi, former Tunisian Ambassador to Japan for his interest in the topic of this book, for the pertinent Japanese papers' articles which he used to send from Tokyo and for allowing me to borrow his own books. That is not surprising from a distinguished academic and a professional researcher.

I was also fortunate enough to receive one research fellowship and three Fulbright scholarships, respectively, to the University of Pittsburgh, PA; the University of Arcadia, PA; and North Central College, IL. They were precious opportunities that provided me with a timely window into the realm of research, including chances to meet with great scholars like **Interviwee 1**, a prominent political scientist, the founder of a notable school of thought in political science, and **Interviwee 2**, an internationally recognized academic authority on Korean affairs. Words can hardly convey how much I owe them. Their courtesy and their insights support this book's claim of originality.

To the memory of my dear brother, **NEJEH**

Introduction

I.1 Background to the Study

The post-Cold War United States-Japan-China[1] triangle, during the first two decades after the disintegration of the former Soviet Union, stood for the pivot of Asia-Pacific politics. From 1990 and up to the end of the post-Cold war second decade, the power relations between China and Japan, and the rules of their respective interaction with the United States were critical in determining the outcome of this interaction among the three parties. Interaction outcomes are usually governed by a variety of variables, primarily the power and security calculations of each side, and of a couple of decisive drivers in East Asian politics, such as the U.S.-Japan alliance and the rising economic and military power of China, which are dialectically interrelated. Now, as the new international order of the US unipolarity was a post-Cold War reality, the balance of power and the quest for power among these drivers, together with their respective security calculations, structurally influenced East Asia's complex security situation where the United States claimed it was playing a positive role through the U.S. forward military presence in the region, which was controversially perceived by regional actors.

On the one hand, nations, like Japan and South Korea, were officially receptive to the U.S. claim of being a stabilizing factor in a volatile East Asian security environment. On the other hand, countries like China, North Korea and, to some extent, Russia, were not comfortable with what they used to perceive as an excessive military presence aiming at containing their modernization programs and, in the long run, preventing the rise of a potential

---

[1] China will refer to the People's Republic of China (PRC) established on October 1st, 1949 by Mao Zedong after the defeat of the Nationalists, who fled to the Island of Taiwan, where they declared the establishment of the Republic of China on Taiwan (ROC). Both sides claim that they represent the whole Chinese people, and state that Taiwan is Chinese territory. In the early fifties, Beijing and Taipei sought reunification, but they differed on modalities. Today, however, Taiwan is divided against itself as to the rationale and feasibility of reunification. The island has become an almost de facto independent country, but the PRC has always stressed that it will never allow Taiwan to declare its independence, and will be ready to use force to prevent that. Here, the ROC will be referred to as Taiwan, and the PRC as China.

challenger to a Cold War status quo which was already dominated by the United States in collaboration with allies like Japan, which itself was not immune to American political and economic abuses and sovereignty infringements.

In the United States, the China threat and North Korea's[2] nuclear weapons were the most effective post-Cold War U.S. political weapons, which were manipulated, exaggerated, and marketed in a way that fit the U.S. strategy of fear in East Asia. Frightening vulnerable nations in the region into accepting the claim that the U.S. military presence in East Asia since WWII always played a positive security role especially in Northeast Asia, and did continue to play that role even after the end of the Cold War. In October 2005, the bilateral U.S.-Japan ad hoc Security Consultative Committee (SCC) summed up the post-Cold War United States policy in East Asia, and unveiled the rationale of the U.S. military presence in the region. The most recent was that of October 2005, unofficially known as the ATARA Report, wherein the SCC opines that "to maintain an effective military presence in Asia and honor alliance commitments there, Washington must maintain a forward presence to reassure friends and allies of its ability to respond to crises and dissuade others from acting in ways that harm U.S. interests" (Wright and Hague 60-64).

Moreover, at the China Conference of April 28-29, 2006, at the University of Chicago, I asked the former U.S. Assistant Secretary of Defense in 2006: "you said that the American forces and military deployments in East Asia are aimed at deterring conflicts. My question was, what kind of conflicts were you expecting?."[3] He argued that "I think the rest of the world, looking at China and

---

[2] Hearings of the Committee on National Security of the House of Representatives of the One Hundred Fourth Congress, March 20, 1996, "Security Challenges Posed by China", p.1, 2, 35. For more on this see also, Hearing Before, The Committee on Armed Services House of Representatives of the One Hundred Sixth Congress. 2nd Session, July 19, 2000, "Military Capabilities of the Peoples Republic of China", Washington: U.S. Government Printing Office, 2001.

[3] "China and the Future of the World", April 28-29, 2006, Chicago Society, University of Chicago. Among the guest speakers were His Excellency Wang Guangya, Permanent representative of the People's republic of China to the United Nations; Peter W. Rodman, U.S. Assistant secretary of Defense for International Security Affairs, Christopher R. Hill, U.S. Assistant Secretary of State for East Asian and Pacific Affairs; Ambassador Wu Jianmin, Former Chinese Ambassador to France, the United Nations in Geneva, and current President of China Foreign affairs University; **Interviewee 1**, a prominent political science professor, a founder of a new school of thought in political science and

the immense power that is accumulating, is hypersensitive to uses of force by China" (Ibid). As a matter of fact, the United States was more worried about what China would do with its "accumulating power" than about East Asia's security which it was claiming it was defending. This actually did shed clouds of doubt about the credibility of this claim, which made it difficult to accept such a claim at face value.

Therefore, the triangular dimension and dynamic of the U.S.-Japan-China equation could be seen, for instance, in China's reaction to the October 2005 the U.S.-Japan SCC ATARA Report, which ostensibly aimed at negating the ongoing Chinese military modernization program and touched upon China's Achilles Heel-Taiwan. Reacting to the ATATRA Report, Beijing passed the March 2005 Anti-Secession Law a couple of weeks after the report stated for the first time that Taiwan was now "a common security challenge" both for Washington and Tokyo. From a Chinese perspective, such a declaration showed that the United States, taking advantage of its overwhelming military power in East Asia, and with Japanese complicity, was going hegemonic (Walker 19). While suspicion that was fraught with historical rivalry prevails between China and Japan, the United States remained committed to a strategy that was seeking to secure its continued dominance for economic, political and strategic predominance" (Zhao 23-28), shedding doubts as to the reality of the U.S. military presence in East Asia. And this is exactly what fits into the political prescription of animus dominandi, that is the pursuit of power as the ultimate objective of states, a pursuit that is manifested through the American "empire of bases" (Ch. Johnson 151) in a crescent-shaped alliance structured around China, starting from Japan in Northeast Asia and going down to India in Southwest Asia.

Therefore, during the first two decades of the post-Cold War era, Japan and China, together with the United States, were going to shape the contours of twenty-first-century East Asia security. At that time, Japan was not only the world's second-largest economy with a well-equipped and competent military, but also stood as the pivot of the U.S. "hub and spoke" strategy in post-Cold War East Asia[4]. But China in its turn, was a rising power which was confusing the United States and Japan as to its unclear intentions regarding the half-

---

currently co-director of a program on international security policy at a major university in Chicago.

[4] U.S.-Japan Alliance: Transformation and Realignment for the Future. October 29, 2005, Bruce A. Wright & Mark o. Hague, "The U.S.-Japan Alliance: Sustaining the Transformation" JFQ / issue 44, 1st quarter 2007, 60-64.

century regional status quo established by the United States in the wake of the Japanese WWII defeat in 1945. China and Japan, combined, account for almost three-quarters of East Asia's economic activity and more than half of the region's military spending (Przystup et al. 1).

Despite their deep economic ties and a doubling of their bilateral trade in the previous five years[5], however, the Sino-Japanese strategic relationship was most of the time strained mainly in the post-Cold war era, with inevitable implications for the U.S. relationship with both of them. As American efforts to improve relations with one side strained ties with the other, relations between Japan and China substantially influenced U.S. policies in East Asia. The implications of the China factor on Japan's security calculus, for instance, had a significant impact on the U.S.-Japan security relationship (Przystup, "China and the U.S.-Japan Alliance", Lecture 2000). U.S. Undersecretary of State Robert B. Zoellick substantiates the interrelatedness of the three nations' security calculations. Zoellick said: "China is big, it is growing, and it will influence the world in the years ahead... the essential question is how the emphasis on Japan reflects an alliance-centric approach for managing change that invites a larger Japanese role in support of international order."[6] But what is the "order" that was conducive to more stability in a volatile security environment as it existed in East Asia during the last decade of the twentieth century?

With respect to the full equation of the U.S.-China-Japan triangle, clashing political cultures and incongruent security interests during the two decades after the end of the Cold War highlighted differences between the three countries in the post-Cold War era. Tensions and conflicts in the region, such as North Korea's launch of a Rodong 1 Missile and a Satellite projectile over Japan respectively in 1993 and 1998, the North Korea controversial nuclear program and, last but not least, South Korea's security hazards emanating from the possible extension of the US nuclear umbrella to Seoul, all resulted from the power relations among and respective security calculations of the United

---

[5] "WORLD ECONOMIC SITUATION AND PROSPECTS 2007", Department of Economic and Social Affairs (DESA), The United Nations. January 2007, Full Text available at: <http://www.un.org/esa/policy/wess/wesp2007files/wesp2007.pdf>

[6] The U.S. Undersecretary of State Robert B. Zoellick. "Whither China: From Membership to Responsibility?" Remarks to National Committee on U.S.-China Relations, New York, NY, September 21, 2005. Also see Robert B. Zoellick's testimony before the House International Relations Committee, May 10, 2006.

States, Japan, and China (*Asia Survey* 1067). Moreover, the 1997 Defense Cooperation Guidelines of the U.S.-Japan alliance, China's 2005 threat to use force if Taiwan declared independence, and the April 2001 U.S. EP-3 plane incident between the U.S. and China, were the most immediate causes of tension in the East Asia-U.S. relationship in the post-Cold War era. These tensions were addressed according to the power relations between the three nations concerned, and the interaction outcome was usually an accurate unit of measurement of power. China, for instance, interrupted its exercises in 1996 and 2000, and withdrew from the Strait of Taiwan, which meant that the then balance of political and military power was not in Beijing's favor.

Dialectically, American power could be exercised to threaten the security of China and defend that of Japan; China's power could be applied to defend the interests of the People's Republic, from a Chinese point of view, but to threaten the security of Japan and the strategic interests of the United States, from an American-Japanese perspective. A potential exercise of power on the part of China against Japan regarding their latent territorial disputes over the oil-rich Senkaku Islands in the East China Sea, for example, would almost certainly involve the United States as the 1951 U.S.-Japanese Security Treaty and its related defense guidelines stipulate. Also, the Taiwan-China conflict was, and still is, the hottest security issue in post-Cold War East Asia, and its resolution was becoming more and more complicated because Washington and Tokyo declared that the Taiwan problem was now a "common security concern" among them, instead of a domestic Chinese question[7]. When the Taiwan reunification issue became a regional security issue rather than a sovereign Chinese matter, the chances of conflict between the United States and Japan, on the one hand, and China, on the other, also became considerably higher. However, the potential for less security and more animus dominandi[8] in East Asia transcended the future of Taiwan to mutual allegations of hegemony and domination between China and the United States-Japan alliance.

China used the large U.S. military presence in East Asia and the 'conspiratorial' aspects of the U.S.-Japan alliance as evidence that the United

---

[7] Ministry of Foreign Affairs of Japan, "Joint Statement: U.S.-Japan Security Consultative Committee", February 21, 2005.

[8] Animus Dominandi: a Latin phrase meaning the quest for power which has characterized international relations since the 1648 Westphalia arrangement. It was originally used by realists as well as neo-realists such as Hans Morgenthau in Politics Among Nations (1948) and Kenneth Waltz in Man, the State, and War (1959).

States was intent on East Asia domination, and was thus providing security only to its own interests and to its satellites in the region, which made the U.S. military deployments in the region a negative security factor. The United States and Japan, however, kept arguing that the rising power of China should command caution and invited suspicion in view of China's 'threats' against Taiwan, China's endless territorial disputes with virtually all of its neighbors (Valencia 8-49) and, more strategically, Beijing's aspirations of ascendancy and even hegemony in East Asia.

But the conceptualization of power[9] is a significant factor in the study of states' interaction, which is generally governed by the quest for power either for hegemony or as a result of an obsession with security. Moreover, competition between two states seeking an alliance with the third, or the suspicion that two are conspiring against one, has characterized this post-Cold War triangle. It was either Japan or China seeking to develop a better relationship with the U.S. at the expense of each other, or the U.S. and Japan collaborating to "contain" China and prevent a prospective Chinese ascendancy in Asia. Accordingly, during the first two decades in the post-Cold War period, the three-way Sino-American-Japanese interaction was basically governed by the distribution of power among them, and by the U.S.-Japanese special security relationship that was always perceived by the Chinese as an alliance seeking to contain China's rising power in the twenty-first century. Indeed, "many Chinese still view[ed] the United States as a major threat to their nation's security and domestic stability" (*Jisi*, "China's Search for Stability with America" 39).

Even if power is a vague and abstract term which can exist between at least two states, it still can be quantified or measured by the success or failure of state A to deter state B from adopting a certain policy regarding a specific issue. Power, in international relations, is the epicenter around which the actions and reactions of the units revolve. It is the means and the end at the same time; the means to achieve security in its broad sense, be it physical, economic, societal, and environmental, and to coerce other states into acquiescence without the actual use of force, and the end to dominate others militarily, politically, economically, and even culturally. Power is the "ability to influence the behavior of others in accordance with one's own ends" (Organski 96). So, power

---

[9] Conceptualization is the "process of specifying what we mean by a term. In deductive research, conceptualization helps to translate portions of an abstract theory into testable hypotheses involving specific variables. In inductive research, conceptualization is an important part of the process used to make sense of related observations" (Schutt 65).

is the central variable in the study of international relations; its level of distribution among the actors concerned, that is the *balance of power* among them, affects the conduct of relations between states, and also dictates their interaction outcomes.

As the balance-of-power system works, some states seek to keep the status quo of rough equilibrium while others could engage in a zero-sum or a win-lose game[10] to advance their own interests. States usually tend to accept the status quo position of the scales rather than try to gain ascendancy and ultimately be destroyed by the combined efforts of the rest of the states, which have a vested interest in keeping the balance undisturbed (Schelling 92-121; Rosenau qtd. in Williams et al. *Classic Readings* 491). The combined reaction of the rest of the units does not mean that they are satisfied with the existing system; it simply means that "the decision-makers of all states perceive that any change would make them less able to get as much of what they want than they could get if the system stayed as it was" (Reynolds 215). Applying the same logic to the triangle under study, "the balance of power will be the main security determinant of Asia for the foreseeable future" (Dibb 55) in the absence of a set of internationally agreed norms, that is anarchy[11], to regulate the growing strength of the Asian great powers in the twenty-first century, and to reconcile that with the already established preponderant power in the region- the United States. The danger of having one element of the system trying to dominate its competitors has always been real as far as Asian politics is concerned, particularly since the end of the Cold War.

---

[10] A Zero-sum game is a contest between two rivals competing for the same objective, making the gain of A an automatic loss for B, and vice versa. This term, originally used in game theory, gained wider usage in international relations to depict a standstill situation where one of the adversaries must lose, so that the other can win; thus making the resolution of the conflict very difficult. The U.S.-Soviet Union Cold War competition for world dominance is a good example of zero-sum game conflicts. It was U.S. Secretary of State George Shultz who warned in 1987 that "Foreign Affairs is not always a zero-sum game. We do not necessarily advance our vital interests at another nation's cost" (Williams 737).

[11] Anarchy as defined by Reynolds is here to be understood in its strict sense of absence of government, not in its more general sense of disorder or chaos. For more on the political science meaning of anarchy, see Hedley Bull, The Anarchical Society, 1977, London, Macmillan Press, and Kenneth Waltz, Man, the State, and War. New York: Colombia University Press, 1959, 159.

Therefore, the stability of the international system depends heavily on the number of the units involved and their power relations. A balance of power between two states or two groups of states tends to be self-destructive in an environment of anarchy where there is no overriding international government. The zero-sum game, which the competing sides tend to play, makes an arms race almost inevitable, since each side perceives any move, even defensive, from state A as an attempt to change the distribution of power in its favor, and therefore to gain more ascendancy at the expense of B (Boulding 41-51). This was the case of Japan and China towards the end of the 19th and the first half of the 20th centuries when competition for power and regional hegemony between these two countries soared (Hunt 123). But the balance of power was in Tokyo's favor. Then, Japan was a developed and industrialized country, armed with American weapons and trained by American experts; China, an underdeveloped country, was the only 'obstacle' for Japan to dominate East Asia, especially after the surprising defeat of Russia in the 1905 Japanese-Russian War. China, therefore, became Japan's regional enemy, which stood against Tokyo's ambitions of power projection in the region (Liu 93-98). The examples of Rome and Carthage which fought three successive Punic Wars from 264 to 146 B.C for the dominance of the Mediterranean, and the U.S.-U.S.S. R contest for spheres of influence during the second half of the twentieth century, are also good reasons to think that binary states' systems are inherently self-destructive (Reynolds 207-16). Hence, the idea of self-destruction is a basic characteristic of an international two-state system.

If the number of units is three within a system, however, as was the case of the post-Cold War U.S.-Japan-China triangle, it does not necessarily make the system more stable. On the opposite, there is a high probability of having two states aligning against the third because states' insatiable appetite for wealth and power usually leads to struggle over the possession of resources (Mathoma 45). Decision-makers in state A tend to fear the intentions of decision-makers in state B, and therefore proceed to take measures to defend their security by approaching state C. When state B becomes suspicious of the intentions of state A, it feels compelled to take precautionary countermeasures to prevent state A from being tempted to annihilate state B (Reynolds 217-18). In fact, each state usually tries to protect its own security, but in the attempt to do so, states paradoxically invite suspicion from each other, and thus trigger a chain of action and reaction in the system, that is a built-in escalation or an arms race.

Applying the same logic of the balance of power to post-Cold War U.S.-Japan-China, one can see that while:

some Chinese analysts [have] complained that now there [was] no regional balance of power, and that their military growth could restore a balance, Americans [had] warned against changing the balance of power. Each country employed a different but longstanding meaning of the term: China's usage referred to a roughly equal distribution of power; American usage referred to the existing distribution of power (Nye, *The Nye Report* 96)[12].

The relative equalization of economic and political power, but not the military one, between China and Japan in the first decade after the Cold War (Bergner 132) created a more equal and balanced competition between these two nations. As China was gaining economic strength and Japan was playing a bigger political and military role in accordance with the 1997 U.S.-Japan New Defense Guidelines, Sino-Japanese competition intensified. The Sino-Japanese rivalry during the 1990s, and especially in the 2000s decade, led to more tension and less security in the region, gave more momentum to the importance of power relations between them, and paradoxically "legitimized" Washington's claim that the US military presence in East Asia was a positive security factor.

As for the United States' place in the Sino-Japanese rivalry over regional influence, the U.S. geopolitical strategy aimed at balancing Japan and China in order to gain more leverage over both of them. The inherently incongruent interests between the two Asian rivals geopolitically served America's interests in East Asia to divide and rule. This is representative of how geopolitics works in an anarchical state system (Nye, "'The Nye Report': Six Years Later" 65). The paradox of geopolitics is that, on the one hand, while each state is seeking to maximize its gains at the expense of the other, yet each is keen to maintain an equilibrium in the distribution of power among them, so that none would be tempted to dominate the rest and disturb the existing balance (Reynolds 256-72).

Patrick E. Tylor called for a. major U.S. geopolitical and strategic objective in post-Cold War East Asia that is to ensure that no rival developed. In a Pentagon planning paper entitled "U.S. Strategy Plan Calls for Ensuring no Rivals Develop", Taylor argued that it was a vital necessity for the United States to

---

[12] This reference format to The Nye Report as a primary source is meant to distinguish it from Nye's 1999 article "'The Nye Report': Six Years Later". The 1995 Nye Report was written by Harvard Professor Joseph S. Nye who was asked in February 1995 by the U.S. Department of Defense to carry out a thorough review of the rationale and the utility of the U.S. alliance with Japan. It will be referred to heretofore as The Nye Report.

"account sufficiently for the interests of the large industrial nations to discourage them from challenging America's favorite regional status quo or seeking to overturn the established political or economic order" (17). The U.S. old-new strategy of preponderance aimed to perpetuate a post-Cold War geopolitical dominance, and Asia is one of the areas in which the United States has always sought to maintain a dominant position (Preble 8-28). To achieve this objective, the United States used its power attributes, and took advantage of the post-Cold War realities of power distribution, which were clearly in America's favor, given Japan's dependence on America's protection, and China's inherent inability to compete with the U.S. over regional or global domination. Accordingly, Japan was heavily discouraged from seeking an independent foreign policy, though it was paradoxically pressured to build a more independent military deterrent or at least pay a higher share of the U.S. protection bill. At the same time, China in its turn was warned against aspiring to a new assertive posture[13].

Preventing the re-emergence of a new rival in Asia that could pose a "threat" similar to the one posed by the Soviet Union was always the ultimate U.S. objective in East Asia after the end of the Cold War. Secretary of State James Baker said in 1991: "The enduring diversity of regional interests and security concerns stand out with even greater clarity. What was a secondary aspect of our Cold War-era security presence is becoming the primary rationale for our defense engagement in the region: to provide geopolitical balance" (Baker 5), that is, a balance which was conducive to a permanent U.S. preponderance in East Asia, where more than 70,000 American soldiers were stationed in Japan and South Korea alone (Ch. Johnson 151-86). America's bottom line, therefore, was to keep its instrumental alliance with Japan alive, and as a viable deterrent against potential Chinese attempts to challenge the regional American-led order, but at the same time to follow what is called the "hedge policy" towards Beijing (Przystup et al. 3), that is hoping for the best but preparing for the worst. The best for Washington was the rise of a "peaceful and responsible"[14] China, but the worst would be the rise of a competitive and revisionist China that was bent on East Asia domination.

---

[13] Hearings of the Committee on Armed Services of the House of Representatives, the One Hundred Sixth Congress. "Security Challenges Posed by China." July 19, 2000.

[14] "China and the Future of the World". Chicago Society, the University of Chicago, April 28–29, 2006. Opening Keynote by Ambassador Christopher R. Hill, United States Assistant Secretary of State for East Asian and Pacific Affairs. For Full Text.

As far as the U.S.-Japan connection was concerned, this complex bilateral relationship was not problem-free. Japan was an American ally, yet a fierce economic rival especially since the end of the Cold War (Yabunaka 6-17). During the Cold War, Japan's dependence on the United States for protection against the Sino-Soviet axis meant that economic rivalry was held in check (*The Economist* 35). Now, though the China 'threat' still existed and was on the rise, from a Japanese perspective, the U.S.-Japanese economic competition became more openly divisive, partly due to Washington's exploitation of its preponderant security position to obtain Japanese acquiescence in bilateral trade disputes[15]. The increasing American-Japanese friction over a host of security and economic issues could open the door for the possibility that the Japanese would seek to rely on their own military capabilities and exploit their own potential in the future. Jeffrey I. Bergner argues that "whether the pro-American LDP [Japan's Liberal Democratic Party] retains power, Japan will move toward a more independent position vis-à-vis the United States" (164).

Since the end of the Cold War, a series of questions relating to the security treaty with the United States were gaining momentum in Japan, which shed doubts about its raison d'être. Questions ranged from asking why 37.000 American soldiers, subsidized by Japanese taxpayers' money, needed to remain in Japan, to the reason for having to satisfy all of America's political and even trade demands. Also, Tokyo was uncertain about the future of its alliance with the United States. The Japanese felt that the United States was playing fast and loose with its special relationship with Japan. Opinion polls in Japan suggested that a majority of Japanese did not believe that the U.S. would offer massive assistance if Japan came under attack, and only 12 percent of the Japanese believed that the post-Cold War U.S.-Japan security treaty was "beneficial" to Japan's security needs (DiFilippo 149-50). Only 27 percent of the Japanese also believed that the treaty was "useful" to the safety of Japan (Ibid). There was strong evidence that Japan's doubts about America's intentions in East Asia fueled Tokyo's security concerns and strengthened Japan's right-wing calls to "move toward a more independent position vis-à-vis the United States" (Bergner 164).

Moreover, Japan was already a major economic power, yet was being held to a second-rate status on the world stage, which created a disequilibrium between Japan's economic and political global status. This was shown in the paradox of being the world's main benefactor of a series of international organizations, such

---

[15] Japanese Subcommittee on Unfair Trade Policies and Measures, 1998 Report on the WTO Consistency of Trade Policies by Major Trading Partners.

as the International Monetary Fund (IMF) and the United Nations (U.N.), and its two-decade failure to win a permanent seat on the U.N. Security Council. Furthermore, Japan was worried about China's emergence as a world power. "For Japan, China was a next-door problem, and stability in China is paramount. This was true for Japan's commercial and economic interests, as well as its national security" (Przystup, "China and the U.S.-Japan Alliance", Lecture 2000).

China, in its turn, viewed Japan as a potential "American tool" to contain the PRC. In the aftermath of the Cold War, China alternately feared that Japan would either be drafted into a U.S.-led strategy to counter Chinese rising power, or would be driven by a diminished American regional presence to confront China with its own nuclear force. China clearly alleged that the main objective of the American military presence in the region since 1945, in collaboration with Japan, was to contain China, negate its program of military modernization, and most of all prevent the reunification of Taiwan with the motherland (Song 23). The U.S. reaction to China's military exercises in 1996 and 2000 across the Strait of Taiwan, together with the U.S.-Japan SCC February 2005 declaration regarding their common stance towards the security of Taiwan, clearly substantiated the Chinese allegations.

While the official policy of the United States was one China, and no independence for Taiwan, China's attempts to regain its sovereignty over what it calls a "renegade province" was marketed by the United States, and with full political backing from Japan, as tendencies of regional hegemony on the part of China. The Taiwan issue in the security and power equation between Japan, China, and the United States after the Cold War was a determining factor in the respective power calculations of the three nations. Though the U.S. publicly supported the "One China Policy", it made it very clear that it would not be passive, should there be a Chinese invasion of the island. An American military intervention in a China-Taiwan conflict would almost automatically involve Japan in view of the 1997 New Defense Guidelines between Tokyo and Washington and their 2005 declaration in this respect, which opened the door for a wider Japanese military and logistical support of potential U.S. interventions in "the areas surrounding Japan" (Nye, "'The Nye Report' Six Years Later" 65).

According to the revised terms of the new U.S.-Japan alliance for the twenty-first century, "Japan's military objectives [were] no longer targeted solely at defending Japanese territory and territorial air and sea space, but to role-sharing with the United States" (Bergner 183), a legion of "responsibilities" such as a probable Japanese involvement in Taiwan, the South China Sea, the Spratly Islands, and the Strait of Malacca. As a consequence, China's deep-rooted fear of

Japan, which had emotional and historical dimensions as well was on the rise. Beijing responded quickly to the September 1997 American-Japanese New Defense Guidelines, which widened Japan's political and security prerogatives in East Asia. The Chinese Foreign Ministry Spokesman, Shen Guofang, warned that "any attempt to have a security arrangement going beyond its bilateral character would certainly be cause for vigilance and concern by other Asian nations" (Mufson 16). More recently, China perceived the February 2005 U.S.-Japan SCC declaration regarding Taiwan as an unwarranted interference in China's domestic affairs, and reacted by enacting the March 2005 Anti-Secession Law, which precluded any legal attempt on the part of Taipei to secede, and pledged a Chinese military reaction in such an eventuality.

On another note, as this work seeks to demonstrate, the reference to Taiwan and North Korea in the US-Japan-China triangle did not make it a pentagon equation, because Taipei and Pyongyang, though they were, and still are, core issues in East Asia's politics and the most immediate security menaces in the region, were not seen as major regional actors like China or Japan. North Korea's problem or the future of Taiwan's status was dealt with in this work as part of the power and security game between the United States, China, and Japan because Pyongyang's security threat, which its missile and nuclear programs allegedly pose to the stability of the region, would not be addressed without having Beijing's interests and power/security calculations met. This is true in view of China's special and historical relationship with the North Koreans, and the political and economic dependence of the latter on the former. The same logic applies to the Taiwan issue, which is not a bilateral dispute between Beijing and Taipei anymore; on the contrary, the peaceful or the military solution to the Taiwan problem would not be feasible without the full involvement of the United States, given the 1979 Taiwan Relations Act, and Japan, in view of Tokyo's commitment since the 1969 Sato-Nixon Declaration till the February 2005 U.S.-Japan SCC statement that Taiwan was a common security problem between Washington and Tokyo. Moreover, Russia would be referred to throughout this work whenever it is relevant, as in the case, for instance, of Moscow's dissatisfaction with Japan's participation in an American-sponsored missile program in Asia called the 1993 Theater Missile Defense (TMD)[16] system, or when dealing with Pyongyang's nuclear standoff with the United States, given Russia's historical leverage on North Korea.

---

[16] TMD stands for the 1993 U.S.-Japan Theater Missile Defense program which aimed at building a missile shield in Northeast Asia including Japan, Taiwan, and South Korea, to

Finally, on the one hand, the United States claimed that its post-Cold War military presence in East Asia was subject to a robust consensus among the majority of the region's nations, both in Northeast and Southeast Asia, which were suspicious of China's strategic intentions to project its coercive power against them. On the other hand, this book argues that one of the root reasons why the U.S.-Japan-China triangle was quite unstable was the controversy over the U.S. military presence in East Asia; a presence that was viewed differently by regional actors, according to their respective power and security considerations on which basis the three parties interacted. Although there was some evidence that nations such as Japan, the Philippines, Thailand, Indonesia.... etc, were indeed more comfortable with an American hegemony than with a would-be Chinese one (Crock 46), one can argue that in no way could this relative regional consensus on the need for a preponderant and "stabilizing" power be a majority consensus. On the contrary, it was widely perceived that the bulk of the Asia Pacific peoples' aspirations were always "threatened by the U.S. imperialism. Tensions and instabilities, particularly in the Korean Peninsula, between China and Taiwan, and other hot spots in the region [we]re heightened because of U.S. interventionism" (Tuazon, "Current U.S. Hegemony in Asia Pacific", Lecture 2003).

I.2. Statement of the Problem

During the first two decades in the post-Cold War era, the United States argued that without the US political and military involvement in East Asia, power competition between Japan and China could be highly risky for the region's security[17] (Hearings, "Security Challenges Posed by China" 1996, 23, 38). Hence, Washington was playing a positive security role in the region because relative stability was successfully maintained over the previous fifty years or so[18]. The U.S. claimed that its military presence in East Asia was always a hedge against a potential Chinese invasion of Taiwan, and a deterrent against another Korean war that would paralyze the region's outstanding economic success, and the

---

protect them from potential North Korean, Chinese, and Russian missiles. Actually, the idea of a TMD shield had been a direct reaction to the 1993 North Korean launch of the Rodong 1 missile in the Sea of Japan. The TMD program was frozen because of Japan's reluctance to participate, fearing a regional arms race with China and North Korea.

[17] Hearings Before the Committee on National Security of the House of Representatives of the One Hundred Fourth Congress. 2nd Session. March 20, 1996, "Security Challenges Posed by China". Washington: U.S. Government Printing Office, 1996.

[18] Ibid.

free flow of oil from the Arabian Gulf to America's key allies in the region, namely Japan and South Korea. The United States supported its claim by the success of the existing regional order, which was measured by the absence of wars since the Vietnam War in East Asia.

The notion of security, however, did not necessarily mean the same thing for China and the U.S. or even Japan. Tokyo viewed the U.S. military presence in East Asia as a "positive" factor in providing security for Japan in particular and for the whole region at large (Bernstein and Munro 184), which was in accordance with the U.S. official justification of its military presence in East Asia. But from a Chinese perspective (Song 33), China's territorial security was still incomplete as long as Taiwan did not come back to the "embrace" of the motherland. Reunification with Taiwan had always been part of China's basic security objectives and even national honor (Chong-Pin Lin 18-53). Moreover, Beijing argued that the U.S. military presence in East Asia was rather destabilizing because it kept generating one crisis after another. The list of crises included the 1994 U.S.-North Korean standoff over Pyongyang's nuclear program, the 1996 and 2000 U.S. military deployments into the Strait of Taiwan, and the annual U.S.-South Korean military exercises along the Demilitarized Zone (DMZ) along the North-South Korean borders. Accordingly, this was not the military presence that was conducive to more security; it paradoxically led to more tension in East Asia, which exacerbated the region's already volatile security environment. Therefore, the U.S. military presence, when looked at from a different angle of vision, was a negative security factor in East Asia. Indeed, those who were critical of the U.S. intentions in the region such as the Chinese, the North Koreans, and the Russians, argued that Washington was just seeking more power and domination, instead of providing more security in their respective neighborhoods.

I.3. Research Objectives

The major purpose of this work therefore is to explore the question of whether the U.S. East Asia policy, basically its military presence, did contribute to the stability of the region under study. This would be achieved by demonstrating how power and security calculations governed the rules of interaction between the U.S., Japan, and China since the end of the Cold War, and how interaction outcomes among them revealed the reality of their power relations. The study of the two dependent variables of power and security in the U.S.-Japan-China triangle is the means to understand the rationale of these interaction outcomes. Interaction is therefore the variable "that most critically affects the maintenance of the system" (Reynolds 221), because when it is in process, we see the units moving from one direction to another, allying with one and conspiring against the other; states as concepts become mobile units in action, showing that there is no "natural harmony" of interests between any two of the three nations concerned (ibid). Each state has had its own security concerns and power ambitions, and each of them has tried to maximize its power either for the sake of power, or because of security concerns.

The major question now is what security role was the United States playing in East Asia in the first decades following the end of the Cold War? Was it the role of a stabilizer in an unstable security environment or one of domination? Was the U.S. acting as a hegemonic empire, or a partner that is altruistically working with Japan and China to deal with East Asia's post-Cold War security challenges? Was it an exercise of power beyond U.S. borders for its own self-interested purposes? Was the United States playing the role of a primus inter pares that is first among equals or more equal than others? Hostile reactions to the United States' policies, suspicions about America's strategies in East Asia, and allegations that the United States was misusing its enormous power and abusing its overwhelming military presence in East Asia, all resulted in an unstable security situation in the region. This is the definition of what Michael Mandelbaum calls the "Goliath"[19] phenomenon (50-56).

Moreover, this work seeks to analyze the concept of security in international relations and how this can apply to the post-Cold War U.S.-Japan-China triangle. A series of guiding questions is asked: Are security and power dialectically or chronologically related to each other? Is it inevitable to endanger others' security when one state seeks to secure itself? How does the distribution of power among the three states affect their respective actions and reactions to each other?

As far as the methodology is concerned, this book adopts a consistent combination of three theoretical models for international relations throughout that is Realism, Neo-Realism, and Offensive Realism. The three approaches were pioneered in the twentieth century respectively by Hans Morgenthau, Kenneth Waltz, and John Mearsheimer. They commonly accept struggle as an innate feature of life in the current international system of nation-states due to

---

[19] Goliath: In the Bible, Goliath is a Philistine giant who was slain by David (1 Sam.17). Politically, the term has always stood for powerful and hegemonic states which frighten others into acquiescence by all means of coercion, including a natural penchant to the use of military force even if such a use violates domestic and international laws.

the anarchic nature of a system composed of units (sovereign states) without a central ruling body (Williams et al. *Classic Readings* 183-95). The adoption of such a combination of the three models was motivated by the fact that "the concept of interest defined as power imposes intellectual discipline upon the observer, infuses rational order into the subject matter of politics, and thus makes the theoretical understanding of politics possible" (qtd in Williams et al. *Dictionary of 20th Century Politics* 428).

Within this theoretical model combining realism, neo-realism, and offensive realism, this book seeks also to address the following theoretical questions: First, since power is the determining variable, this work intends to develop an understanding of this crucial concept, and its role in dictating and influencing interaction outcomes within the post-Cold War U.S.-Japan-China triangle. This work assumes that the main units of action are sovereign states and their exercise of power is dictated by their respective military, economic, and political attributes of power (Singer 77-92). It also assumes that security could be achieved either by a set of defensive measures or by taking an offensive posture vis-à-vis others.

I.4. Research Questions

Underlying the above analysis and the theoretical framework of this book is the following research question: Under what conditions was the post-Cold War U.S. military presence in East Asia a negative or a positive security factor?

Thus, the research undertaken here would attempt to ascertain whether the United States did contribute to the stability of East Asia after the end of the Cold War, and/or to the tension and unrest which the region witnessed during the period under study.

I.5. Research Hypotheses

In analyzing this question, three hypotheses were addressed:

H 1: The U.S. military presence in East Asia after the end of the Cold War was a negative security factor.

H 2: The post-Cold War U.S. military presence in East Asia played a positive security role.

H 3: A combination of negative and positive security calculations maintained a relative balance between U.S. interests in East Asia and the concerns of the region's major actors - Japan and China.

I.6. Structure of the Book

This book is divided into five parts: an introduction, four chapters, and a conclusion. The introduction should provide the background of the work, the main question to be researched, and the purpose of this study as well as its structure. Chapter I reviews the literature about how power and security are dialectically interrelated in order to apply the findings to the main question of this work as to the nature of the U.S. military presence in East Asia in the post-Cold War era. It attempts to demonstrate the inseparability between security and power in international relations as seen from different standpoints, which will lead this work to tackle one of the perplexing questions in international relations as to the blurred limit between a defensive and an offensive posture. Moreover, security is not only military readiness but also economic security based mainly on securing energy supplies for an economy to continue to operate competitively. In the process of highlighting the importance of energy security to states, this chapter deals with the Sino-Japanese dangerous but so far quiet dispute over the sea-bed oil resources in the Senkaku Islands in the East China Sea as a case study. The selection of this case was motivated by the fact that this dispute brought China and Japan to the brink of confrontation on many occasions, in 1995, 1999, 2000, and 2008, and continued to be a major source of friction in the Sino-Japanese relationship with considerable implications for their respective interaction with the United States.

Chapter II explains the theoretical framework, the analytic model, and the research design. The theoretical framework that guides this book is based on the recognition of power realities in East Asia and power politics in international relations. The following section presents the analytic model which puts forward the possibility of a link between "Power" and "Security" in the interaction between the U.S., Japan, and China since the end of the Cold War. The last section of this chapter depicts the type of research design, which basically includes the selection of the data used to answer the research question.

Chapter Three analyzes the drivers in post-Cold War East Asia which have governed the power relations between the U.S., Japan, and China. These drivers include the study of the post-Cold War U.S.-Japan alliance on the basis of the power and security calculations of both countries. Also, China's rising economic and military power and its implications on the security and power calculations of Japan and the United States will be studied in depth in order to pave the way for the analysis to move to the next and last chapter, whereby this work will try to highlight who is threatening whom, and which side is seeking to maximize its power at the expense of others-that is hegemonic, and which side is security-conscious more than power-obsessed.

Chapter Four seeks to answer the central research question of whether the post-Cold War U.S. military presence in East Asia played a negative or a positive security role. This was achieved by looking at the U.S.-Japan-China triangle through the prism of hegemony, so that this work could come up with a final judgment of the reality of the U.S. military presence during that period. Hegemony is dealt with, first, from a theoretical and historical point of view, and then the findings are applied to the U.S. position today in East Asia in relation to Japan and China.

The research into the American strategic mindset regarding the U.S. perception of the 'China threat' should reveal the "doublespeak"[20] that Washington was using when talking about welcoming "a peaceful and responsible" China, while working to prevent China's rise to ascendancy in the region. To achieve this purpose, primary sources are used such as U.S. Congress Hearings, declassified U.S. official documents, and personal communications with Assistant Secretaries of State and Defense, the twentieth-century founder of "offensive realism" third school in political science[21], as well as interviews with think tank experts in Korean affairs[22]. The same findings about hegemony would also be applied to the case of Taiwan, which became a "common security challenge" between Washington and Tokyo during the early post-Cold War decades. According to a March 2005 Chinese Anti-Secession Law, Taiwan's move towards de facto independence would almost certainly trigger a Chinese military response, which put the three countries on a collision course because of the complexity of the issue to Beijing. The Taiwan problem is dealt with as a case study of hegemony which tries to show if the U.S.-Japanese shift of policy regarding the future of Taiwan was indeed meant to be a practice of hegemony, or was a result of their common concern about regional security and stability.

Finally, the conclusion consists of three sections. First, the findings section presents the final results of the main argument of this work about the post-Cold War controversial U.S. military presence in East Asia. Second, the implications section will try to highlight the significance of this work to academic scholarship, and how it could be helpful in researching a post-Cold War new

---

[20] For the meaning of terms like 'Doublespeak', 'Newspeak', 'Old speak', 'Duckspeak', see, George Orwell, *1984*, Penguin Books, Ltd. London, 1949.

[21] Hereafter referred to as Interviewee 1.

[22] Hereafter referred to as Interviewee 2.

triangle which has become the focus of international relations scholarship, as it will define much of the future of the world throughout the twenty-first century. Nevertheless, this book does have its own limitations, as any academic work, which will be put forward in the last section of this conclusion.

In the course of this research, several individuals were interviewed to gather insights and perspectives relevant to the topics discussed in this book. However, to protect the privacy and confidentiality of these participants, the names of the interviewees have been anonymized.

Chapter 1

The Duality of Power and Security: A Review of the Literature

1.1. The Pursuit of Power (Animus Dominandi) and the Quest for Security (Animus Securitas)[1]

Since the Westphalia Treaty[2], states have been in a constant chase of power *(animus dominandi)* to dominate each other (Morgenthau), but Kenneth Waltz's neo-realism opines that the primary concern of states is not more power, but more security *(animus securitas)* (Waltz). John J. Mearsheimer's offensive realism, however, argues that states not only do seek but also should seek more power because the structure of the system, and not human nature, as Morgenthau advances, pushes them to do so (Snyder, 2002, 149-173) The major difference between Morgenthau and Waltz is that they have different answers for the question why states pursue power? Morganthau, conversely, argues that states are interested in power mainly because there is a will to power that is instinctive in human beings. It is an animus dominandi in every individual, and of course, states are dominated by individual policymakers who are born with that animus dominandi. Therefore, the competition for power among states in Morgenthau's approach is largely a consequence of human nature. Waltz, however, believes that states pursue power because the structure of the international system leaves them with no choice. Waltz's argument is that in an anarchic system, states concerned about their survival have no choice but to pursue power, but not too much power. So, a kind of "animus dominanadi" for Waltz is an obligation for survival and not a choice to make.

---

[1] Animus Securitas means almost the opposite of animus dominandi, that is an obsession with security, and the intent to seek to guarantee one's security by all means available in international relations including building one's military, economic, and political attributes, and also entering into alliances.

[2] The Treaty of Westphalia was signed by Germany, Austria, France, the Netherlands, and Spain in 1648 in Westphalia, Germany. The treaty ended the Thirty Years War 1618-1648 within the Holy Roman Empire, and established what is today called the nation-state system of international relations.

In my interview with **Interviewee 1** at the University of Chicago on April 28, 2006, he told me that the difference between him and Waltz is that Waltz believes that states should not pursue too much power, whereas he believes that states should maximize their power. He said:

> I think that there is one similarity, one important similarity and one important difference between me and Waltz and Morgenthau specifically. I agree with Waltz that states are largely motivated by the structure of the system. I am a structural realist like Waltz. I follow in Waltz's footsteps in the sense that the principal reason that the states pursue power is because the structure of the system leaves them no alternative if they hope to survive. That is what Waltz and I have in common. The difference between me and Waltz is that Waltz believes that states should not pursue too much power whereas I believe states should maximize their power. I believe that states should pursue hegemony. Waltz believes it is foolish for states to pursue hegemony[3].

Interviewee 1 also talked about his difference with Morgenthau. He says that he differs from Morganthau regarding the latter's argument that states are interested in power because it is the consequence of human nature. **Interviewee 1** does not agree with the human nature approach in terms of the drive for power. But he agrees with Morganthau that states want to dominate other states in the system. States want to be the hegemon. "So, I am a structural realist like Waltz who believes like Morgenthau that states pursue domination" (See Footnote Below).

Therefore, looking at international relations exclusively through the prism of *only* one of these three theories yields only half the answer because seeking more security and more power are dialectically as well as chronologically linked

---

[3] Personal Communication: My Interview with **Interviewee 1** who is Professor of Political Science at the University of Chicago. He is a founder of his own school of political science called 'offensive realism' which borrows from Hans J. Morgenthau's realism and Kenneth N. Waltz' neo-realism, but is known for its own approach to international relations. Among his works are The Tragedy of Great Power Politics, New York: Norton, 2001, Translated into Chinese, Greek, Italian, Japanese, Korean, Portuguese, Romanian, and Serbian; Liddell Hart and the Weight of History, New York: Cornell University Press; London: 1988; Conventional Deterrence, New York: Cornell University Press, 1983. The interview took place on April 28, 2006. For a full text of the interview, please contact the Vernon Press.

to each other. States tend to build enough force to guarantee their physical security because "all states must constantly be ready either to counter force with force or to pay the cost of weakness" (Waltz 160). Then, states tend to look for more power because individual, as well as national appetites for more power in its broad sense, are almost as innate in people as in states. International relations are a blend of a quest for security and a pursuit of power. "It is important to realize that such a competition between states for security, and hence for power, is a basic situation which is unique with men" as well as with states (Herz 232). When states feel relatively secure, they usually seek to maximize their security guarantees by building more power until they become stronger than other states and eventually the strongest, which consequently invites similar countermeasures from their potential enemies.

In the absence of an effective law-enforcing international body, power rivalry has been a pattern that has bedeviled international relations. States have been united only by common interests or common dangers, instead of common values of peace and justice. The primacy of interests takes priority over the primacy of values. It is a zero-sum game; what is won by one country is almost automatically lost by another. And when there is no "supreme authority, there is then a constant possibility that conflicts will be settled by force" (Waltz 188). This is like a chess game; maximizing one's gains is achievable only at the expense of one's adversary who, in turn, becomes antagonized by others' advances, and thus creating a vicious circle of action and reaction that is escalation. Some states focus on the chessboard; others on the chessmen; the former take into account the weight of the different pieces and their impact on the chessboard, and the latter believe that what is important is the moves of the chessmen rather than the nature of the chessboard itself (Waltz 201-10), evoking Woodrow Wilson's words that "everyone's policy depends on everyone else's" (Waltz 226).

As anarchy has been a basic characteristic of international relations, nations balance each other whenever possible and, in many ways, make up for their respective weaknesses. Though the balance of power is a nineteenth-century model of politics, it is "a concept which recurs with great frequency throughout the literature but is used to mean different things by different people, or by the same people at different times" (Reynolds 210-11). The balance of power concept can be tested in a simulation of a three-unit state system, borrowing Kaplan's and I.L. Claude's arguments and following Reynolds' model of the three-unit state system. Applying such a concept to the East Asian triangle under study, for instance, the balance of power concept could have two different meanings. First, if the three units concerned- the U.S., Japan, and China- try to balance against each other, then the system has an inherent probability of self-destruction. If "the decision-makers in state A, observing states B and C, perceived a development suggesting an increase in C's capabilities, or an apparent improvement in relations between B and C", they would approach B, pointing out the danger (Reynolds 217). "B's decision-makers, learning of this approach, will fear that A and C are planning to use their combined power to destroy and divide B up between themselves" (218), and subsequently, state B "will accordingly make urgent approaches to A and C suggesting to each joint action against the third state" (217).

Now, if we use a mathematical deconstruction of the post-Cold War U.S.-Japan-China triangle, let us assume that State A stands for the United States, State B for Japan, and State C symbolizes China. Then an equation as such could have three probable outcomes of alignment and conflict: first, A+B against C, that is, the U.S. allying with Japan against China, and thus playing a negative security role, since it would be taking sides and inviting security suspicion from China; second, A balancing B and C, and trying to maintain the status quo because it serves its own interests; and third and the least probable, B approaching C (or vice versa) to contain and dislodge A, which means Japan and China coming together to counter a perceived or real U.S. hegemony in East Asia. The fourth probability is A and C allying against B, that is, the U.S. and China joining efforts against Japan, is not included here because it is believed to be a very far-fetched eventuality, at least as long as China is a communist country and Japan is the major American ally in Asia around which the U.S. preponderant position in the region revolves.

The first case of A+B against C could happen if Japan sees that China has become too strong militarily or economically, and that it is threatening Japan's security by its increasingly assertive behavior in the region, manifested through China's attempts, for instance, to dominate the contentious Senkaku and Spratly Islands conflict respectively in the East China Sea and South China Sea, or Beijing's threats against Taiwan. A Sino-Taiwan conflict could close the Taiwan Strait and choke Japan's economy by preventing the shipment of oil on which the Japanese economy heavily depends. All these probabilities would be a good reason for Japan to conclude that China has become a serious threat, and needs to be dealt with by joining efforts with the United States to redress the disturbed balance of power in the region. As a reaction to a perceived alignment of A and B against C the latter "will accordingly make urgent approaches to A and B suggesting to each joint action against the third state"

(Reynolds 217). In such an eventuality, C, China, could approach B, Japan, to stand against A's hegemony, but this probability is very low, given the history of mistrust and suspicion between the Chinese and the Japanese, deeply rooted in their interactions during the 19th and 20th centuries as explained in Chapter Three of this work. That is why this study has excluded the fourth possibility of C and B conspiring against A. In short, the more probable eventuality is to see C going back to A; China starting to ingratiate itself with the United States, making concessions on bilateral issues of contention such as the future of regional order, more flexibility in trade issues and an increasing pressure on North Korea to dismantle its nuclear and missile programs.

A perceived rapprochement between China and the U.S., however, could alarm Japan and push it to change its tactics to prevent an American tilt towards China at the expense of the American-Japanese special relationship. This was the case between the three countries during the second Clinton term, but for a different reason: trade and economic reforms in Japan. Following the 1997 financial blackout in Asia[4], together with Japan's reluctance to reform economically, the U.S.-Japan-China triangle witnessed a Sino-American rapprochement symbolized by China's president Jiang Zemin's visit to the U.S. in October 1997, and President Clinton's visit to China in June 1998, which gave a real boost to their bilateral relations, perceived by the Japanese as a Chinese attempt to drive a wedge between the United States and Japan, and an American signal that it was trading China for Japan in its new East Asia strategy (Funabashi 31-32). The fact that Clinton did not stop in Japan on his way to China, for instance, to brief the Japanese about his visit to Beijing, led Japan to establish a crisis committee to

---

[4] The 1997/98 East Asian currency crisis, or what is locally but pejoratively called the IMF crisis, started in July 1997 in Thailand when the Thai currency collapsed overnight in a way that reminded the world of the Black Thursday of October 1929 in the New York Stock Exchange. The Thai currency crisis affected later currencies and stock markets in several Asian countries which used to be called East Asian Tigers. Indonesia, South Korea, and Thailand were the countries most affected by the crisis. Malaysia, Hong Kong and the Philippines were also hit but relatively less. China, Taiwan, Singapore and Vietnam were slightly affected. As a result, many businesses collapsed and millions of people fell below the poverty line in 1997-1998. The economic crisis also led to political upheaval, and even to the fall of old regimes like that of Suharto in Indonesia and Chavalit Yongchaiyudh in Thailand. For more on this subject, see Ngian Kee Jin, *Coping with the Asian Financial Crisis: The Singapore Experience*, December 13, 2005, available at <http://www.iseas. edu.sg/vr82000>, and Rajnish Tiwari, Post-crisis Exchange Rate Regimes in Southeast Asia, Seminar Paper, University of Hamburg, 2003.

monitor a developing situation of a perceived American "disengagement" from its strategic commitment that Japan was America's number one partner in East Asia (*Pittsburgh Tribune Review*, July 26, 1998).

In view of the panoply of possibilities emanating from the movement of the United States, Japan, and China as sovereign units moving towards each other or against each other, the end game, therefore, is that at least one side of the triangle will inevitably feel threatened, that is the odd man out. The variety of interaction outcomes reminds us of a situation which fits Reynolds' point that "which pairing emerges from the various approaches will depend on bargaining skills and on the ways in which the rewards and costs of each course of action are perceived by the decision-makers in each state, but the result of the exchange is that one of the three states is [threatened] by the combined action of the other two" (217). But as an old-world order of bipolarity just disintegrated after the demise of the ex-USSR, and a new one of unipolarity was then taking shape, old concepts such as alignment and balancing were losing many of their old meanings and acquiring new ones (Eldridge).

As a matter of fact, the end of the Cold War revealed that a new world order emerged in which the old relative balance of power among states no longer existed. The demise of the old international order between the United States and the Soviet Union as the world's two superpowers created a new era characterized by new security concerns resulting from America's perceived appetite for more power and domination, and other nations' sense of uncertainty about their security and interests, that is an opposition between an alleged American *animus dominandi* versus other states' *animus securitas*. Power realities of East Asia, for example, then showed an unequal distribution of power between the United States, China, and Japan, leading their triangular interaction to be conducted on the basis of their respective power and security calculations. But as Bergner put it, "this is not the kind of neighborhood that one could properly describe as a community" (206); it is not also the right neighborhood where the United States military presence could play a positive security role, as the U.S. used to claim (Ministry of Foreign Affairs of Japan, "Joint Statement: U.S.-Japan Security Consultative Committee", February 21, 2005). This power/security interconnectedness, however, increased the chances of regional instability, and created higher probabilities of power competition, especially in the post-Cold War early decades.

Equally important, in view of the significance of the notion of security in determining the quality and the outcome of interactions between states, it is almost inevitable to endanger other states' security when one state seeks to increase its own security. This is what John Herz calls a "security dilemma"[5] (231-35), which refers to a situation in which one state takes action to enhance its security only to have this action seen as threatening by other states; the result is that they engage in "defensive" countermeasures which intensify the first state's sense of insecurity (Buzan 83). The dilemma arises from the fact that because of this process, actions taken to enhance one's security can paradoxically end up diminishing it. There is a dilemma for the second state in that if it regards the first state's action as offensive and takes no countermeasures, it leaves itself vulnerable, whereas if it responds vigorously, it will exacerbate the first state's insecurity (qtd in Williams et al. *The Dictionary of 20th Century Politics* 601).

Although the security dilemma is a feature of anarchy in international relations, it can be exacerbated by perceptions based on false information or on inherent bad faith, which has generally characterized international relations. Accordingly, states tend to dismiss conciliatory overtures by other states as either tricky or a sign of weakness, rather than as a genuine desire for peace (Weltman). Consequently, a security dilemma usually leads to what Barry Buzan calls a "security complex". It is a situation where "a group of states whose primary security concerns link together sufficiently closely that their national security cannot realistically be considered apart from another" (Buzan 62). Here, it is imperative to remember that the state of anarchy in the international political system[6] is not automatically conducive to total chaos because of the existence of international norms of behavior, though not necessarily observed, mainly by strong countries, but stipulated in legal conventions between states called International Law[7], though this law has

---

[5] A security dilemma situation is when state A takes action to enhance its own security, but paradoxically endangers the security of other states which in their turn react by engaging in countermeasures which would be construed as threatening by State A.

[6] The International Political System is the system governing relations between sovereign states which could be stable or unstable depending on stability factors such as conventional international law, and instability ones like the distribution of power among states. It is "derived from systems analysis in which international politics are seen as a system that is either stable or unstable" (Williams et al. 366). For more on the international political system See George Modelski, "Agraria and Industria", in K. Knorr and S. Verbal (eds) The International System, Princeton, Princeton University Press, 1961.

[7] International Law: Though Hugo Grotius is considered the father of international law, the term was first coined by Jeremy Bentham in Principles of Morals and Legislation, 1780. It refers to all the treaties, customs, and agreements between sovereign states, which could be defined as international public law that is administered by a host of

always been an expression of the ideology of the "satisfied" powers. But in dealing with cases of lack of observance of international law and the practice of power politics in international relations, states tend to align themselves with the strong members of the system.

Moreover, one of the conditions for the stability of a three-unit system or a triangular interaction is the flexibility of alignment (Reynolds 217) between the actors concerned, a condition which has not existed in the U.S.-Japan-China interactions in the post-Cold War era. According to two primary sources, among others- the Hearings of the Committee on National Security of the House of Representatives of the One Hundred and Fourth Congress, March 20, 1996, and the Hearings of the Committee on Armed Services of the House of Representatives, the One Hundred and Sixth Congress, July 19, 2000- one can easily see that in this triangle there has been a fixed, instead of flexible, alignment between A and B respectively standing for the U.S. and Japan. There is one floating unit C, standing for China, which is trying to maximize its benefits from its interaction with both A and B, but trusting neither of them because of historical and geo-strategic considerations. In his testimony before the House National Security Committee on Security Challenges on March 20, 1996, Arthur N. Waldron, Professor of Strategy and Policy, said: "We must forge strong alliances with our friends—and particularly with Tokyo."[8] Back in the 1970s, President Nixon said, in his 1972 Report to Congress entitled "United States Foreign Policy for the 1970s: The Emerging Structure of Peace", "Japan is our most important ally in Asia. It is our second-greatest trading partner. It is an essential participant, if a stable world peace is to be built. Our security, our prosperity, and our global policies are, therefore, intimately and inextricably linked to the U.S.-Japanese relationship", (Excerpts from President Nixon's 1972 Report to Congress, 1).

Regarding the C corner, and according to the same source of Hearings, "China's clear intention [has been] to divide the United States from its Asian

---

agencies such as the United Nations, and the International Court of Justice. One of the weaknesses of international law is the lack of an aggressive mechanism to enforce judgments, which makes their observance an optional matter, most of the time depending again on how powerful the defendant state is.

[8] Hearings before the Committee on National Security of the House of Representatives of the One Hundred Fourth Congress. 2nd Session. March 20, 1996, "Security Challenges Posed by China". Washington: U.S. Government Printing Office, 1996, 73.

allies", namely Japan[9]. The history of Sino-Japanese wars since the 1894/95 Pigtail War until Japan's WWII behavior in Asia, such as the memories of the 1937 Rape of Nanking, has minimized the chances of seeing a real and genuine Sino-Japanese positive strategic relationship (See Chapter Three). This has made it more difficult for both nations to see each other as partners, instead of competitors for regional hegemony.

Reynolds argues that "the less the flexibility of the system, the more likely it is to break down" (222), but this is not an inevitable outcome regardless of the "costs-gains calculus." The Mutually Assured Destruction (MAD)[10] deadlock, for instance, eliminated most probabilities of war between the United States and the Soviet Union because the costs-gains calculations were nil. In this context, Wohlstetter said that if "peace were founded firmly on mutual terror, and mutual terror on symmetrical nuclear capabilities, this would be ... 'a melancholy paradox'; nonetheless a most comforting one" (qtd in Williams et al. *Classic Readings* 284).

Furthermore, the nature of the Communist government in Beijing, which the Americans distrust, together with the problem of Taiwan at the heart of the Sino-American-Japanese interaction, has always been an obstacle for the trilateral relationship to mature and develop. Richard D. Fisher of the Jamestown Foundation said in his testimony before the Armed Services Committee of the U.S. House of Representatives, "as long as the PRC remains governed by a Communist Party there is likely to be growing friction with the U.S. over Taiwan, missile defense, Washington's leadership in Asia, and the South China Sea."[11] The American anti-communist attitude probably confirms the argument that "similarity of ideological outlook may make some

---

[9] Hearings before the Committee on National Security of the House of Representatives of the One Hundred Fourth Congress. 2nd Session. March 20, 1996, "Security Challenges Posed by China". Washington: U.S. Government Printing Office, 1996, 71.

[10] MAD: This acronym depicted a superpower nuclear standoff in the mid-1960s when the Soviet Union and the United States had enough nuclear weapons to destroy each other, notwithstanding who strikes first. The second-strike capability which Moscow and Washington developed, assured that striking first by nuclear weapons was no longer an advantage, as the aggressor knows that the enemy will always the capability to retaliate in a deadly way. In a MAD situation, the assured unacceptable cost of damage which the Soviet Union could inflict on the United States in a second strike, precluded the chances that Washington would gamble with an all-out nuclear showdown.

[11] Hearings of the Committee on Armed Services of the House of Representatives, the One Hundred Sixth Congress. "Security Challenges Posed by China." July 19, 2000, 78.

alignments easier to achieve, but strong ideological antipathy may make some alignments impossible" (Reynolds 222).

Thus, the negative flexibility in Sino-Japanese and Sino-American interactions has meant that China has been perceived by Washington and Tokyo as the potential disturber of the status quo system, and not the U.S., which has been seen by the Chinese as an intruder into East Asia's affairs. The mutually negative perceptions between China and the United States are inextricably linked to the third corner of the triangle-Japan-which has chosen to ally with the latter allegedly to contain the former. And since Japan and the U.S. "began to work out guidelines for Japanese support in time of crisis [it] meant that China could not play a Japan card against the U.S., or try to expel the Americans from the region" of East Asia (Nye, "China's Re-mergence and the Future of the Asia Pacific" 39).

Successful alignments can be achieved either through bilateral security agreements such as the 1951 U.S.-Japan Security Treaty, or through collective security forums, that is, multilateral alliances like the North Atlantic Treaty Organization (NATO) or the now moribund Warsaw Pact. After the Second World War, the United States relied on what Inis L. Claude calls "collective security" such as NATO, NATO's Asian counterpart, the Southeast Asia Treaty Organization (SEATO), the United Nations, etc. Therefore, collective security is a military doctrine that is based on the perception of a common enemy whom one state cannot deal with individually. Members of a collective security apparatus are supposed to identify their respective interests closely with the general interest of their alliance. This does not amount to asking that national interests be abandoned, but that they simply be harmonized with the collective interests of the alliance members. States "must be willing to accept commitments which involve the sacrifice of their freedom of action or inaction in the most crucial ... situations" (Claude 226).

Moreover, for a collective security thesis to be credible, members of the alliance usually stand ready to use force in the face of threats either to one of them or to their alliance as a whole. Theoretically, the primary and major purpose of collective security is purely defensive, such as the Cold War NATO policy not to attack first, and to respond collectively against aggression against one or all of them. The no-first-attack, however, was not observed in the 1990s when NATO's air force bombed the former Yugoslavia in 1994 and 1998 to protect respectively Bosnians from Serb forces, and to force Yugoslavia to withdraw from the dominantly-Muslim Kosovo enclave. Notwithstanding NATO's military or political objectives, it marked a radical change in the alliance policy from defensive to offensive, and hence from "peacekeeping" to "peacemaking".

Collective security is meant to provide collective action to counter aggression, as the United Nations Charter, for instance, stipulates. The U.N. theoretically provides the bounds of international supervision. Member states are supposed to abdicate their sovereign control over some elements of national power, taking reassurance about their security from the stipulations of the U.N. charter. Thus, a state "exposes itself to obligations determined by the community for dealing with situations, which" could be triggered by "irresponsible" behavior or by an uncompromising position (Claude 225) of another state or group of states. In return, this international law-enforcing body would act impartially to preserve the territorial integrity of its members, great or small, strong or weak, and poor or rich. Therefore, collective security permits no inter-alliances, and no help for traditional friends rightly or wrongly. This is in harmony with "the basic proposition of collective security [that] whoever commits aggression is everybody's enemy; whoever resists aggression is everybody's friend" (Claude 231).

The success of collective security, however, hinges upon the relative equalization of power between member states. If one or two states command the bulk of the alliance, as is the case of the United States within NATO or the U.S.-Japan Alliance, the chance of having an impartial enforcement of international law in the face of threats is slim. If the major power behaves in a threatening or an aggressive manner towards a weaker state, the amassing of a credible force against it becomes almost impossible. The Anglo-American war on Iraq in March 2003, which was opposed by the overall majority of NATO members, especially France and Germany, proved that when there was a preponderant power within a collective security apparatus like NATO, the concept and the will of collective security depends heavily on the decision and interests of the leading member.

Therefore, the security-power equation, which has been the basis of state interactions since 1648, is dealt with in this work in different ways, depending first on the relative power of each member and second on the power relations within the system. To compensate for power imbalance, states tend to ally themselves with stronger members, or enter into international forums of collective security. Since the 1951 U.S.-Japan security treaty, Tokyo has trusted the United States with the provision of security for Japan. This is uncommon from a realist standpoint because states usually do not trust each other with issues of survival as such. I asked **Interviewee 1** why, in political science, a state would trust its former enemy for its own survival. He offered two points. First, is that Japan will trust the United States in good part because Japan knows that the United States has the best interests in containing China. The security situation here is very similar to the U.S.-Western Europe security relationship during the Cold War. Then, England and France trusted the United States because they knew that Washington had a deep-seated interest in containing the Soviet Union.

Second, the same logic applies today to U.S.-Japan security. The Japanese have figured out that because the United States does not want China to dominate Asia, Washington will continue to value its security alliance with Tokyo. So, the U.S. is protecting Japan because it is in its best interest to do so, and not out of trust or compassion towards the Japanese. But Japan has been doing all sorts of things to build its own military deterrence. "They will rely on the Americans for good points but they will also do a lot to protect themselves. The Japanese will surely figure out that this is a self-help war. I would not be surprised if at some point in the next 20 years Japan moves to acquire nuclear weapons especially if China rises or continues to rise."[12]

The following question that arises is that if the system leaves no option for states but to seek or to maximize power and hegemony, why would we blame states that seek domination and hegemony, which also leads to another question about which side to blame for decisions to make wars and seek domination. One of the possible answers is that even if the international system of anarchy encourages wars not only for security's sake, but also for dominating others, the decision to go to war also depends on a lower system, that is domestic factors such as the political system of each nation which allows or does not allow for opposite views regarding the decision to go to war, and whether it is a "just" war, or even the leader's personality himself. This view is based on a systemic approach of international relations in the process of seeking an explanation of why states make wars against other states, and who is to blame for the decision to go to war.

The correlation between states and human beings in explaining the roots of international anarchy has been a bewildering question for the last four centuries. To what extent can we incriminate the innate evil in man who takes the decision of war, instead of shifting the burden to the existing anarchical

---

[12] Personal Communication: My Interview with **Interviewee 1** at the University of Chicago on April 28, 2006.

system or to the nature of power relations between states? As a matter of fact, the analogy between the State and Man was expressed by Montesquieu when he said that "the life of governments is like that of man. The latter has a right to kill in case of natural defense: the former has a right to wage war for their own preservation" (qtd in Waltz 165).

As a "man cannot begin to behave decently unless he has some assurance that others will not be able to ruin him" (Rousseau 221), it could also be applied to nations interacting within a state of anarchy where there are no limits on the practice of power politics. The antithetical character of states' interests precludes good chances that they "behave decently" in an anarchical international system of self-help. In the absence of a law-enforcing body that can judge contentions and compensate the victim, states would not tend to "behave ethically" because they are the judges of their own affairs. Therefore, conflict between autonomous states is a chronic feature of international relations, since looking for "a continuation of harmony between a number of independent, unconnected sovereigns in the same neighborhood, would be to disregard the uniform course of human events, and to set at defiance the accumulated experience of ages", as John Jay put it two centuries ago (Jay 33-40).

Moreover, states, like men, before they choose confrontation, would deliberate on the assets and potential liabilities of engaging in conflicts. Bismarck, the German father of modern realpolitik[13] or political pragmatism, argues that "fools learn from their own experience, wise men learn by others' experiences" (Williams et al. *The Dictionary of 20th Century Politics* 564-65-66). Authoritarian regimes, however, are compared to those who are driven by sentiments instead of reason and, therefore, national affairs are run by personal decisions. Waltz substantiates this assumption when he writes, "States... are

---

[13] Realpolitik: a mid-19 century German concept championed by Karl Otto von Bismarck. It is a version of political realism. Realpolitik's argument about game theory in international relations gained momentum in the study of political science. It was the first to introduce the "fail safe" strategy as a way of conducting international politics. It relies on what was termed as "the best-case scenario" which minimizes potential losses. (Robertson, David. The Penguin Dictionary of Politics, 1993, Penguin Books, Ltd, New York, 410). Realpolitik ought not to be confused with Machtpolitik which is a German translation of one of the interpretations of political realism which stresses the idea of "an aggressive foreign policy which substitutes threats and the actual use of military power for international law" (Williams et al. The Dictionary of 20th Century Politics 546). The 2003 Iraq war could be an example of Machtpolitik because it was waged without a UN sanction, as France and Germany argued last year.

like men; they display both an urge to live and an inability consistently to order their affairs according to the dictates of reason" (italics added) (Waltz 162).

The correlation between men and states becomes more important not only in their common goal of seeking security, but also in deciding about war and peace. Cobden said in 1849: "As you find the population governing themselves- as in England, in France, or in America - there you will find that war is not the disposition of the people, and that if Government desire it, the people would put a check upon it" (qtd in Waltz 161). Woodrow Wilson also confirmed Cobden's view that in drawing a distinction between peaceful and aggressive states, democracies tend to prefer peaceful coexistence more than authoritarian regimes because despotic governments are more prone to go to war in order to play the card of nationalism and consequently turn domestic attention away from questioning the legitimacy of its rule. But this is not always true because even democracies do tend to dominate weaker states and "even good men and good states resort to force occasionally in their dealings" with other states (Waltz 187). Democratic England, for instance, waged a war against totalitarian Russia in 1857.

Another historical example: Francis I, known for his constant wars with his brother-in-law Charles V, explained that the reason for the permanent state of belligerency between them was "simple"; he said: "None whatever. We agree perfectly. We both want control of Italy" (Schuman 261). Furthermore, Senator Robert Taft wrote in 1951 that "history shows that when the people have the opportunity to speak, they as a rule decide for peace if possible. It shows that arbitrary rulers are more inclined to favor war than are the people at any time" (Taft 23). However, the case of Athens, a fifth-century B.C. democracy, does not corroborate Taft's argument. Athens demanded that the Mellians, a colony from Sparta, accept Athenian rule and domination. They told them that "if we were on friendly terms with you, our subjects would regard that as a sign of weakness in us, whereas your hatred is evidence of our power" and popularity (Thucydides 358).

Moreover, in times of insecurity and uncertainty, life for states, as for human beings, takes priority over justice. In the absence of order there can be no importance for justice or for freedom. "Men need the security of law before improvement in their moral lives is possible" (Waltz 163). While the individual surrenders his natural rights to the state in order to obtain security, states make sovereignty concessions to regional or international forums to gain security in return. This applies, for instance, to members of the European Union that are moving towards a European superstate in the form of a confederation. At the broad international level, the same rationale can also apply to members of the

United Nations which provides, at least theoretically, for the physical security of some of its members through political and sometimes military means.

Thus, the attempt to account for the roots of war betrays the simplicity and the complexity of the question because the interplay of men, the national system and the international environment have been behind most conflicts. Therefore, it would be wrong to assume that the Japanese Emperor, for instance, was personally responsible for Japan's WWII military actions in Asia, since such a partial account of a conflict like the Second World War would yield only half an answer. The inclusion of the nature of Japan's politics and existing power relations with its neighbors in the 1940s is likely to provide a better explanation of phenomena like WWII and of terms like defensive and offensive wars.

Finally, this section has tried to conceptualize the core concepts of power and security by using a combination of a Realist approach to power relations, leading to the conclusion that power is the end game for states as for human beings. The tendency to dominate the other is an inherent characteristic of an anarchical international system which is ruled by a counter system of balancing among states to make up for their respective weaknesses. If weak states do not ally or align themselves with stronger partners or alliances, and in the absence of an international legal body, they would pay a heavy price for the failure to readjust themselves to a system of a permanent security dilemma. Moreover, states are ruled by men, and the insatiable appetite for power is innate in human beings before it is the case in the international system. Since this system is made by men themselves, one can assume that men can be responsible for the war. The last part of this section has tried to show that the decision to go to war cannot be explained by one single level of the system, but only a comprehensive systemic view can help identify why states governed by men may decide to go to war whether to defend one's interests or to attack others.

1.2. Defense Vs. Offense

Robert Jervis, a prominent political scientist, suggests a way to distinguish between defensive and predatory intentions of states by advocating an offense-defense balance thesis. Jervis believed that "states can make themselves more secure without gravely endangering others" (qtd in Williams et al. *Classic Readings* 197-98). Rough equality of power between states could assuage their mutual suspicion of each other. A state can reassure its neighbors that its efforts are directed at increasing its own security rather than seeking domination, and thus dissuade them from reciprocating by taking extra precautionary military measures. The purpose then would be to protect oneself, and not to conquer others and expand into foreign territories. This could be realized only by pursuing a defensive policy, instead of an offensive one, which could be manifested mainly by the quantity as well as the quality of the weapons procured. A state that buys more weapons than it needs, or that seeks to introduce offensive weaponry in its armed forces clearly invites suspicion because "mobilization [is] a declaration of war; [and] to mobilize [is] to force one's neighbor to do the same..." (Vagts 398). In its effort to consolidate its defense capabilities, the state would provoke its neighbors to take security precautions by adopting the same policy of acquiring more weapons, thus creating the vicious circle of acting to increase one's security only to find itself more threatened by the reaction of one's neighbors.

As survival has been the major objective of all states, the issue leads the discussion to the inference that states ought not to stop seeking power because increasing security necessitates the strengthening of one's power vis-à-vis potential enemies. This can be achieved by consolidating military capabilities, maximizing economic competitivity to secure resources, and last but not least, balancing unbeatable adversaries by entering alliances; thus getting into the balance-of-power game. States balance each other "not because they enjoy the process of checking each other, but because for each state its power in relation to other states is ultimately the key to its survival" (Waltz 210). Hence, if your own survival depends on the weakness of others, reason dictates that you have to work to keep them weaker than you, which guarantees a state of competition for more power among states, each seeking to achieve survival by acquiring more power than other states. Therefore, and by this token, conquering or even destroying your weak neighbor in a pre-emptive strike becomes an act of self-defense. This is not surprising in an international environment wherein states are eyeing each other with suspicion and fear.

The principle of self-reliance and its attendant sense of mutual distrust between states emanate from the presumption that one's neighbor is a potential threat until it proves that it is not. And till it does so, a state ought to prepare for war, even a pre-emptive one, which is a military attack launched in the belief that the adversary is poised to attack, and that it is advantageous to strike first. Historically, pre-emption is an old concept; there has been no legal requirement that a country wait to be attacked before it can effectively deal with physical threats because the right of anticipatory "self-defense" is older than the nation-state system of the seventeenth century. As far back as 1625,

Francis Bacon wrote in his essay "Of Empire" that: "A just fear of imminent danger, though there be no blow given, is a lawful cause of war" (qtd in Williams et al. *The Dictionary of 20ᵗʰ Century Politics* 709).

If a country does not strike when its potential enemy is weak, it could be struck later when the balance of power shifts in favor of the other side. As long as there is a potential security threat,

> everyone, having no guarantee that he can avoid war, is anxious to begin it at the moment which suits his own interest and so forestall a neighbor, who would not fail to forestall the attack in his turn at any moment favorable to himself, so that many wars, even offensive ones, are rather...for the protection of the assailant's own possessions than a device for seizing those of others (Rousseau 91).

Preventing a potential enemy from getting as strong as you are can guarantee one's preponderant position, and also eliminate security risks in the future. Frederick S. Dunn said: "So long as the notion of self-help persists, the aim of maintaining the power position of the nation is paramount to all other considerations" (13). Thus, it seems that states' offensive actions are dictated by the circumstances in which they all interact. Since September 11, 2001, for instance, the United States seems to have returned to George Shultz's 1984 doctrine, which emphasizes the idea that the U.S. policy toward perceived security threats "should go beyond passive defense to consider means of active prevention, pre-emption, and retaliation" (qtd in Williams et al. The Dictionary of 20th Century Politics 607). Shultz, in this context, said: "If there is a rattlesnake in the yard, you don't wait for it to strike before you take action in self-defense" (11). Even before the 1980s, the United States had contemplated dropping the atomic bomb quickly before a likely opponent had time to make one of his own.

Pre-emptive war, however, should not be confused with preventive war. Actually, there is a thin line of time and will between preventive and pre-emptive action; the difference is essentially one of time. In a preventive war, hostilities are intended to stop not an impending attack but one that is likely to occur in the future. During the Cold War, Francis P. Mathews, U.S. Secretary of the Navy, advocated preventive action in 1950 against the Soviet Union. He said: "A preventive war against the Soviet Union would win for us a proud title - we would become the first aggressors for peace" (qtd in Williams et al. *The Dictionary of 20ᵗʰ Century Politics* 709).

As advanced before, the paradox, which is endemic to international relations, is that in the process of consolidating its self-defense, a state sends alarming signals to its neighbors about its intentions, and therefore arouses in them fear and suspicion. In his account of the Peloponnesian War between Athens and Sparta, Thucydides said: "What made war inevitable was the growth of Athenian power and the fear which this caused in Sparta" (Thucydides 358-59). Although Athenians and Spartans had been allies against the invading Persians, they became arch-enemies simply because Athens' growing power after the defeat of the Persians was taken in Sparta as a warning that the Athenians could direct their military power against the Spartans. Existing side by side without a higher authority to impose standards of conduct, Sparta felt threatened by any actual or perceived increase in Athens' power. A more recent example of how the sense of threat often pushes states to ally with a stronger one to make up for their weaknesses was the 1950 Sino-Soviet Alliance. Mao Zedong wrote in June 1949: "it was the possibility of military intervention from imperialist countries that decided the necessity of China allying itself with socialist countries" (Chen 65).

Once again, the blurred lines between defensive and offensive doctrines, and consequently the possibility of confusing them mainly in times of tension between countries, have always been a factor of instability in international relations. To think of Japan's sense of vulnerability and insecurity within the post-Cold War regional context, for example, one can understand Japan's military and political moves as purely defensive, but taking into account Japan's WWII behavior towards its neighbors, the latter's suspicion about and mistrust of Japan's intentions are also understandable because Japan seems to have departed from its constitutional and legal constraints on armament and defense spending. Therefore, the Japan case study, as a country that has confused between what is offensive and defensive, is worth examining to demonstrate that these are purely subjective terms, though they are well-recognized concepts in political science.

Within the controversy of defensive-offensive weaponry, Japan's Self-Defense Force is an example that speaks for itself. Over the last three decades, military observers (Sasae 8-31) have pointed to the contradiction between the clear meaning of Article 9 of Japan's Peace Constitution, and the invincible force Japan now maintains, which is strong enough to enable Tokyo to project its power, if it chooses to do so, in the Asia-Pacific rim (Bergner 188). Recent Japanese interpretations of Article 9 have made it possible for Japan to undertake "any" military program as long as it is called "defense." Theoretically,

Article 9 reads: "The Japanese people forever renounce war as a sovereign right of the nation and the threat or use of force as a means of settling international disputes ...Land, sea and air forces, as well as another war potential, will never be maintained." Practically, Japan's Self-Defense Force (SDF) numbers nearly 246.000 men. This so-called defense force also includes surface-to-ship and surface-to-air missiles. The Japanese Navy now possesses more than 62 surface combatants, 16 submarines and antisubmarine aircraft, and minesweeping helicopters (Bergner 176-80). Moreover, Japan produces 99 percent of its own naval vessels, 89 percent of its own aircraft, 87 percent of its ammunition, and 83 percent of its firearms (Phillips 104).

Therefore, the question here is how to account for this clear departure from the spirit of Japan's peace constitution, and whether this is going to set a precedent for future Japanese military initiatives. The Japanese argument, however, is that all ground, naval and air forces Japan now maintains are in accordance with Japan's SDF created in 1952 under American dictates, and in harmony with Article 51 of the U.N. Charter, that every nation has the right to self-defense. But this does not answer the contradiction between Japan's actual military forces and the latter's clear interdiction as clearly specified in the Japanese Constitution. And even if the argument of self-defense is accepted, there is still another ambiguity about Japan's military capabilities. Though some military deployments are clearly offensive in nature, such as Hitler's war in Europe, it still needs soul-searching to distinguish between what is offensive and what is defensive. Actually, "the difference between offense and defense is, in the end, more a difference of intention and doctrine than one of capability" (Bergner 173).

However, the quality and quantity of weapons which states procure do not give an accurate sense of others' intentions. Excessive levels of weapons do not necessarily lead states to believe that their respective neighbors are planning aggressive actions against them. It could simply show a level of obsession with security rather than an intention to gain preponderance. But defense budgets do provide some evidence about whether a state's intentions are defensive or disguisedly offensive. Japan, for instance, though its defense expenditure is usually under 1 percent of its GNP, standing at $ 4.795 billion in 1993, for instance, according to the provisions of its "Peace Constitution", comes third in its defense budget after the United States and Russia. China's military spending, however, is approximately 5 percent out of a GNP of $ 554.9 billion (Dibb 26-29). Comparing China's and Japan's defense budgets, it is clear that the Japanese spend at least four to five times more than the Chinese on their military capability. This dichotomy should be viewed in light of the fact that Japan is believed to be on the defensive, seeking to minimize its security vulnerability, whereas China is allegedly said to be preparing for a more assertive posture in East Asia in the post-Cold War era. This is neither true nor accurate because Japan's GNP is almost 7.2 times the size of that of China, making the Japanese 1 percent defense budget much higher than China's estimated 5 percent (Dibb 30-32), which makes the boundaries between what is offensive and defensive more blurred.

Moreover, the consensus that Japan should not spend more than 1 percent of its Gross Domestic Product (GDP) on defense, initially devised to mute criticism over the huge Japanese military force, is a rubber stamp because this principle has not been observed, at least over the last decade or so. Japan's current defense budget at approximately U.S. $ 42 billion is almost 1.5 per cent of its GDP. According to Jeffrey T. Bergner, "leaving China aside, Japan spends more on its military than North Korea, Vietnam, Taiwan, South Korea, Australia, the six ASEAN countries, and all smaller nations in the region combined" (174).

Equally important, self-defense does not allow Japan to sign collective security agreements to defend other nations, but just security agreements that defend Japan only. The 1951 Treaty of Mutual Cooperation and Security between the United States and Japan was signed in the midst of the Cold War to balance the 1950 Sino-Soviet alliance, which targeted the growing American "intrusion" into Asia's regional affairs. But the gap between the wording of a treaty and its interpretation remains subject to political realities which are event-driven in nature. Moreover, the 1969 Nixon-Sato Communiqué was a clear violation of the "only-security-agreements-that-defend-Japan" principle. The communiqué reads, "the security of Taiwan is of utmost importance to Japan", which was an overt Japanese support of Taiwan and an unwarranted intrusion into China's internal affairs, from Beijing's perspective.

Again, such commitment to Taiwan's security was repeated in the February 2005 U.S.-Japan SCC meeting, which declared that the Taiwan problem was now a "common security challenge."[14] For the first time in Japan's post-World War II history, Tokyo expressed such an overt and radical shift in its foreign policy and marked a clear departure from Article 9 of Japan's Peace Constitution not to commit itself to defending any other nation through

---

[14] Ministry of Foreign Affairs of Japan, "Joint Statement: U.S.-Japan Security Consultative Committee", February 21, 2005.

treaties or any other form of alliance. This departure triggered a prompt response from China that Japan's alliance with the U.S. was no longer a defensive treaty but an offensive one that could bring East Asia to the brink of war, given the sensitivity of the Taiwan problem for the Chinese.

In conclusion, the controversy about defensive vs. offensive postures has remained one of the issues that have bedeviled international relations since the early days of nations and communities. It all depends on the intention rather than on the rhetoric or the political discourse of decision-makers. As the debate about whether pre-emptive or preventive wars are right or wrong from legal, moral, and conventional viewpoints, continues, it shows the determining impact of states' security calculations in their dealings with others. It also demonstrates the importance of power relations between units interacting within a system characterized by competition for power and obsession with security.

But security and power as core concepts are not the only reasons for war and conflict; states are also ready to go to war to control energy resources. Oil and arms are almost the only items that have remained outside the World Trade Organization's jurisdiction (WTO). Even states that are self-sufficient in energy have shown an endless appetite for more "dominions" to ensure that supplies continue to flow into their reserves. Among the reasons why Japan attacked Pearl Harbor in 1941, for instance, were the U.S. military measures to block Japan's sea lanes of energy supply (Liu 76). The 1991 and 2003 U.S. wars in Iraq are also two interesting case studies about the importance of and the struggle over oil resources in the Gulf.

1.3. Energy Security

President Franklin D. Roosevelt concluded more than half a century ago that America's welfare depended upon open markets but mainly on free access to energy resources. He said: "…it is our hope…that trade and commerce and access to materials and markets may be freer after this war than ever before in the history of the world" (Winkler 27). Without the free flow of oil, the United States fears the specter of economic depression and military decline (Lemco and MacDonald 290). In the 1970s, the Japanese economy was 60 percent the size of that of the U.S.; by the end of the Cold War, it was more than 69 percent (Bergner 214-16). Thus, ensuring the free flow of energy supplies has become a top national security priority in the post-Cold War era because the U.S. objective in East Asia that no country in the region could equalize America's level of power is not achievable without the control of energy resources.

The energy issue between China and Japan became one of the basic pillars of their relationship after the end of the Cold War because it encompassed economic, security, and political calculations. Japan, as one of the poorest countries in raw material fortunes, largely depended, and still depends, on foreign oil and gas, which further deepened its dependence on the United States to guarantee the continuation of the flow of energy resources from the Middle East across the contentious South China Sea. As for China, its booming economy, rapid urbanization, and the Chinese people's growing appetite for cars increased the country's post-Cold War demand for oil and natural gas. "Twenty years ago, China was East Asia's largest oil exporter. Now it is the world's second-largest importer; last year, it alone accounted for 31 percent of global growth in oil demand" (Zweig and Jianbai 53). As the workshop of the world, China's increasing need for electricity and industrial resources more than doubled from 1990 to the end of the 2000s. "China's combined share of the world's consumption of aluminum, copper, nickel, and iron ore more than doubled within only ten years, from 7 percent in 1990 to 15 percent in 2000, and is likely to double again by the end of the decade" (Ibid).

China's major industrial infrastructure is based on the coast where there are very limited natural resources. It was estimated that China would be a larger consumer of petroleum than Japan by the year 2010, relying on 40% of those needs on overseas imports (Harrison 272). The supply of energy was likely to become a major constraint on China's economic growth. Justin Yifu Lin, Director of the China Center for Economic Research at Peking University, in Beijing, says, "the country's economy could grow at 9 percent per year for the next 20 years" (Zweig and Jianbai 25), so China could continue to feed its 1.3 billion people. To keep pace with its increasing energy needs, China became a net importer of oil in 1993, which accounts for only 25 percent of its energy needs. Since then, Chinese import levels kept steadily growing, passing 1.6 million barrels a day in 2001. China's imports reached nearly 4 million barrels a day by 2010 and 7 million by 2015, close to the United States import level then (Harrison 274).

The enormous untapped oil and gas resources existing in contested areas in the East China Sea and the South China Sea, however, should reduce China's dependence on costly imports from far away and unstable sources such as the Arabian Gulf, Southeast Asia, and even African states. In its hunt for foreign energy resources, China has been courting the governments of these states aggressively, building goodwill by strengthening bilateral trade relations, awarding aid, forgiving national debt, and helping build roads, bridges, stadiums, and harbors. In return, China has won access to key resources, from gold in Bolivia and coal in the Philippines to oil in Ecuador and natural gas in Australia (Zweig and Jianbai 26).

In East Asia today, as China and Japan need growing petroleum imports for their respective economic survival, intransigence on either side regarding pending energy issues can trigger a serious crisis in the Sino-Japanese relationship (Durkee 4). To highlight the importance of energy issues in states' relations, a case study will be undertaken in order to shed light on the Sino-Japanese conflict over the jurisdiction of the Senkaku Islands, or what the Chinese call Diaoyu, which are a group of eight islets 200 miles off the Chinese coast in the East China Sea that are currently occupied by Japan but claimed by China (Harrison 272). The controversy about jurisdiction rights between Tokyo and Beijing, particularly in the East China Sea, clouded the Sino-Japanese interaction with doubts (Prescott 23). The East China Sea, and to a lesser extent, the Sea of Japan, contain rich natural gas and oil reserves (Valencia 8-11). The most promising areas lie in the central portion of the highly contested continental shelf in the East China Sea, where gas and oil reserves are respectively estimated to range from 175 trillion to 210 trillion cubic feet[15] in volume and as high as 100 billion barrels of oil[16] (Harrison 272).

As for coal, which then represented 68 percent of China's energy consumption, whereas its deposits are located in the north and west, China's energy demand is centered in the southern and eastern coastal provinces (Ibid). Beijing started seeking to raise the share of natural gas in its energy mix to 10 percent by 2020 through increased domestic gas production (Winterford 369-98). China's drive for more gas as its economy rises explains why Beijing dramatically stepped up its sea exploration and production in the East China Sea in the 2000s decade, where geological assessments indicate that the massive reserves in the area consist largely of gas (Harrison 277).

---

[15] Saudi Arabia has "proven and probable" gas reserves of 21.8 trillion cubic feet, and the United States, 177.4 trillion, Far Eastern Economic Review, 26 Apr.1990, 8.
[16] Saudi Arabia has "proven and probable" oil reserves of 261.7 billion barrels, and the United States, 22 billion, Far Eastern Economic Review, 26 Apr.1990, 8.

A 1968 United Nations survey mission had reported a "high probability that the continental shelf between Taiwan and Japan may be one of the most prolific oil and gas reservoirs in the world" (The United Nations Convention on the Law of the Sea', U.N. Doc. A/CONF 62/121, Art.76, 10 December 1992). But the bitter controversy between China, Taiwan, and Japan over seabed jurisdictional rights was always a major obstacle to exploration in the contested areas. Despite the July 2002 Taiwan-China agreement to start joint exploration in the Taiwan Strait, the China-Japan dispute over jurisdiction in the areas concerned held latent danger to regional stability.

Therefore, the energy stakes in East Asia would inevitably have a deep effect on the intraregional interaction, and the only way out for Japan and China was to resort to their "respective" offshore oil and gas fields in the East China Sea around and under the oil-rich Senkaku Islands. Since November 1980, China had claimed that the "entire East China Sea continental shelf, extending eastward nearly all the way to Okinawa, as a "natural prolongation" of the Chinese mainland", as defined in the U.N. Law of the Sea Treaty (Calder 130), while Japan asked for a median line, almost 100 miles west of the Okinawa. Historically, Japan was the first Asian country to occupy the chain in the early years of this century (Harrison 272). Japan also claimed the Senkaku chain, based on its "discovery" of the islets in 1884. Tokyo had annexed these islands in 1895, roughly at the same time it took Taiwan from China after the 1894/95 Pigtail War.

A Japanese government survey estimated that "well over 94.5 billion barrels of quality oil were trapped in the area to the northwest and south of the Senkakus" (ibid), whereas Chinese drilling activity found that abundant petroleum riches lie in contested areas, inviting potential tension between the two countries over areas regarded as vital by the Chinese and the Japanese alike, and leading to a standstill similar to that between Francis I and his brother-in-law Charles V when their desire for a common goal made war between them inevitable. The major reason for the permanent state of belligerency between them, Francis I once explained, was "simple"; he said: "None whatever. We agree perfectly. We both want control of Italy" (Schuman 261)

Given the high economic and political stakes involved in the quiet struggle over seabed petroleum resources, especially in the East China Sea, the China-Japan conflict over the Senkakus testified to the complexity of East Asian post-Cold War dynamics. Beijing has mounted its pressure on Japan for negotiations on joint exploration and development arrangements which would give China a share of the petroleum resources on the Japanese side. Japan, however, still insisted on a median line, and did not budge from its position. As for China, when diplomatic leverage failed to pay off, Beijing responded by sending survey ships across the hypothetical line, stirring diplomatic contentions between the two countries.

In the 1990s, China even used military force to seize the Senkakus, as Beijing was acutely aware of its vulnerability as an oil importer, while geological surveys suggested the presence of substantial oil and gas reserves around the islands (Harrison 273). The recurrent sovereignty standoffs over the East China Sea jurisdiction controversy brought China and Japan to the brink of a military showdown in 1995 and 1999. In a law unilaterally defining its maritime boundaries, Beijing formally incorporated the Senkakus as Chinese territory, and sent, in August 1995, Chinese fighter planes on a patrol mission over the islands; an act that was immediately encountered by Japanese jets, triggering a tit for tat episode in an already fragile Sino-Japanese relationship (Harrison 277). In May 1999, after Japanese rightist groups planted a Rising Sun flag on the Senkakus, Beijing encircled the islands with 10 naval vessels for a week, accusing Japan of seeking hegemony in the East China Sea (Ibid). Moreover, from January 1998 through August 2000, according to Japan's Maritime Self-Defense Forces, China sent 16 ships into areas on the Japanese side of the median line on 22 different occasions.

More recently, in November 2004, a Chinese nuclear-powered submarine intruded into Japanese waters near Okinawa for more than two hours, "ostensibly by accident" (Calder 130). Later, in September 2005 and on the eve of the Japanese parliamentary elections, Chinese warships started patrolling one of the most controversial gas fields, the Chunxiao field (Ibid). Although Beijing has declared its readiness to explore cooperative arrangements with Tokyo for the joint exploration and development of contested areas, China continued to claim the entire continental shelf as its own, rejecting Japanese proposals to negotiate "a median line" in accordance with principles stipulated by the 1994 U.N. Law of the Sea Treaty. Indeed, China proceeded with its own exploration and development program in contested areas, while periodically reminding Japan of its claim to the entire shelf by sending survey vessels across the hypothetical line close to the highly contested seabed surrounding the Senkaku Islands.

As for the U.S. stance regarding the Sino-Japanese contest for sovereignty over the Senkaku Islands, U.S. regional interests were another variable to be taken into account, as it might further complicate the chances of a peaceful resolution of the conflict[17]. The 2006 Armitage report places the United States firmly on Japan's side, while Robert Zoellick, the U.S. Assistant Secretary of State, seemed more careful about how Washington should balance its relations with Beijing and Tokyo (Przystup et al., "Visions of Order: Japan and China in U.S. Strategy" 3). As Deputy Secretary of State, Armitage declared that the U.S.-Japan Security Treaty covered territories administered by Japan, extending to the disputed Senkaku Islands. Though acknowledging that the Senkaku Islands did not involve core U.S. interests, the report recommended that the U.S. stood by Japan in its dispute with China, which was manifested by the joint exercises conducted in January 2006 by the U.S. Marines and elements of the Japanese Ground Self Defense Force which focused on the defense of unspecified remote islands. Therefore, China's growing insatiability for energy resources was causing concern in Tokyo and Washington, as it could tell where China's energy strategies were heading.

Thus, the resolution of seabed jurisdictional disputes will depend on broader political developments in the region and power relations among the three major corners of East Asia's post-Cold War triangle, but especially those between China and Japan. As Sino-Japanese economic interdependence further deepens, the prospects for seabed petroleum cooperation could improve considerably, and political and military tensions between Beijing and Tokyo over the controversy of jurisdiction in the East China Sea might ease in the long run, if spared foreign intervention in their bilateral differences, and if they started to look at each other's neighbors that would inevitably have to work together, instead of working at cross purposes.

The oil-rich Senkaku/Diauo Islands case study demonstrated the complexity of the issue of energy security in states' relations, particularly in the Japan-China connection and subsequently in the full equation of the post-Cold War U.S.-Japan-China triangle. It shows that the resolution of energy contests depends to a large extent on the power relations between the parties concerned. The fact that China took unilateral measures in the South or East China Sea meant that the regional balance of power was in China's favor, as the United States would hardly go to war against China because of Sino-Japanese

---

[17] For more on the U.S. interests in both the South and East China Sea, see 'United States Security Strategy for East-Asia Pacific Region', U.S. Department of Defense, Office of International Security Affairs, Washington D.C, 27 Feb. 1995. See also 'the United States Government Policy on the Spratly Islands and the South China Sea', American Enterprise Institute, Washington D.C, 1999.

skirmishes over the Senkaku jurisdiction. But the diplomatic cover-up of China's moves in the South and East China Sea substantiated Beijing's prudence in pushing too far, because U.S. energy and security interests in the region were very important in China's power and security short-term as well as long-term calculus. As China was seeking to boost its bilateral relations with resource-rich states, and sometimes striking deals with unfriendly nations to the United States such as Iran and the Sudan, Washington and Tokyo were more and more looking at the issue from the "spheres of influence" perspective, which was a divisive discourse reminiscent of the Cold War Soviet and American spheres of interest.

As a matter of fact, the "Oil-slick" Sino-American equation is another variable to consider in the energy triangular contest between China, on the one hand, and the United States and Japan, on the other hand. More than 45 percent of China's 2004 oil imports came from the Middle East, America's energy turf (Zweig and Jianbai 28). By the first decade of the twenty-first century, Iran alone accounted for more than 11 percent of China's whole oil imports. Tehran and Beijing agreed that Iran would supply China with 150,000 barrels of oil per day for 25 years and at market price (Ibid 29). In Africa, Beijing embarked upon what was called "China's Safari Diplomacy" to expand its traditional connections with the Third World, which it claimed it represented for 20 years (Kurlantzick 1). As of 2004, the three African nations of the Sudan, Angola, and the Congo supplied 28.7 percent of China's oil imports.

In Latin America, Monroe's "Western Hemisphere" doctrine, and in Canada, the Sino-American simmering energy contest seemed relentless. In the former, China "was now the main impetus for export growth for many Latin American states", as Beijing allocated $ 20 Billion in new investments for oil and gas exploration during the Chinese President Hu Jintao's visit in November 2004 to four Latin American nations (Ibid). In Canada, China sought access to Canadian energy resources in places such as the massive tar sands of Alberta, which the American Vice President Dick Cheney emphasized as vital to U.S. energy security in his 2001 report Zweig and Jianbai 31). In 2004, Beijing and Ottawa signed a package of energy agreements whereby China was granted the right to develop Canada's gas, oil, and uranium deposits, which was interpreted by the U.S. State Department as China "treading on what Americans perceive as their turf and vying for resources they also covet, [and] Beijing was stepping on some very sensitive toes"; certainly, America's energy toes (Ibid).

In conclusion, as China continued to rise economically, its energy needs kept increasing in proportion. And as China needed more and more energy, it would continue to work to secure energy resources across continents and deep in the seas, leading to more simmering energy competition between the US and Japan, on the one side, and China, on the other side. Subsequently, the energy contest between the three legs of East Asia's twenty-first-century triangle almost necessarily resulted in more security problems, adding to the region's security complexities, as the hunt for energy among the three nations pit them against each other in the Middle East, Africa, Latin America, and even in North America. While China was building strategic trade and energy relationships along the sea lanes from the Middle East to the South China Sea, the United States was said it occupied Iraq in order to dominate its energy resources and use them to undermine OPEC's politicized oil prowess, while Japan relied on American guarantees to secure oil shipments to the Japanese economy.

1.4. Summary

Since this chapter was meant to provide a review of the literature on the power and security concepts as the two main dependent variables around which this book revolves, it also expanded into revisiting some controversial terms like defensive and offensive posture in international relations. Furthermore, it is an opportunity to revisit the three major schools of thought in political science, which are realism, neo-realism, and offensive realism, respectively pioneered by Hans J. Morgenthau, Kenneth Waltz, and John J. Mearsheimer. These are the schools that provide the theoretical framework of this book and guide the analysis of the post-Cold War triangle of the United States-Japan-China from the prism of their respective power and security calculations in order to explore the nature of the U.S. military presence in East Asia as a negative or positive security factor in the region.

The findings of this chapter should clarify the understanding of the major differences between the three main schools in political science- realism, neo-realism, and offensive realism. My personal communication with **Interviewee 1**, the founder of offensive realism, which not only calls on states to seek just power but also to seek hegemony as well, ought to provide significant theoretical insight into Chapter Four as to why the United States went hegemonic in East Asia. This chapter also expands the scientific scope of this work because it paves the way for the structure as well as the theoretical framework of the next chapter, as it discusses a second school of political realism that does not agree with Morgenthau's argument that states seek power because human nature is selfish and predatory. Otherwise, the limitation of the theoretical framework to only classic realism and neo-realism, without expanding the analysis into offensive realism, would have distracted from the effort to revisit controversial concepts such as offensive and defensive wars, for example. This chapter shows that the difference between such vague concepts is one of intention rather than of military preparation.

Finally, the case study of the fermenting China-Japan conflict about sovereignty issues over the oil and gas-rich Senkaku Islands in the East China Sea highlighted the fact that security was not only physical and military, but it also encompasses energy security, which was as vital to economies bereft of natural resources like the Japanese economy, as to increasingly demanding economies like the Chinese. Serious sovereignty issues interwoven by historical enmities, and exacerbated by political and security antithetical calculations, were indeed a liability, rather than an asset, to East Asia's security. This was the security that the United States claimed it was protected by its military presence in the region, and by its alliance with Japan, as Washington was claiming it was playing the role of a pacifier in the early decades after the Cold War, which prevented another Korean war or a military conflict across the Strait of Taiwan between Taiwan and Communist China.

Chapter 2

Theoretical Framework and Research Methodology

2.1. Introduction

As the literature review in Chapter One explored the dialectical link between the key concepts of power and security, and has shown the limitations of looking at the post-Cold War U.S.-Japan-China triangle through the prism of one single theory, this work adopts a combination of a realism-based analysis which stresses the power variable in states' interactions, and at the same time highlights the priority of the security variable in states' strategic calculations. It has, therefore, demonstrated the need for looking at this triangle through a model of qualitative and exploratory methodology using a combination of realist, neo-realist, and offensive realist approaches to international relations. It also develops an analytic model to explain the factors and motives that account for the U.S. policies in East Asia with respect to Japan and China since the end of the Cold War. The analysis of these factors should, in the end, clarify whether the post-Cold War U.S. military presence and its attendant political leverage in East Asia has played a positive or/and a negative security role in the region under study.

The first section of this chapter provides the theoretical framework which guides this work. It is a framework that is based on a recognition of power realities and power politics in international relations. The following section presents the analytic model that puts forward the possibility of a link between power and security in the interaction between the U.S., Japan, and China in the post-Cold War era. The last section of this chapter depicts the type of research design including the methodology of reading the data collected for this work.

2.2. Theoretical Framework: Power in a State System

As this book adopts a realist approach, it recognizes that power is the hinge of international relations. The adoption of this approach has been motivated by the fact that "the concept of interest defined as power imposes intellectual discipline upon the observer, infuses rational order into the subject matter of politics, and thus makes the theoretical understanding of politics possible" (Morgenthau qtd in Williams et al. *The Dictionary of 20th Century Politics* 456). It is an approach that also recognizes that the struggle for power acquisition is an innate feature of life in an international system of nation-states due to the anarchic nature of a system composed of units that are sovereign states, without a central ruling body.

This work adopts Hans J. Morgenthau's assumption that "international politics, like all politics, is a struggle for power. Whatever the ultimate aims of international politics, power is always the immediate aim. Statesmen and peoples may ultimately seek freedom, security, prosperity, or power itself" (Morgenthau 29). The concept of power, therefore, is central to Morgenthau's analysis whereby the essence of interactions between sovereign states in a system of anarchy is a "struggle for power". Morgenthau argues that, "the statesmen think and act in terms of interest defined as power" (Morgenthau 12). Accordingly, human nature is innately selfish and constantly engaged in a struggle for power. This would push "relations among nations, where the problems stemming from the inherent nature of human beings are compounded by the dynamics of a competitive environment" (Morgenthau qtd in Williams et al. *The Dictionary of 20th Century Politics* 455), to an unstable arena which is ripe for a constant contest for more power and more security.

John R.P. French and Bertram Raven suggest, in "The Bases of Social Power", that there are five major bases of power (Cartwright 1959). First, "expert power" is based on the perception that the leader possesses some special knowledge or expertise; second, "referent power" is based on the follower liking, admiring, or identifying with the leader; third, "reward power" is based on the leader's ability to offer rewards to the follower. Fourth, "legitimate power", which is based on the follower's perceptions that the leader has the legitimate right or authority to exercise influence over the other; and fifth, "coercive power"[1], which is based on the fear of the follower that noncompliance with the leader's wishes will lead to punishment. The relevance of this *deconstruction* of power

---

[1] Coercion: it is the step before using actual force to get what you want. It is the exertion of influence (not moral) through threats to inflict harm. Coercion can be direct or indirect. Direct coercion is the explicit threat to coerce the other into acquiescence. Indirect coercion is the implicit threat to make others change their behavior in the desired fashion. The U.S. blockade on Cuba in effect since the 1962 Missile Crisis is a kind of coercion. Chinese military exercises in the Strait of Taiwan can be considered as coercion.

stems from the fact that the third and the fifth definitions of power will be applied to the analysis of the power variable and its inextricable link to the second dependent variable of security in dictating the quality and the outcome of the interaction between the three-unit system composed of the United States, Japan, and China since the end of the Cold War.

In exercising power in East Asia, for instance, the United States has played the carrot and stick[2] game with China since the end of the Cold War, which applies the third and fifth kinds of power as defined by John R.P. French and Bertram Raven. The reward kind of power includes the carrot policy, and the coercive one encompasses the stick policy. In the 1990s, Clinton's "constructive engagement"[3] prescription was based on the vision of engaging the Chinese by talking to them instead of boycotting and trying to contain them, that is, giving them a stake in a positive interaction from which China would draw a great deal of economic benefits such as the badly-needed technology transfer and the then Most-Favored Nation status (MFN).

The United States was in a position to mediate rewards for China, such as highly needed technology transfer. Acquiring Western technology was one of Deng Xiaoping's Four Modernizations, which paved the way for the 1970s Sino-American détente. The U.S. provided China with "a direct stake in a beneficial relationship with the United States by offering it access to American production of technology" (Harding 163). In return, according to the Congressional Hearings Committee on National Security of the House of Representatives of the One Hundred Fourth Congress, March 20, 1996, which dealt with the "Security Challenges Posed by China", China was asked to put on hold exporting missile technology to the Middle East, refrain from coercing Taiwan, and pressure North Korea into a more accommodating posture regarding

---

[2] Carrot and Stick: It is an old-new term describing a U.S. foreign policy that is based on a reward/punishment vision. If the target state "cooperates", it will receive economic, political or even military rewards. If it refuses to acquiesce, it has to be coerced into compliance. The carrot and stick policy includes coercion and inducement.

[3] Constructive engagement: this term refers to the U.S policy towards the Apartheid regime in South Africa in the 1980s. President Reagan argued that doing business with Pretoria, that engaging its political leaders, would lead to policy change from within the regime. It was later used by Clinton's National Security Advisor Anthony Lake in a Speech at the Johns Hopkins School of Advanced International Studies on September 21, 1993.It is the "pragmatic policy of engagement, of expanding areas of cooperation with China while confronting differences openly and respectively", Foreign Policy Bulletin, January/February 1998, vol.9, no.1, p.39.

Pyongyang's nuclear programs, which were perceived as a threat to American allies in the region, particularly to Japan.

The U.S. Secretary of State in the 1970s, Henry A. Kissinger, said: "Power is the ultimate aphrodisiac" (*New York Times*, October 28, 1973). This definition of power takes the analysis back to the fifth base of power of coercion and hegemony advanced by French and Raven because it can apply to the context of the U.S.-Japan-China triangle in the post-Cold War epoch. The United States, as the only remaining superpower has used its political power to coerce the Japanese economically by extracting from them economic concessions relating to tariffs, the car industry, and the large American trade deficit with Japan. "We got rooked a bit on commerce from time to time…they still have a very large trade surplus with us, and they got big hard foreign exchange."

Indeed, "trade and economic frictions are certainly not new in the post-Second World War history of Japan-U.S. relations" (Sasae 32)[4]. It was clear to the U.S. that Japan, partially dependent on American security guarantees in a region having the biggest number of territorial disputes and historical enmities in the world[5], was in no position to stand against the will of its protector. "For Japan, North East Asia remained a volatile and dangerous region, one in which Japan lacks real friends. For the United States, the alliance was the foundation of its regional and global strategies- the ability to project power and meet security commitments to Japan" (Przystup, "China and the U.S.-Japan Alliance", lecture 2000). Using one's political leverage to extract concessions in other areas willingly and unwillingly was a use of power politics or coercive power to dictate the direction of the U.S.-Japan interaction in favor of the United States.

As a matter of fact, the view of the United States using coercive power in East Asia was also advanced in China during the 1990s and after. According to James J. Przystup, China believed that the main objective of the American military presence in the region in collaboration with a half-a-century alliance with Japan was to contain China and negate its program of military modernization. Przystup said:

---

[4] For more on the analysis of Japan-U.S. economic frictions from a Japanese negotiator's perspective, see Yabunaka, Mitozi. Economic Negotiations with the U.S.: Real picture of Frictions. Tokyo: The Simul Press, 1991.

[5] For a detailed study of the origins and consequences of East Asia territorial claims, particularly in the South China Sea, see Marwyn S. Samuels, Context for South China Sea, 1982, London, Methuen. Also, "The Republic of China's (Taiwan) Sovereignty over the Spratly Islands", a document issued by the government of the ROC, 30 April 1993.

Since the [1996] Clinton-Hashimoto summit, the Revised Defense Guidelines, the agreement to cooperate on Missile Defense Research, Beijing is coming to see the intensifying alliance security cooperation as serving ultimately as a constraint of China's freedom of action... in East Asia (Ibid).

Japan's official pro-alliance stand, however, perceived the U.S. military presence in East Asia as an essential factor in providing security for Japan, even though the American military presence there since the end of the Cold War served America's interests of ensuring a constant U.S. dominance in the region by checking China's growing power and holding Japan in a dependent position. But it is safe to argue that one of the main reasons why China was deterred from invading Taiwan in March 1996, for example, was the sending of two U.S. aircraft carriers – the Independence and the Nimitz-into the Strait of Taiwan after China fired M-11 missiles at targets close to Taiwan's two busiest ports. A senior Chinese foreign affairs specialist said in an interview with Richard Bernstein and Ross H. Munro in 1996, "in history, the Chinese leaders have believed in force...it is realpolitik" (Bernstein and Munro 152). A few years after the collapse of the Soviet Union, "some Chinese analysts complained that now [1996] there was no regional balance of power, and that their military growth could restore a balance" in the region (Wolf, "Don't Give in to China's Tantrums" qtd. in Nye, "The Nye Report: Six Years Later" 96). Moreover, the 37,000 American soldiers along the demilitarized zone between North and South Korea have deterred another Korean war, which could paralyze the region's outstanding economic success and the free flow of oil from the Gulf states to Japan and South Korea. Accordingly, the U.S. military presence in East Asia since the early 90s may be a positive security factor, as the success of a political order is usually measured by the absence of actual wars.

In line with this theoretical framework, the U.S. claim that it played a positive security role in relation to Japan and China since the early 90s could mean different things for the three nations concerned. For the United States, a balance of power in East Asia meant a balance in America's favor, which implicitly referred to a state of "imbalance" for China, North Korea, and Russia (Mathisen 80-144); for the Chinese, however, the United States was not balancing Japan and China but it allied with Japan to contain a potential Chinese ascendancy to power in the region. Japan, in its turn, did not see things from the same angle of vision. For Tokyo, the American military presence in East Asia was a legal issue because the U.S. was, and still is, legally bound by the 1951 Security Treaty to protect Japan, by the 1953 Korean truce to secure South Korea, and by the 1979 Taiwan Relations Act to defend Taiwan's security.

As Interaction outcome, another explanatory variable, is usually determined by the relative distribution of power between the U.S., Japan, and China (Dibb 54), it depends heavily on the "degree of coercion that could be exercised by the parties on each other" (Burton 230). As the anarchic nature of the international system is the most important cause of war, Waltz argues that "with many sovereign states, with no system of law enforceable among them, with each state judging its grievances and ambitions according to the dictates of its own reason or desire--conflict, sometimes leading to war, is bound to occur" (159).

Moreover, Kenneth Waltz argues that the balance of power within the international system has a major impact on both the stability of the system and the actions of the units within it (Waltz 198). The balance of power invokes the idea of an equal amount of quantifiable and non-quantifiable variables between two states, like China against Japan, or two groups of states, such as the U.S. and Japan against China. The state of balance of power or terror during the Cold War between the U.S. and its allies, and the USSR plus its Eastern European satellites, is also another example.

This would lead one to think of a balance of capabilities, but the concept of balance of power is much wider than this interpretation. This concept could also refer to an "external" balancer trying to maintain a state balance of power, be it military or economic, between two states or two groups of states so that the balancer would gain more leverage on both sides that do not trust each other but accept a "neutral" judgment in case of contentions between them (Williams et al., *Classic Readings* 206). This means that the balancer needs to create an imbalance, that is, a balance in its favor, in accordance with T. Mathisen's argument that the "basic strategic interest, notably for great powers, is to work for a favorable balance of power" (126); a balance that is certainly favorable to their own strategic interests.

Therefore, since this book is a study of the U.S.-Japan-China triangle as an international-relations case, it is methodologically imperative that it proceed by looking at this triangle from the prism of concrete action and reaction within the theoretical framework of alignment of the three nations concerned. China, for instance, reacted to the revision of the U.S.-Japan alliance in 1997; Chinese Foreign Ministry Spokesman, Shen Guofang, warned that "any attempt to have a security arrangement going beyond its bilateral character would certainly be cause for vigilance and concern by other Asian nations"(Mufson 16). Also, Japan became nervous about North Korea's 1993 and 1998 missile tests because "the North's Scud-derived missiles now ha[d] an extended range - the latest being tested [wa]s able to cover most of Japan. And if the North could fit this missile with a nuclear warhead, the implications for Japan's security would be very serious" (Sasae 4-5). A Japanese commentator said to the *New York Times*: "Japan alone cannot handle China, Japan alone cannot handle a unified Korea, and Japan alone cannot protect its sea lanes - so for all these reasons [Japan] has needed the U.S. alliance" (Bernstein and Munro 167). Therefore, it is safe to assume that the security interests of individual states in East Asia in the first two decades following the collapse of the ex-USSR were inextricably linked to each other, which is not unusual in an interaction between a group of states operating within a chronically-unstable environment.

As a conclusion, it is significant for this work to have revised the concept of power, and highlight its significance in governing relations between sovereign states interacting within an environment of anarchy. Doing so has helped this book understand more deeply and analyze further how power and security calculations governed the United States-Japan-China triangle in the post-Cold War first two decades. Going through Raven's five categories of power and applying them to the U.S.-Japan-China interaction, should bring a better picture of the workings of the triangle under study, leading to the need to explore the linkages between the concepts of power and security, which are here the key dependent variables of this book.

2.3. The Analytic Model

The main assumption underlying this model is that power and security are key variables to understand the rationale and the logic of interactions within the three-unit system of the post-Cold War U.S.-Japan-China triangle. States interact on the basis of the distribution of power among them (Burton 1986), and on how they perceive their respective security interests. An equal distribution of power between states could make their interactions more balanced and more prone to compromise. As a result, in the pursuit of their own interests, states generally recognize the "need for joint action in order to achieve [a modus vivendi] in circumstances wherein neither party feels able merely to impose his own demands upon the other" (Gulliver 181). The resulting "strategic interdependence" from a theoretical parity of economic, military or political power between the United States, Japan, and China, for instance, would make "the ability of one participant to gain his ends, dependent to an important degree on the choices or decisions that the other participant will make" (Schelling 5). Strategic interdependence, however, does not necessarily substantiate the idealists' argument about the "natural harmony" of interests between states, as advanced by the Kantian universalist tradition, which sees at work in international politics a potential community of mankind (Williams et al., *The Dictionary of 20th Century Politics* 20).

2.3.1. The Argument

This work argues that power and security are crucial variables in determining the quality and the outcome of interactions between states within an international system characterized by an absence of an overriding central authority. The distribution of the inventories of power, (or the balance of power), and the security calculus, together with the parties' perceptions of each other, are determining factors in international relations in general and since the end of the Cold War in particular [6]. This reminds us of the old Chinese aphorism which reads that "the country that has no enemy in mind will perish" (Mao Tse-Tung 13).

Accordingly, the perception of their respective interests and the realities of the balance of power between the United States, Japan, and China since the end of the Cold War had a deep impact on the behavior as well as the outcome of interaction between them[7]. These are the key variables that, in interconnection, have dictated the rationale and the outcome of interactions between the three states under study. In short, this work offers a power-political or a realist and security-first (neo-realist) explanation of the U.S.-Japan-China relations in the post-Cold War epoch[8].

---

[6] The White Paper on China's National Defense issued by the State Council, July 1998, qtd. in "The Chinese Armed Forces in the 21st Century" edited by Larry M Wortzel, Strategic Studies Institute, U.S. Army College, December 1999, 7.

[7] For more on this, See Yimin Song, "On China's Concept of Security", UNIDIR, Geneva, 1986, U.N. Publication Sales No.GV.E.86.0.1.

Hearings of the Committee on Armed Services of the House of Representatives, the One Hundred Sixth Congress, July 19, 2000, and the National Security Strategy of the United States of America, September 2002.

"Public Opinion In America and Japan" by Everett Carl Ladd and Karlyn H. Bowman, 1996, the Roper Center for Public Opinion Research , University of Connecticut, Storrs, Connecticut.

[8] See Joseph S. Nye, "The Nye Report: Six years Later, International Relations of the Asia Pacific, Vol.1, 2001, and Paul Dibb, "Towards A New Balance of Power in Asia", ADELPHY PAPERS, Paper no. 295, 1994.

2.3.2. Dependent Variables: Power and Security

The dependent variables of the model adopted by this work relate to the shape and the rationale of the post-Cold War U.S.-Japan-China triangle, with a focus on the first decades after the end of the bipolar international order. Power as a non-quantifiable variable refers to the elements of strength combining military, economic, and political degrees of leverage on other states to make them change their policies or behavior. It also includes the important element of how the units concerned perceive their power relations and how they seek to perpetuate a system of a balance of power that is in their own favor. Moreover, the security variable plays a determining role in foreign policy design for states. After all, survival, instead of power acquisition or projection, has always been the priority of nations since the 1648 Westphalia Peace Order (Waltz 159-60, 167-70, 183-84).

The process of simulating power and security in a three-unit triangle like the one between the United States, Japan, and China can result in either stability or disturbance, and in more or less security. Stability occurs when the three parties can find common ground for compromises through the process of bargaining about issues relating, for instance, to the U.S.-Japan strategy to anticipate China's intentions as a rising power, Japan's growing military involvement in world affairs as the 1997 revised version of the U.S.-Japan 1951 Security Treaty clearly shows, and China's intentions on how to deal with a potential Taiwanese declaration of independence. This can happen only "when the actors adjust their conduct to the actual or anticipated preferences of others, through a process of "policy coordination" (Miller qtd. in Mathoma 62).

Interactions resulting in the stability of the system could be measured by an agreement on a bilateral or a trilateral issue, such as the reduction of the U.S. military presence in Japan or South Korea, China's controversial behavior in the East China Sea, and China's posture across the Strait of Taiwan. The disturbance of the existing system of power distribution, however, is the diametrical opposite of stability; it occurs when the actors fail to reach an agreement about a critical issue regarding the continuity of the system. Power is therefore dichotomous; states seek power either to maintain a favorable status quo, or to change the existing one. The second dependent variable of security is indeed dichotomous, since taking defensive measures to enhance one's security could be perceived by others as threatening offensive behavior (Lebow).

2.3.3. Independent Variables: The Balance of Power, and Interaction Outcome

The independent variables relating to power and security questions include first the balance of power between the actors concerned as a relative measurement of strength, physical and economic security within the existing international and regional environment (Lieber; Viotti and Kauppi), and second interaction outcomes in view of a power and security equation.

In dealing with the difficulty of measuring power, this work has adopted Jeffrey Hart's three approaches to measuring power in terms of its inventories: 'power as control over resources', 'power as control over actors', and 'power as control over events and outcomes' (Hart). Because states are involved in a struggle whose objectives are "to increase power, to keep power, or to demonstrate power" (Rourke 32), the independent variable of the balance of power, which explains how powerful one state is in relation to others, and therefore how much proportional leverage it has over them, is a determining factor in explaining the dependent variable of power as a core concept. Indeed, the distribution of power among states does explain their respective behavior as well as the nature of their interactions with each other. Both power politics and bargaining are considered a "power struggle with the outcome determined by the relative strengths of the parties in context" (Gulliver 187). Therefore, the post-Cold War U.S.-Japan-China interactions during the period under study will be analyzed through Hart's approach of quantifying and measuring power. The three states are seen as units involved in a struggle to 'control resources', 'control each other', and 'control events and outcomes' of their interactions with each other.

Perceived threats to the physical and economic security of Japan, China and the United States are a major explanatory variable used in this analytical model. Security as a subjective concept depends on the perception of who is threatened. Sometimes, states misunderstand their security environments by exaggerating their security risks or overreacting to perceived threats (Reynolds 44-5, 49, 54-57). "For some states, such as Switzerland, for example, security consists solely in defense of the metropolitan territory. For others security includes the defense of interests outside the metropolitan territory thought to be vital to its existence or to the welfare of its people" (Reynolds 55).

The U.S. war on Iraq in March 2003 is a good example of which the Bush administration tried to sell as a war against "terrorism" to defend American national security against alleged "weapons of mass destruction". In accordance with the realist theoretical framework adopted by this book, it is Hans J. Morgenthau's definition of security as "the survival of a political unit...in its identity as the reducible minimum, the necessary element of its interests vis-à-vis other units...its content...encompasses the integrity of the nation's territory, of its political institutions, and of its culture" (qtd in Olson and Sondermann 244).

Accordingly, the Sino-Japanese contest in the East China Sea, for instance, or over the problem of Taiwan, the U.S. attempts to "export" democracy to China, and the westernization of Hong Kong, all could be considered by Beijing as threats to the security of China (Kim 11), and therefore could be a good reason for the Chinese to take assertive measures to defend China's interests relating to these issues.

The judgment that states A is seeking power projection capabilities, or it is simply taking purely defensive precautions against perceived or real threats, is not possible without having the state concerned acting with or reacting to another state or an alliance of states. Interaction outcome between states is the second independent variable whereby we can simulate the first two variables of power and security to make them interconnect and interact so as to result in a desired outcome of cooperation or confrontation, and of bargaining or coercion. The study subsequently adopts Reynolds's definition of the notion of 'interaction' as the relative power of the unit, the costs-gains calculus, and the freedom of alignment (Reynolds 219).

2.3.4. The Proposed Linkages between the Independent Variables (the Balance of Power and the Interaction Outcome) and the Dependent Variables (Power and Security)

This work tries to relate the phenomenon to be explained (the dependent variables) to other explanatory phenomena (independent variables) by means of general laws or theories (Nachmias 59). "When we say that variable X and variable Y are related, we mean that there is something common to both variables" (Ibid); they go together and change together in a systematic way, which means that they co-vary, or it is a case of co-variation. "Establishing a relation in empirical research therefore consists of determining whether the values of one variable co-vary with values of one or more other variables, and measuring those values" (Ibid).

As far as this book is concerned, the combination of the inventories of power and the states' perception of their respective security interests in relation to the security environment where they interact hypothetically leads to the following assumptions:

1. States' interactions are governed by the distribution of power between the major actors and by the latter's perception of potential security risks.

2. The more powerful a state is, the more likely it is that it will adopt a competitive posture in interacting with others.

3. The weaker a state is, the more likely it will be willing to settle contentious issues diplomatically.

4. The more leverage a state has on other states, the more likely it is that it will play the role of a hegemon.

5. The more a state looks hegemonic, the more it becomes a negative security factor in the system.

2.4. Research Design

2.4.1. Introduction

The two basic purposes of any research design are to provide answers to research questions and to control variance. Therefore, the research design that this work adopts combines the descriptive approach and the structured, focused design (George qtd. in Mathoma 58). S. Isaac and W. Michael, in *Handbook in Research and Evaluation*, present the different purposes of these methods of research methodology.

First, the descriptive research aims at "describ[ing] systematically the facts and characteristics of a given population or area of interest, factually and accurately" (79), which should be used in dealing with the impact of the main drivers in East Asia, such as the U.S.-Japan alliance and the rise of China on the security equation in the region. Describing "factually and accurately" the inventories of power among the three countries concerned would help identify which side is seeking domination and which one feels it is threatened by the concerted effort of the other, or by the combined efforts of the other two sides. Finally, the structured, focused comparison approach combines "some features of the historian's methodology for intensive, detailed explanation of the single case" and the "aspects of the political scientists' conception for the requirements for theory and his procedures for scientific inquiry" (George qtd. in Mathoma 61). This method should be used in making a series of comparisons throughout this work between, for example, China's and Japan's significance to the U.S. strategic objectives of preventing the rise of regional hegemons, which may try to dislodge the United States from an allegedly preponderant position.

To address the principal question whether the U.S. presence in East Asia was a positive or a negative security factor during the post-Cold War first two decades, this work has mainly adopted the comprehensive method of structured, focused comparison "to study intensively the background, current status and environmental interactions" (Isaac and Michael 19-33) between the

U.S., Japan, and China interacting within "an unstable three-unit system" (Reynolds 217-18). Moreover, structured, focused comparison provides a theoretical focus, and thoroughly investigates each case by raising a combination of standardized as well as general questions. It therefore provides a guide for research throughout the two processes of data collection and data analysis (Mathoma 49).

These research objectives could only be achieved by formulating a set of guiding questions that will provide the appropriate framework for the process of explaining the impact of the two dependent variables of power and security on the interaction of the three units of analysis- the United States, Japan, and China- during the early decades after the end of the Cold War. The following questions will guide the examination of the post-Cold War U.S.-Japan-China triangle:

1. What were the main drivers in East Asia in the early post-Cold War decades? Who were the major actors in the region?

2. What were the respective interests and calculations of these major actors? What were the means available for each of them to achieve these interests? What was the actors' propensity for risk-taking policies to defend their interests?

3. What was the distribution of power among them? What were their power relations? What are their respective resources and capabilities? How powerful did the main actors see themselves then? How did they perceive their respective opponents?

4. How insecure did each one feel? Why? What did the terms "security" and "defense" mean for each actor?

5. What was the main source of the actors' clash of interests?

6. What was the main variable that governed their interactions with each other? Was it the maintenance of the existing system, the pursuit of more power at the expense of others, or the guarantee of their own security, be it economic, political or physical?

7. How strongly did they feel about unresolved regional issues?

2.4.2. Units of Analysis

Barry Buzan gives a definition of the units of analysis as "locations where both outcomes and sources of explanation can be located" (204). Although "international relations is heavily determined by the structure of the legal system and the decision-making apparatus within a nation, by role definitions, by power considerations, by external influences and by real conflicts of interests" (Kelman 2), this work adopts the state level of analysis, and uses Philip Alan Reynolds' model of the three-state system (Reynolds 217) in order to explain the interrelatedness as well as the interconnectedness between power acquisition and perception, and the quest for security among the United States, Japan, and China in the post-Cold War era. The choice has been motivated by the fact that the study of international relations as an academic discipline has been demarcated and considerably marked by two major historical developments that have stressed the idea of an international state system. Those historical events were the Westphalia Treaty and the Settlement of Vienna, respectively, in 1648 and 1815. The former established an international system of nation-states based on the principle of what later became known as Castlereagh's idea of "just equilibrium" or balance of power between a group of states to prevent any power or group of powers from gaining ascendancy (Gooch 390-93). It was for the first time that the 'State' was recognized as the determining factor in international relations, and thus made it possible to use the 'State' as a unit of analysis in political science research (Kaplan 16 qtd. in Reynolds 208). Reynolds wrote: "A system conceived as consisting of states as units and the interactions among them will, if skillfully defined and analyzed, assist in understanding the greater part of international occurrences" (207).

The focus, therefore, is on the 'State' as the unit of analysis which should enable this work to conceptualize the existing international system. Accordingly, this book examines the impact of the two core concepts of power and security on the interactions among the U.S., Japan, and China in the post-Cold War era: a triangle representing a sample of state system, with each state standing for one subsystem. The goals of the subsystems, which are critical variables in the study of the different state system models, cannot be achieved in a vacuum. States have to interact with each other in order to achieve their respective policy objectives.

This means that states' behavior is basically influenced by the environment in which they interact. If states exist in a stable and unthreatening context, they will probably try to seek more power to control and dominate each other. But if states exist in an environment of security risks, they will first try to fortify their own defenses and build their respective security. Thus, the different modes of interaction are normally dictated by the varying number of units, the varying unit capabilities, and the different foreign policy objectives of the units, that is, by the external environment within which states interact. Therefore, the use of variables such as power and security to analyze different levels of analysis, or the use of the independent variables of the balance of power and interaction outcome to explain the dependent ones, will be used throughout this work.

In short, this work assumes that the main units of action are sovereign states, and their exercise of power is dictated by their respective military, economic, and political strength in relation to each other. It also assumes that security can be achieved either by a set of defensive measures or by taking an offensive posture vis-à-vis others. So, what are the power relations or the distribution of power between the three countries concerned (balance or parity)? How does the distribution of power between the three states affect their respective actions and reactions to each other? How does power perception by the parties concerned influence their relative propensity to take risks of disturbing the existing system of power relations?

2.4.3. Data Collection

The sources of data required for the investigation of the research question include professional publications and literature in the form of books, articles and research projects in professional journals and prominent magazines such as *Foreign Affairs, Journal of International Affairs, International Relations, World Politics,* and *American Political Association.* Primary sources include a series of significant personal communications like interviews with the founder of the third school in political science, offensive realism, referred to hereafter as **Interviewee 1** and a prominent international scientific authority on Korean affairs at the University of Chicago, referred to hereafter as **Interviewee 2**. Primary sources also include meetings and discussions with His Excellency Wang Guangya, Permanent Representative of the People's Republic of China to the United Nations; former U.S. Assistant Secretary of Defense for International Security Affairs in 2006, former U.S. Assistant Secretary of State for East Asian and Pacific Affairs in 2006; Ambassador Wu Jianmin, Former Chinese Ambassador to France, the United Nations in Geneva, and former President of China Foreign Affairs University. The discussions took place during the China Conference at the University of Chicago on April 28 and 29, 2006. Available unclassified U.S. Congressional Hearings and Government Documents on the U.S. priorities and stakes in East Asia in general, and in relation to Japan and China in particular, can also be used as government documents and therefore, as official positions.

The U.S. Congressional Hearings include those of the Committee on National Security of the House of Representatives of the One Hundred Fourth Congress, March 20, 1996. This document deals with the "Security Challenges Posed by China"; it includes statements by prominent experts in Sino-American Affairs from the American Enterprise Institute and the U.S. Naval War College. The second government document used in this study is the Hearings of the Committee on Armed Services of the House of Representatives, the One Hundred Sixth Congress, July 19, 2000. These Hearings, which are taken from the Monthly Catalogue of U.S. Government Publications, related to the Chinese military capabilities as perceived by the United States. Some witnesses invited for this session included Douglas MacArthur from the U.S. Army War College and Dr. Bates from the Brookings Institution.

The choice of the data is dictated by the importance of the U.S. Congress in the foreign policy decision-making process. Section 8 of Article I of the American Constitution states that "Congress shall have power to ... provide for the common defense and general welfare of the United States.....[and] to raise and support armies...." As this quotation states very clearly the decisive role of the legislature in influencing and making American foreign policy by using the power of the purse or the appropriation prerogative, it is safe to assume that foreign policy making in the United States is a shared constitutional prerogative between the executive and the legislative, instead of being the exclusive responsibility of the National Security Council, although it is the latter that usually initiates and designs foreign policy ideas and plans.

Moreover, for the sake of diversifying data sources, the Pentagon's official view of the Chinese military capabilities and their implications for the balance of power in East Asia is studied here. The Pentagon's Army War College Strategic Studies Institute has provided military data on China and Japan, which has considerably influenced the post-Cold War U.S. policies in the region. The U.S. Army War College, in collaboration with the Strategic Studies Institute (SSI), publishes a monthly series to update the national security community on the research done on national and international security issues, and forthcoming publications as well as upcoming conferences sponsored or organized by the SSI. I have found these publications and monthly newsletters quite relevant to this research because of the great deal of influence that the SSI and its components of the U.S. Army College and the U.S. Naval War College have had on U.S. foreign policy and on America's strategic views of conflicts all over the world.

Furthermore, the American Enterprise Institute for Public Policy Research in Washington, D.C (AEI) and the Hoover Institution on War, Revolution and Peace in California have published a series of studies dealing with policy problems of current and future interest to the United States to evaluate courses of actions available to policy-makers. The AEI-Hoover policy studies have explored the question of whether Japan will rearm, and if it should rearm with nuclear weapons. The relevance of such a study to this work is so obvious that some reference to this study will be made from time to time.

Moreover, the data includes a document by the Journal of the Japan Association of International Relations, which is one of the main sources of information and advice for Japan's Prime Minister's Office. Japan's famous 1976 National Defense Program Outline (NDPO) marked a turning point in the pacifist post-World War history of Japan, and has put into question the credibility and the raison d'être of article 9 of the Japanese Constitution.

Finally, the use of multiple sources of evidence or what Lawrence Neuman calls "triangulation" is intended to enhance the construct validity of the data (Neuman qtd. in Mathoma 57). Triangulation should ensure construct validity by providing multiple measures of the same phenomenon, and thus enabling the researcher to examine an issue from various viewpoints. Besides, triangulation should improve the reliability of the measures by securing the "convergence of information from different sources" (Yin 96).

2.4.4. Data Analysis

Since the major purpose of this book is an exploratory one, it adopts a qualitative inductive research strategy. It begins with specific data and then develops general ideas to explain patterns in the data. As conceptualization is an important part of the process used to make sense of related observations, core concepts of power and security are broken down into manageable explanatory variables like the breaking of the inventories of power into military strength, and the defense-offense contrast.

A comprehensive outline of the phases of qualitative data analysis involves the description of the data and the processing of data collection, the organization/categorization of the data into concepts, the connection of the data to show how one concept may influence another, and the legitimization of the research hypothesis by evaluating alternative explanations and disconfirming evidence and searching for negative or null cases. The representation of the account (reporting the findings) is the last stage in the qualitative research process (Schutt 17-18-19).

Furthermore, developing 'theory' is a vital part of the process of qualitative research, occurring explicitly in interaction with data analysis (Coffey and Atkinson qtd. in Schutt 23). The goal of many qualitative researchers is to build up inductively a systematic theory, which is "grounded" in the observations, which are summarized into conceptual categories, and tested directly in the research setting with more observations. Over time, as the conceptual categories are refined and linked, a theory evolves (Glaser and St Huberman qtd. in Schutt 297).

Qualitative research approaches measurement[9] in a way that tends to be more inductive. Instead of deciding in advance which concepts are important for a study, what these concepts mean, and how they should be measured, qualitative research begins by recording what they see during observational sessions (Schutt 20). Once a variable's level of measurement is identified, how cases vary on that variable should become more comprehensible. The nominal level of measurement[10] (also referred to as categorical), which is qualitative in nature, identifies variables whose values have no mathematical interpretation, such as power and security, but they can vary in kind and quality. In fact, it is conventional to refer to the values of nominal variables as "attributes" instead of values. Although the attributes of categorical variables do not have a mathematical meaning and are known to be monolithic, they must be carefully conceptualized or broken down into manageable attributes such as the inventories of power (Reynolds 256-57-58).

Finally, this work also has the characteristics of descriptive research, which starts with data and then proceeds to the stage of making empirical generalizations based on those data. More importantly, descriptive motive means choosing the appropriate descriptive research strategy, which can be either qualitative or quantitative. The distinction between quantitative and qualitative methods basically depends on the type of data collected and on the research motive. Quantitative methods are most often used when the motives for research are explanation and description. They are based on deductive

---

[9] Measurement is a cornerstone of scientific research. To know a variable's level of measurement can help the researcher understand better how cases vary on that variable. It is the kind of precision "with which the values of a variable can be expressed" (Schutt 85). There are four levels of measurement: nominal, ordinal, interval, and ratio.

[10] The nominal (or categorical) level of measurement is most often used in qualitative research. It is used to identify variables whose values or attributes have no mathematical interpretation; they vary in kind or quality but not in amount (Schutt 86).

hypothesis-testing research, which proceeds from general ideas, deduces specific expectations from these ideas, and then tests the ideas with empirical data. Exploration, however, is most often the reason for using qualitative methods. Exploratory motive implies an inductive research strategy that begins with specific data and then develops general ideas to explain patterns in the data. However, researchers can use these methods for descriptive and evaluative purposes (Gubrium and Holstein qtd. in Schutt 17). Indeed, "explanations derived from qualitative research will be richer and more finely textured than they are in quantitative research, but they are likely to be based on fewer cases from limited area" (Schutt 45).

2.5. Summary

To conclude, this chapter presents the theoretical framework of this book. Equally important, it also states the analytic model and the argument of this work. Moreover, this chapter outlines the research design that is adopted to answer the research question of this work. The next chapter puts the post-Cold War U.S.-Japan-China triangle in the early decades of the new world order of unipolarity in its geostrategic context, within which we are now considering how the determining variables of power and security ruled the interaction between the three countries whose power and security calculations kept shifting after the end of the Cold War, and hence their respective positions on the chessboard of this triangle.

Chapter 3

East Asia's Major Drivers in the Post-Cold War Early Decades

3.1. Introduction

This chapter seeks to study the main drivers in the power-security calculus in the post-Cold War U.S.-Japan-China triangle, with a focus on the first two decades of the unipolar world order. These drivers primarily included the U.S.-Japan security alliance, and the military and political complexities it then added to East Asia's security dynamic, together with the China factor and its implications on the triangle under study. From a political science standpoint, when a security environment fundamentally changes or dramatically improves, alliances become irrelevant, and therefore tend to disappear (Organski 282-83, 286-90). But this is not necessarily true all the time; alliances can and do survive radical security developments, depending on the will and the interest of the parties concerned to invent a new rationale for their alliances. The post-Cold War U.S.-Japan security alliance is an interesting case study of how alliances can outlive their raison d'être, as it has outlived the Cold War itself, and kept gaining momentum despite the dissatisfaction of Japan's neighbors, namely China, North Korea, and even Russia (Garrette and Glaser). Unlike Japan's neighbors' expectations, the US-Japan alliance became stronger even after the end of the Cold War. It, therefore, elicited distrust and suspicion among major East Asian powers, which exacerbated, instead of improving, the post-Cold War security environment in the region.

But the major question was whether this alliance equally served the interests of both parties, that is, providing *security* to Japan and the United States alike against perceived regional threats emanating from North Korea's nuclear program, China's rising power, and to some extent Russia's nuclear remnants from the moribund Soviet Union. On the one hand, Japan felt under threat because it was handcuffed by Article 9 of its peace constitution, which prohibited Tokyo from having a standing army; on the other hand, the United States emerged as the sole superpower on earth after the demise of the Soviet Union officially in 1991, leading to an international security system of unipolarity rarely experienced before (Ikenberry, "Illusions of Empire" 144).

Moreover, given the 75,000 soldiers it still maintained in South Korea and Japan alone, the United States was then perceived by many nations in East Asia as a dominating power (Tuazon, "Current U.S. Hegemony in Asia Pacific", Lecture March 1, 2003). So, how could an alliance between the most powerful country in the world and a country that was dependent on the latter's security guarantees equally serve the interests of both sides?

3.2. The U.S.-Japan Alliance in the Complexity of the Triangle

3.2.1. The Paradox of More Power and Less Security

The history of the U.S.-Japan security relationship went back to the post-World War II period when the United States decided to end its direct military occupation of Japan in 1951. But Washington continued to dominate Japan's foreign and security policies through a series of security treaties and guidelines which, each time renewed or consolidated, provided Japan with less security and America with more power and preponderance in the Asia-Pacific region. The 1951 Treaty of Mutual Cooperation and Security between the two countries clearly stipulated that the United States was to provide security for a disarmed Japan. Article V of the treaty reads that "each Party recognizes that an armed attack against either party in the territories under the administration of Japan would be dangerous to its own peace and safety and declares that it would act to meet the common danger in accordance with its constitutional provisions and processes" (Japan's Defense Agency, "Basic Policy for National Defense, Tokyo, May 20, 1951), which was not consistently observed by the Japanese in view of Tokyo's expansion of its military and security prerogatives to Japan's "surrounding areas"[1] to the detriment of Article 9 of Japan's Constitution. Moreover, the 1978 U.S.-Japan Guidelines for Defense Cooperation stated that "the United States w[ould] maintain a nuclear deterrent capability" to defend Japan against a direct military attack, a blockade, and any other coercive actions, which also ran against a longtime Japanese public stand that it would not make, use, or allow nuclear weapons on its territories.

---

[1] See the 1996 U.S.-Japan New Defense Guidelines, the 1997 Clinton-Hashimoto Declaration, and he February and September 2005 U.S.-Japan Security Consultative Committee (SCC) statements. All these documents renewed the 1951 Security Treaty between the two countries, further consolidated their security relationship regarding the security situation in East Asia, and expanded Japan's security prerogatives from solely defending Japan's territory to Tokyo's full involvement in the "areas surrounding" the Japanese archipelago.

The end of the Cold War, however, exacerbated Japan's security problems because Tokyo was now facing a security dilemma whether to support a regionally controversial alliance with Washington, or to seek an independent solution to its own security shortcomings. If Japan chose the former, then it needed to justify such a posture for its suspicious neighbors. If Tokyo chose the latter, it would have to deal with a myriad of highly sensitive issues, such as Article 9 of the country's Peace Constitution, which states that "the Japanese people forever renounces war as a sovereign right of the nation and the threat or the use of force as a means of settling international disputes...Land, sea and air forces, as well as other war potential, w[ould] never be maintained." Equally important, Japan's neighbors' reaction to the prospects of Japanese rearmament and probably a revival of militarism like that of the 1930s, paradoxically complicated Japan's security calculus, and led to less security for Japan. But, "rather than developing policies that [we]re consistent with popular interests, Tokyo [was] working hard to convince the public to accept extensions to the Cold War security regime" (DiFilippo 21).

In the aftermath of the Second World War, Japan's defense policy rested on three basic principles: first, its peace constitution, and namely Article 9, which prohibited Japan from raising an army or developing offensive weaponry. Second, Japan adhered to the Charter of the United Nations, which was considered in Japan as a parallel constitution, but dealt with threats "on the basis of Japan-U.S. security arrangements, pending effective functioning of the United Nations in the future deterring and repelling" of security threats to Japan (Japan's Defense Agency, "Basic Policy for National Defense, Tokyo, May 20, 1957). Third, the security alliance with America was a basic pillar of Japan's defense policy to maintain regional stability for the foreseeable future. However, this section argues that this alliance paradoxically brought about less security for Japan and more power for the United States.

The post-Cold War security relationship between the United States and Japan was inextricably linked to the WWII outcome- Japan's WWII surrender to the United States. As a result, the U.S.-Japan relationship was always characterized by inequalities and asymmetries (Green 13-14), resulting in an unequal relationship that put Japan in the uncomfortable position of supporting an alliance that provided Tokyo with less security, given Japan's neighbors' opposition to this alliance, but provided the U.S. with more power and leverage in East Asia (Hiroshi 44-69). Now that the Soviet threat had disappeared, the United States came up with new threats in order to justify the continuation of the alliance and to keep Japan on board (Ch. Johnson 152). Since the early 1990s and well into the twenty-first century, Washington followed the tactics of fear and exaggeration to magnify the combined Sino-North Korean threat to Japan and to the stability of East Asia at large. Accordingly, China and North Korea were labeled as potential threats to Japan's security and to U.S. regional interests alike (Cossa 6).

As a matter of fact, if the U.S.-Japan alliance aimed at maintaining stability in East Asia, stability remained a mirage for more than five decades during the Cold War. On the opposite, tension, overt military confrontations, blockades, and eventually an arms race characterized the lifetime of the alliance in question. From the Korean War, which dragged over two years after the 1951 U.S.-Japan Security Treaty, to the 1964-74 Vietnam War, and the 1964 Chinese nuclear bomb, along with the Sino-American proxy military confrontations over Taiwan and the Quemoy and Matsu Islands (Rehaiem 28-52), the U.S.-Japan alliance exacerbated the already precarious security situation in East Asia. This clearly made it a destabilizing variable in the region's political and military equation, leading one to conclude that it was indeed a negative rather than a positive security factor in East Asia. After all, the U.S.-Japan alliance did not prevent North Korea from developing nuclear weapons programs publicly and clandestinely despite the 1994 U.S.-North Korea Agreed Framework. Pyongyang eventually tested its first nuclear bomb on October 6, 2006, leading to more security risks not only for Japan, but also for East Asia at large.

Moreover, the U.S.-Japan alliance did not slow down Pyongyang's relentless efforts to develop and "proliferate" missile technology, and launch in August 1998 a projectile over Japan. It also did not stop the Chinese from firing mid-range missiles across the Taiwan Strait during a series of military exercises aimed at disrupting Taiwan's 1996 and 2000 presidential elections, leading President Clinton to dispatch two aircraft carriers to the area, which conversely could have posed further threats to Japan's security in particular and to the region's stability in general, had a Sino-American military confrontation across the Strait of Taiwan taken place.

As a matter of fact, the U.S.-Japan alliance was always asymmetrical, for the American-Japanese relationship was not equal either in principle or in practice. "Because Japan's dependence on the U.S. was almost total in the security area and also heavy in the economic field, America was in a position to be able to exert a decisive influence on that country's international policy" (*Shinbun* 6). The alliance was distracted from Japan's sovereignty and prevented the country from having an independent foreign policy that was conducive to a more secure Japan and a stable Asia, regardless of Japan's potential militaristic tendencies.

For more than sixty years, it was the U.S. that took the initiative in planning and dictating security policies in the Asia-Pacific region. Ever since the 1951 U.S.-Japan Security Treaty and through the 1997 New Guidelines for the U.S.-Japan Defense Cooperation, notwithstanding the degree of incrementalism in Japan's discretion regarding Tokyo's security prerogatives over the years, Japan gained less security, but paid more funds for America's perceived protection, and got less leverage in bilateral economic and trade disputes. Paradoxically, Japan was at the same time the object of increasing suspicion from its neighbors, namely China and North Korea. "Beijing [was] emphatic about its belief that the strengthening of the U.S.-Japan security arrangement introduced instability and imbalance in the Sino-American-Japanese relationship" (DiFilippo 9-10). Besides keeping Japan in a dependent position, the asymmetries in the American-Japanese connection created more security risks for Japan, given the Sino-North Korean perception of Japan's association or even complicity with the dominant United States as threatening to their security interests, leading Beijing and Pyongyang to adjust their respective security calculations and behavior (Shambaugh 59-79) to the changing character of the US-Japan alliance.

The 1990s versions of the U.S.-Japan alliance consolidated the U.S. upper hand in Japan's security matters and subsequently further strengthened Washington's preponderant position, at least in East Asia. The 1995 and 1997 revised versions of the U.S.-Japan security treaty, though expanding Tokyo's security responsibilities and discretion, did not touch upon the core of the asymmetrical nature of the bilateral relationship between the two nations-Japan's dependency on security and foreign affairs. Moreover, some Japanese revisionists argued that the expansion of Japan's security responsibilities in the region was a mixed blessing because it further antagonized Japan's neighbors, mainly China, North Korea, and Russia. Consequently, Japan's newly acquired security prerogatives made the country a more potential military target should an American military confrontation with Pyongyang over the latter's nuclear programs, or with Beijing across the Taiwan Strait, take place ("Militarism Brewing in Japan", *China Daily*, September 25, 2000).

Furthermore, the expansion of Japan's regional role according to the 1997 New Defense Guidelines to include the provision of logistical and even military support to future American wars, even in "areas surrounding Japan" ran against the spirit and the letter of Article 9 of Japan's Constitution. Thus, Japan's peace constitution unequivocally emphasized not only a Japanese commitment not to have a standing army, but also not to participate in regional or world conflicts, whether with or against the United States. Certainly, this constitutional and moral contradiction had its political, security, and economic costs for Japan in the post-Cold War era, such as more security hazards from North Korean missiles and potentially more rapid military modernization in China.

Substantial improvements, however, in the security environment in East Asia took place during the 1990s, first between the United States and North Korea, following the signing of the 1994 nuclear Agreed Framework, which averted an American-North Korean military showdown in Northeast Asia; second, between Japan and China after the Chinese President Jiang Zemin's historic visit to Japan in 1998, and third between Tokyo and Pyongyang in March 1995, when members from key Japanese and North Korean political parties met in Pyongyang and called for a resumption of normalization talks.

However, Washington traditionally sought to maintain a regional threat environment during the 1990s and well into the first decade of the twenty-first century simply because a stable Asia was not in America's strategic interest of perpetuating a U.S.-dominated status quo. From the U.S. perspective, "unifying the Korean Peninsula, [for instance], and improving relations among the United States, Japan, [China], and North Korea [would] made it difficult to maintain American troops" in East Asia (DiFilippo 8), leading to the conclusion that the U.S. military presence and stability in East Asia were indeed incompatible in the American power and security calculus.

Regarding regional interaction, the U.S.-Japan alliance maintained a self-complacent and even introverted posture regarding East Asia's attempts at multilateralism. The alliance kept the same Cold War mentality of distrust and, more importantly, an exaggerated reaction to Japan's neighbors' policies as well as an uncompromising approach to their respective security concerns. Though Japan and the U.S. officially supported ASEAN's 1994 security apparatus–ASEAN Regional Forum (ARF)[2], for instance, which comprised 23 nations then,

---

[2] ARF was created in 1994 by member states in the ASEAN. After the inclusion of Cambodia in 1995, India and Burma in 1996, Mongolia in 1999, and the Democratic People's Republic of Korea in 2000, ARF's membership stood at 23. ARF has officially sought to "foster constructive dialogue and consultation on political and security issues of common interest and concern.... and to make significant contributions to efforts towards confidence-building and preventive diplomacy in the Asia-Pacific region" (Association of Southeast Asian Nations Web site at <www.aseansec.org/3530.htm>). As ARF has failed to play the role

including the United States, Japan, Russia, China, South Korea, and North Korea, Tokyo and Washington made very little effort to strengthen or endorse the ARF because they attached more importance to their bilateral alliance than to any other regional security mechanism which could undermine or replace the preponderant U.S. security role in the area. This showed a U.S.-Japan agreement that "multilateral security in the Asia-Pacific region [was] something to support publicly; it [was] not something that either Washington or Tokyo ha[d]gone out of their way to promote and develop" (DiFilippo 7).

One can go further to argue that the United States even abused Japan's security vulnerability to increase its military power and political leverage in Asia. Since Washington always needed a new raison d'être for its future military presence in East Asia, it had to find or invent a new regional threat in order to justify both the continuation and the expansion of its alliance with Japan (Ch. Johnson 152). Tokyo, however, believed that its alliance with the United States could be a deterrent against imminent threats, probably from North Korea, but it turned out that the existence of the alliance per se, let alone its consolidation since the end of the Cold War, paradoxically provoked more tension with North Korea and China, which threatened Japan's security, rather than promoted stability in East Asia.

To substantiate America's interest in keeping a threat environment alive in East Asia, two Pentagon Reports in January 1992 and February 1995 ought to be highlighted. Regarding the former, it was believed that North Korea's January 1993 decision to deny access to the International Atomic Energy Agency (IAEA) inspectors to two main sites suspected of being used for nuclear waste was indeed a reaction to the bellicose 1992 Pentagon Report towards Pyongyang. The report stated that North Korea's "quest for nuclear weapons capability continu[ed] to be the most urgent threat to security in Northeast Asia" (Office of the Assistant Secretary of Defense, 'A Strategic Framework for the Asian Pacific Rim', 1992).

These allegations, however, were rejected by Pyongyang, which argued that the United States was inventing excuses to rationalize an attack against North Korea, with Tokyo's financial and logistical support (*Korean Central News Agency*, December 2, 1998). North Korea "consistently charged complicity on the part of Japan and South Korea in that both countries have been willing to

---

of that of NATO in Europe as a stabilizing forum, it has been used by the United States to talk to 23 participating foreign secretaries on the same occasion.

support the military plan of the United States to take control of North Korea" (DiFilippo 81). A couple of months after the 1992 Pentagon Report, and on March 12, 1993, North Korea announced its intention to withdraw outright from the Nuclear Nonproliferation Treaty (NPT). Two months later, Pyongyang launched a Rodong missile, which landed in the Sea of Japan, indicating North Korea's sophisticated delivery capabilities, and creating security repercussions in Tokyo.

What was disturbing for the Japanese were the contradictory accounts of Japan's Defense Agency's conclusion that the missile did not fly over Japan, and the U.S. confirmation five years later that the missile might have crossed over Japanese territory (*Japan Times Online*, October 23, 1998). This was in line with the consistent policy on the part of the United States to exaggerate perceived threats in order to ensure Japanese compliance, while paradoxically putting Japan's security in jeopardy (*Japan Times Weekly International Edition*, March 30-April 5, 1998, 3).

The second Pentagon Report of 1995, generally known as the Nye Report, was issued less than three months after the October 21, 1994, U.S.-North Korean Agreed Framework. According to this framework, Pyongyang agreed to freeze its nuclear program. In return, the United States would provide financial assistance for the construction of two civilian light water reactors in North Korea, and lift its economic embargo on Pyongyang. According to this report, China and North Korea were transformed not only to a major justification but also to the major justification to continue the U.S.-Japan security alliance. The report also recommended that Washington and Tokyo had to be on the alert for all signs of Beijing's attempts to destabilize East Asia or threaten American security interests in the "areas surrounding Japan". Situated more than 5000 miles away from China and North Korea, one would wonder how U.S. security can be directly threatened by the Chinese or North Koreans; if they really posed a security threat in the first place, it would be to Japan's security, and not to that of America. In short, the U.S.-Japan alliance put Japan's security in jeopardy, as Tokyo lost more chances of a peaceful modus vivendi with its neighbors (J. Wang 29-44).

Moreover, the 1995 Nye Report, besides asking for greater transparency in China's military intentions and political strategies, characterized North Korea as a potentially destabilizing security factor in East Asia. The report stated:

North Korea's history of aggression, threats to peace, and exports of missile technology created a context in which its development of nuclear weapons would be an extremely dangerous threat to security on the Peninsula, in Asia, and for global non-proliferation. At the same time, North Korea's conventional military threat to the Republic of Korea did not abate, and requires continued vigilance and commitment of United States forces [3].

Nevertheless, Japan still wanted to ally itself with the United States, perceived by Pyongyang and Beijing as hegemonic, threatening, and arrogant (Mufson). Japan did not show so far any sign of voluntary disengagement or at least keeping the alliance status quo as it was during the Cold War, or expressed readiness to work with its neighbors in matters relating to the region's complex security issues. On the opposite, Japan continued to share American views on East Asia politics that the Cold War containment policies had to give way to measured *diplomatic* engagement of China, and to a hardline approach to North Korea's nuclear and missile programs, which continued "to be the most urgent threat to security in Northeast Asia" according to the February 1995 Nye Report. Thus, Japan's neighbors' negative reaction to its alliance with Washington resulted in more tension, rather than more stability, which was against Washington's goal to market its alliance with Tokyo as a stabilizing security factor in the region.

Moreover, North Korea's security concerns arising from the hostile premises of the U.S.-Japan alliance led to a serious nuclear standoff in 1994 between the Clinton administration and Pyongyang, which almost brought the region to the brink of a military confrontation that could have involved other Asian countries such as Japan and South Korea[4]. The North Koreans, afraid of America's military presence in the region, and seeking to ensure a modicum of security, started drawing fuel from the Yongbyon nuclear reactor[5], raising more suspicion about its nuclear intentions, and triggering another security problem for Japan

---

[3] Office of the Assistant Secretary of Defense for International Security Affairs-East Asia and Pacific region- 'United States Security Strategy for East Asia-Pacific Region, Washington D.C., Department of Defense, February1995, p.18.

[4] "U.S.-North Korean Confrontation Causing Rifts in Tokyo and Seoul", Asia Intelligence Update: Red Alert, Austin, TX: Stratfor, a private intelligence-gathering company, December 9,1998.

[5] U.S. Department of defense, "United States Security Strategy for the East-Asia pacific Region", Report of Office of International Security Affairs, Washington, D.C.: Government Printing Office,2000.

because of its link to an alliance which North Korea suspected of preparing an invasion against its territory under the code name of "Operation Plan 5027."[6]

Though the October 1994 Agreed Framework between the United States and North Korea, brokered by former President Jimmy Carter with the full sanction of the Clinton administration, led to a period of calm, it was an accord without teeth because it lacked good faith. Pyongyang did not trust America's words, and Washington again had no interest in taking the pressure off North Korea or in easing tension in the region. Anthony DiFilippo said that "despite the existence of the Agreed Framework and KEDO, Washington continued to paint the picture of a nuclear weapons threat from North Korea" (31). It was a concerted U.S. effort to continue to exaggerate allegations about Pyongyang's threat to the security of East Asia in general and to Japan in particular, and subsequently to justify the need for the U.S.-Japan security alliance.

For North Korea, it was not a mere coincidence that this accusatory report mentioned that "Japan's new global role involve[d] a greater Japanese contribution to regional and global stability" (DiFilippo 10), and paved the way for possible Japanese involvement in future regional military conflicts, leading Pyongyang to conclude that Tokyo was becoming an American accomplice to dominate East Asia and threaten the security of North Korea. Thus, Japan became a potential target of North Korean missiles and even nuclear weapons due to its association with a suspicious alliance with the U.S., whereas America's power in the region was further reinforced by a stronger Japanese commitment to this alliance, a commitment that was expressed by many Japanese officials such as the President of Japan's Military Academy Makota Iokibe (Iokibe, "Japan- the U.S.- China: Toward a True Partnership", Lecture 2007).

While the end of the Cold War prompted Japan to seek an international political and military role commensurate with its economic and technological prowess, Tokyo's decision to move closer to the United States, instead of looking out to its neighbors for an inclusive and comprehensive regional security management, was detrimental to Japan's security. The North Korean and Chinese perception of Japan conspiring with the United States to dominate East Asia resulted in less security for the Japanese, and more power leverage for Washington. The anti-Japan perception in East Asia was further deepened by the concerted U.S.-Japan efforts during 1996 and 1997 not only to strengthen

---

[6] "Operation Plan 5027", Korean Central News Agency, December 14,1998; "'Operation Plan 5027' Carried into Practice", Korean Central News Agency, December 20,1998.

their bilateral alliance but also to review the 1978 Guidelines for the U.S.-Japan Defense Cooperation, which so far governed the alliance rules and the security relationship between the two nations (Walker 20). The June 1996 twenty-second meeting of the U.S.-Japan Security Consultative Committee (SCC) apparently answered Japan's quest for more security responsibility by expanding Tokyo's regional security role, but certainly secured more American political and military power. Moreover, the 1997 Guidelines for U.S.-Japan Defense Cooperation stipulated that "both Governments w[ould] conduct bilateral work, including bilateral defense planning in case of an armed attack against Japan, and mutual cooperation planning in situations *in areas surrounding Japan*" (italics added).

These new guidelines expanded the scope of Japan's maneuvering room in matters of military and security responsibilities because they opened the door for Japan for the first time since WWII to support American troops in future wars in Asia, thus shifting the forty-year Japanese commitment from protecting a disarmed country to *maintaining regional stability* in "the areas surrounding Japan." But, as this chapter partly tries to demonstrate, Japan's new security responsibilities, sometimes called 'privileges', were detrimental rather than beneficial to the country's security[7].

Tokyo's new role in the 1997 defense guidelines was fiercely opposed by Japan's neighbors, mainly North Korea, China, and Russia. Those countries felt that Japan's working with the United States was a rejection of regional security arrangements such as the Association of Southeast Asian Nations (ASEAN), whose initial aim was to safeguard the region against great power rivalry, and to act as a forum for the resolution of intraregional differences. "Both China and North Korea [have] become deeply concerned with what they perceived as a potential military threat emerging in Japan. South Korea also became quite uneasy with these changes, as would Russia" (DiFilippo 42).

China emphasized its position that the United States was indeed seeking to exercise hegemonic control over the East Asia-Pacific region, and alleged that Japan was being enlisted to support this effort. Japan's alleged support of a U.S. 'hegemonic' role in East Asia was perceived in Beijing as a prelude to the resurgence of pre-WWII Japanese militarism. "Tokyo's reaffirmation of the security alliance with the United States increase[d] Chinese angst by bestirring

---

[7] Joint Statement, U.S.-Japan Security Consultative Committee, Completion of the Review of the Guidelines for U.S.-Japan Defense Cooperation, New York, September 23, 1997.

bad memories in Beijing of Japan's militarist past, and specifically, its military aggression against China" (DiFilippo70). China viewed that Washington and Tokyo together presented a far more destabilizing challenge to Chinese regional security interests than any other country, and always expressed deep concern over Japan's expanding security role in areas surrounding Japan after the end of the Cold War. China's President Jiang Zemin said that "Taiwan should not be covered by the new guidelines" (*Beijing Review* 42, no.41, October 11, 1999). China's security concerns included primarily the problem of Taiwan, its territorial disputes over the Spratly Islands with more than ten Asian nations, and over the Senkaku Islands with Japan. Moreover, Beijing feared that Japan's new role could increase the chances of a potential American intervention in a China-Taiwan military confrontation.

The security reverberations which terms like "situations" and "surrounding Japan", etc. in East Asia, were more threatening to Japan's security than to America's because they prompted fears in Pyongyang that Japan's new regional responsibilities would provide the United States with discretionary power to play the role of a hegemon in the region (Asia/Pacific Research Center, Stanford University, May 1998). Pyongyang accused the U.S. and Japan of coercion. The North Koreans alleged that Washington and Tokyo "entered a phase of attaining their wild design on a full scale to gain supremacy over Asia by means of a military solution" (*People's Korea*, October 8, 1997).

Interpreted by North Korea as a step in the direction of Japan's new posture of remilitarization, "Pyongyang became very worried and... reacted harshly to the new guidelines for defense cooperation between Japan and the United States" (DiFilippo 47). On August 31, 1998, North Korea stunned the Japanese and the Americans as well when it suddenly, and without prior notice, launched a missile that flew over Japan, though Pyongyang later announced that it had launched a civilian satellite and not a missile.

While the North Koreans initially withheld any information about the incident, Washington and Tokyo jumped to the conclusion that the projectile was a Taepo Dong 1 missile. As late as the end of October 1998, Japan's Defense Agency still maintained that the launch was a ballistic missile, despite the fact that two weeks after the incident, the Pentagon secretly informed the Japanese that the launch was indeed a North Korean attempt to put a satellite into orbit. Though it turned out that the launch was indeed a projectile, the incident per se scared the Japanese, but was exploited by the United States to remind Japan of the future need for the alliance to protect the country, thus maintaining the favored condition of a threat environment.

Japan's Former Prime Minister Keizo Obuchi admitted that "the recent missile launch by North Korea, even if it was an attempt to launch a satellite into orbit, poses a serious problem, which directly concerns both Japan's national security and peace and stability in Northeast Asia" (Statement by Obuchi at the Fifty-third Session of the U.N General Assembly, New York, September 21, 1998). It was clear that Tokyo learned how to keep this threat environment, as it continued to argue until very late that it was a missile and not a satellite, and then said that even if it was a satellite, it still posed a threat not only to Japan, but also to the region at large, thus exaggerating the North Korean threat, and consequently increasing the chances of acceptability of the U.S. military presence in East Asia.

In America, "the Department of Defense stressed that, although it was a satellite, North Korea's action should still be seen as a threat since it showed that its technological achievements could present a security problem" (DiFilippo 46), without specifying whose "security problem" it was. But if the incident was ever a "security problem", it was indeed a Japanese problem. From a Sino-North Korean perspective, Japan was responsible for the regional tension and this "security problem" in Northeast Asia because of its link to a threatening alliance with the United States; a country perceived to be seeking more power and hegemony in the region (Korean Central News Agency, September 26, 2000). This supports the claim of this chapter that the post-Cold War U.S.-Japan alliance brought about more security problems for Japan because it was perceived by its neighbors as an American tool to bring East Asia under control by maintaining the same threatening impression in order to keep a frightened Japan on board. Therefore, the Pentagon's confirmation that North Korea's launch was a satellite with no evidence supporting a military objective clearly contradicted the U.S. emphasis on the North Korean threat to the stability and security of East Asia, which leads the discussion to point out to a definition problem, instead of a "security problem" between the United States and Japan's neighbors.

It was not clear, however, who represented a threat to whom, because China, North Korea and Russia believed that the U.S. military presence in East Asia was a negative security factor (DiFilippo 13-33). "Since the U.S.-Japan security alliance was a bipolar rather than a multipolar structure- which was advocated by China, Russia, and North Korea– it represented a real or at least a potential threat to them....it [is] increasingly perceived by China, North Korea, and Russia as a destabilizing, or at least threatening, regional force" (DiFilippo 13). Washington, however, maintained that its alliance with Japan was a stabilizing rather than a threatening security factor in the region, since the alliance had succeeded in preventing a Chinese military invasion of Taiwan, and a North Korean attack on South Korea.

Furthermore, the joint military exercises in East Asia in 1998 by the U.S., South Korea, and Japan had their security repercussions all over the region. Those exercises took place in the midst of an inspection crisis in October/November 1998 when Washington asked for unrestricted access to North Korea's underground nuclear sites, which was interpreted by the North Koreans as a prelude to the implementation of an American secret war strategy dubbed as "Operation Plan 5027" to invade North Korea, with military and logistical support from Japan and South Korea. During President Clinton's 'suspicious' visit to Japan in November 1998, the Japanese newspaper *Shankei Shimbun* reported that Bill Clinton confidentially told Japan's Prime Minister Obuchi that in case Pyongyang refused to allow full and free inspections, Washington was ready "to consider military action against [North Korea]'s threat" (*Asia Intelligence Update*, December 9, 1998).

Clinton's visit, characterized by the North Koreans as a "final checkup" mission, created a security crisis which, regardless of Clinton's secret or declared purpose, again revealed how much security issues in East Asia were intermingled. Following bellicose signals from the United States, North Korea emphasized the fact that security problems ought to be looked at comprehensively, instead of trying to isolate or neutralize one country politically or militarily. Pyongyang made it clear that in case the U.S. carried out Operation Plan 5027, North Korea would target not only the "U.S. aggression forces who chiefly execute the 'Operation Plan 5027' but also South Korean authorities who were willing to serve as their bullet shield, and Japan and all others that offer bases or act as servants behind the scenes" (*Korean Central News Agency*, December 2, 1998).

Besides worsening the security situation in East Asia, North Korea's defiant discourse revealed a North Korean understanding of the interrelatedness of security issues in the region. The December 1998 inspection crisis about North Korea's nuclear programs and its subsequent joint military exercises demonstrated that no security problem could be dealt with in a vacuum or in isolation; the security problem in Northeast Asia was a comprehensive and indivisible issue that had been influenced *negatively* by the U.S.-Japan alliance, making Tokyo a pawn in the eyes of its neighbors, and consequently a primary target (*Korean Central News Agency*, December 2, 1998).

Though the North Korean-Japanese relationship witnessed a breakthrough in late 1999 following the historic visit of Japan's Prime Minister Tomiichi Murayama to Pyongyang, North Korea's 1993 and 1998 missile incidents revealed a major variable connected to the interrelatedness of security issues in East Asia. The regional security situation was so inextricably interwoven in such a volatile region that it was very difficult to think of an American-North Korean military confrontation over Pyongyang's nuclear program, or a Sino-American showdown about the Taiwan problem, without implicating Tokyo. Japan was a country perceived by Beijing and Pyongyang as a tool of the U.S. strategic design to dominate East Asia and further consolidate its dominant position in the region.

Regardless of its intention, Pyongyang's 1998 decision to send a satellite into orbit without prior notice to the Japanese that the projectile would be flying over Japan created the impression of provocation. The projectile incident revealed how much Japan was nervous and vulnerable at the same time. It also showed the degree of mistrust and suspicion in East Asia, leading one to conclude that almost any regional security problem could easily be misunderstood and could "spin out of control as long as the U.S.-Japan security arrangement still exists and some countries perceive that it targets them in any way" (DiFilippo 48). The 1998 projectile incident also shed light on the history of the North Korean-Japanese relationship, which went back to the 1894/95 Sino-Japanese Pigtail War when Japan, supported by American guns and counsel, crashed a weak China and occupied all of the Korean Peninsula until Tokyo's 1945 surrender to the United States in the Second World War (Morse 27-55). Historical animosities were further exacerbated by recent mutual allegations that North Korea's nuclear and missile programs are the most imminent threat to Japan's security, and that Japan was committed to an American alliance targeting primarily North Korea's security and wellbeing.

In reaction to Pyongyang's projectile launch, Tokyo announced a series of sanctions against North Korea, including an end to food aid and assistance, and a freeze on efforts to normalize bilateral relations with Pyongyang, in addition to a Japanese decision to revitalize the American-sponsored Theater Missile Defense (TMD) (Japan's Ministry of Foreign Affairs, September 1, 1998). But in response to the controversial TMD project, China's Director of arms control, Sha Zukang, said: "If a country seeks to develop advanced theater missile defense or even national missile defense in an attempt to maintain absolute security, other countries will be forced to develop more advanced offensive missiles" (*Far Eastern Economic Review*, February 4, 2000). Even the United

States recognized the negative security implications a TMD system could have had in Asia in general, and in East Asia in particular. American defense officials became "concerned about the untoward effect the deployment of a TMD system could have on Sino-American relations and considered the possibility of keeping it out of Asia" (DiFilippo 95).

However, the 1998 surprise North Korean launch of a satellite awakened Japan to its security vulnerability, and revived Tokyo's interest in the TMD program, pushing Japan to seek shelter under an American missile program that is already condemned by most major actors in East Asia. It removed most of Japan's hesitation to recommit its resources to the development of a missile shield over Japan that could detect incoming North Korean or even Chinese missiles. The September 1998 U.S.-Japan agreement about the joint TMD program postulated that the United States would construct the interceptor missile, while Japan would develop the radar and satellites (*Japan Times Online*, December 25, 1998).

Again, Japan's decision to develop a cooperative TMD system with the United States further aggravated the security situation in the region because it implicated North Korea, China, and Russia, as it could have triggered a potential arms race that would exacerbate the already precarious security environment in Northeast Asia (*Asahi Evening News*, July 19, 2000). The TMD system, if deployed, would include Japan, South Korea, and Taiwan, which envisions the danger of ballistic missile attacks from China that were portrayed by the United States and Japan as threatening, leading to the inference that the TMD program seeks to negate China's efforts to modernize militarily. Indeed, it was believed in China that the U.S.-sponsored TMD deployments are a "shield to reinforce the U.S. sword", referring to the American hegemonic posture in East Asia (Ibid).

In an attempt to counter the TMD project, the Chinese started thinking of building more and more missiles, as the TMD allegedly sought to neutralize China's military modernization programs. But at the heart of the issue, the United States and Japan had not deployed their TMD shield yet, and were seeking to bargain with China not to deploy 'aggressive' weapons in the region; in return, Beijing ought to behave 'responsibly and peacefully', that is not to challenge the current status quo which was dominated by the United States as the sole guarantor of regional security; a claim which this book seeks to refute. The Chinese were aware that the TMD missile shield, if eventually deployed, could not only "neutralize" China's major military arsenal, but could also functionally take back the balance of power in East Asia to the period of the

1842 Opium War when the Chinese empire was in a weak power position vis-à-vis Western and Japanese powers (Gerson, "Fresh Look: Re-examining the Role and Impact of U.S. Bases in Asia-Pacific", Lecture 1999).

Notwithstanding the delay in the implementation of TMD in East Asia because of the advent of a new Republican administration in 2001 and the 9/11 attacks on New York and Washington nine months later, Tokyo's decision to actively participate in the U.S.-sponsored TMD program, however, highlighted Japan's high technological infrastructure. An infrastructure that could easily be converted into military objectives, triggering a more dangerous security environment because of Japan's neighbors' outright rejection of Japanese full rearmament ("Militarism Brewing in Japan", *China Daily*, September 25, 2000). The prospects of Japanese rearmament brought back the 1930s and 40s memories of Japan's militarism and occupation of its neighbors, besides the human rights violations against civilians, such as the 1937 Rape of Nanking incident or the 1910 annexation of the Korean Peninsula. The perception of a Japanese military power turning to an offensive posture instead of a defensive one could spark an endless arms race, a scenario quite detrimental to the security of East Asia, which could render the U.S.-Japan alliance almost obsolete. As explained in Chapter One, the line between defensive and offensive postures is a matter more of intention than capability, and consequently, the possibility of confusing them, mainly in times of tension between countries, becomes very high.

Indeed, Japan's sense of vulnerability in the post-Cold War era prompted Tokyo to make some military and political moves which are meant to be defensive, but taking into account Japan's WWII behavior towards its neighbors, China's and North Korea's suspicion about and mistrust of Japan's intentions were also understandable. What "really matter[ed] was that sentiment was growing in Moscow, Beijing, and Pyongyang that the United States was exploiting its position as the sole military superpower and that in East Asia, Japan was acquiescing to America's hegemonic plan, perhaps to the point of *readopting its past aggressive behavior*" (emphasis added) (DiFilippo 101). This showed the determining impact of states' security concerns on their interaction, and demonstrates the importance of power relations between these units, interacting not only within a system characterized by competition for power and obsession with security, but also within an environment of historical enmities.

On another note, political realism views that in the absence of an overriding international government that judges conflicts between states and provides security for the weak, nations cannot trust the promises of other states to defend them in times of need. This, however, did not apply to Japan, whose economy was the second largest in the world. From a political science standpoint, states should either seek to become militarily powerful enough to secure themselves, or enter into alliances to make up for their respective weaknesses; and pay the costs of that alliance, which Japan did (Waltz 159-86). It is a wonder from a political science point of view that a country like Japan, almost on parity with the United States economically and technologically, could trust a Cold War alliance, established in a very different geopolitical environment, with its security in a post-Cold War volatile and unpredictable security situation in East Asia. Accordingly, the effectiveness and the relevance of the security alliance to Japan's security triggered a national debate that showed no consensus about whether Japan still needed an "unequal" security alliance with a "hegemonic and untrustworthy" America (*Japan Times Online*, June 28, 1999). Indeed, "opinion polls consistently showed that a notable proportion of the Japanese public was uncertain about the need for the continuation of the bilateral security arrangement" (DiFilippo 106). Therefore, Japan's alliance with the United States offered no security to Japan; it only offered more security problems for the Japanese. Hence came the debate about the relevance of the U.S.-Japan alliance to Japan's security.

Calls for the revision and even the abrogation of the alliance with the United States were accompanied by strong advances to reconsider the appropriateness of Article 9 of Japan's so-called peace constitution. A Japanese parliament member from the Liberal Democratic Party (LDP), Shintaro Ishihara, championed the 'Japan That Can Say No' campaign during the 1990s. His anti-alliance campaign took its name from his bestselling book, in which Ishihara advocated the development of a security structure independent of the United States because Japan, in his view, did not need American protection. Ishihara continued to argue that the series of military, political, and economic asymmetries in the alliance made the latter a legal document that had confined Japan for half a century to a subordinate position, instead of an equal one, because Washington does not mean the alliance to be the basis for an equal partnership (Ishihara 76). Japan accepted a subordinate status because of Cold War security requirements; now that the Soviet Union had disappeared, it was high time that Japan reconsidered the real need for this alliance. Ishihara said in his 1990 book:

> The time has come for Japan to say to the United States that we do not
> need American protection. Japan will protect itself with its own power

and wisdom. This will require a strong commitment and will on our part. We can do it as long as there is a national consensus to do so....From both a financial and technological point of view there are no barriers to accomplishing this goal in the near future. We can develop a more effective defense capability at less than we are paying today (76).

Ishihara's resolute call for a genuinely independent Japanese defense apparatus received further support from an increasingly growing political elite in Japan. They stressed that "Japan should strive for a more independent security policy from that advocated by the United States. There was a sense that we became too dependent on America" (*Far Eastern Economic Review*, August 12, 1999).

The point here is that the U.S.-Japan alliance could have provided some security to Japan, but it provided Washington with more than security; it gave the US more power as a tactical advantage in East Asia. The alliance was used by the United States as a basis to perpetuate its preponderant position in the region, that is, to maximize its power gains at the expense of other East Asian actors such as China, perceived by both Washington and Tokyo as a potential regional hegemon which needed to be contained (Ch. Johnson 151). "From a U.S. perspective, potential threats in the region ha[d] to be neutralized to prevent instability [and]... to forestall any undermining of Washington's power" (DiFilippo 95-96). To guarantee Japanese cooperation, the United States consistently used the strategy of fear to frighten Japan into accommodating America's interest to continue the alliance because, from Washington's perspective, the security stakes in the region were so high that they could be met only by a stronger alliance between the world's sole superpower and the second strongest economy in the world.

Accordingly, China had to be either engaged or contained, North Korea had to be disarmed from any nuclear weaponry, and Russia, though less threatening, still had to be reminded of the strong U.S. military presence in the region. As the only military superpower (Ch. Johnson 156-60), the U.S. sought to remain politically involved and militarily committed in East Asia. Washington's unrivaled power would only be perpetuated by sustaining U.S. military superiority over current and potential rivals. The aspect of unpredictability and the threat impression of North Korea, which the U.S. magnified in East Asia in the post-Cold War era, helped justify why Washington needed to be present in the region. To continue to retain its preponderant position in the region, America claimed that it had the moral and legal obligations to protect Japan against North Korean missiles and against China's hegemonic tendencies, largely exaggerated by invoking Beijing's hard line towards Taiwan's bids for independence.

It was a concerted policy on the part of the United States since 1990 to raise the security fears of Japan, and to exaggerate perceived threats to Japan's security in order to guarantee a continuing Japanese interest in the alliance. A renewed alliance with Japan allowed the U.S. to continue to exercise its self-imposed 'responsibility' of maintaining regional security and indirectly retain a dominant control of the region. Thus, it was safe to assume that the purpose of this alliance for the United States was to gain more power rather than deal with an immediate security threat in the region. While Japan thought the alliance would provide more security in a hostile environment, one can argue that it was paradoxically detrimental to the country's security in the face of a bellicose North Korea and a probably vindictive China.

Finally, as this book tried to argue, security problems in East Asia could not be handled bilaterally because almost every security issue necessarily involved most regional actors, such as the 1998 North Korean launch of a satellite that flew over Japan. Japan's reaction to that incident invited opposite feedback from Beijing, Moscow, and even South Korea, supposedly another key American ally in the region. Moreover, the Chinese-North Korean-Russian reaction to Japan's 1998 agreement to start cooperating with Washington over the TMD program testified to the validity of the argument about the interrelatedness of security in East Asia. It showed that China and Russia, in particular, feel threatened by a prospective TMD missile shield in Northeast Asia, which was perceived as a step in a regional arms race that could only exacerbate the security situation in the area.

Moreover, this section argues that the United States took advantage of Japan's weak negotiating position after WWII in the security alliance to dictate to Tokyo American economic and trade conditions. Over the last two decades or so, there was an impression that Japan was kept in a secondary position even in matters relating to its own security and economic affairs, which was used by Japanese right-wing politicians to mobilize Japanese public opinion in the quest for the outright repeal of the security alliance. Therefore, a brief overview of Japan's acquiescence to American dictated in the economic area seemed to be indispensable to shed light on the hidden side of the "unequal" U.S.-Japan equation before and since the early 1990s.

3.2.2. Japan's Economic Sovereignty in Question

In addition to guaranteeing Japanese security through the formation of the American-Japanese Mutual Security Treaty (MST), the United States sought to integrate Japan into a larger framework of economic relationships and thereby remove the attractiveness of the communist-dominated Asian market. However, unlike West Germany, there were no large neighboring non-communist economies to which the Japanese economy could be anchored. China and North Korea fell to communism, and became Soviet allies, and the American concern that Japan would be attracted to the gravity of neighboring communism pushed the United States to work to prevent that from happening. To overcome the problem of an isolated and vulnerable Japan, the United States took several initiatives. One was to expedite the decolonization of Southeast Asia. Here, it should be remembered that one of the causes of the Pacific War was that European colonial powers had largely closed these economies to Japanese exports. In addition, the United States gave Japan relatively free access to the American market and to American technology (Schaller 70). Furthermore, the United States used its vast financial resources to assist in the rebuilding of the Japanese economy, but it did not demand access to the Japanese economy for its multinational corporations; instead, the *quid pro quo* for American economic concessions to Japan was Japanese permission to use their air and naval bases in order to deter an alleged threat of Chinese and Soviet expansionism.

In return, Washington integrated Japan into the post-Second World War international economic regime of a "free" and market economy. Despite strong West European resistance based primarily on the fear of potential Japanese economic competition, the United States also sponsored Japanese participation in major international financial organizations such as the IMF and the World Bank (Zeng et al.). Japan's accession to the General Agreement on Tariffs and Trade (GATT) in 1954 took place despite the objection of more than half of the then GATT members, including the European and British Commonwealth member states, because of recent war memories. Behind this policy, the U.S. sought to orientate Japan's trade away from China in order to avert the influence of communism which then took hold of China and North Korea (Schaller 86). This marked a crucial step in Japan's economic integration in the West.

Tokyo received the American Most Favored Nation (MFN) status, which exempted Japanese exports from paying high tariffs under the 1930 Smoot-

Hawley Act[8]. Moreover, the U.S. opened up American textile markets in 1962 to Japanese exports, whose excess was absorbed by the United States over more than a decade after Japan's accession into the GATT. Between 1954 and 1960, Japan's exports to the U.S. more than doubled from 450 million dollars to 1.1 billion dollars, which led to the emergence of a booming and competitive Japanese economy, as Japanese exports increased sixfold during the 1960s alone, and its Gross National Product (GNP) kept increasing at an annual rate of more than ten percent (Q.Wang, *Hegemonic Cooperation* 61). Hence came the Japanese economic miracle as the most competitive economy in East Asia for more than four decades, and the second largest in the world after the American economy.

The dominant U.S. role in the international economic system, which helped the Japanese economy rise from under the ashes of the first and most destructive nuclear attack in history, gained America a dominant position in its economic relationship with Japan. Qingxin Ken Wang said that this was also the logical consequence of the U.S.-Japan security alliance, which has now kept Tokyo in a weaker position for more than five decades. "By virtue of its economic preponderance, technological prowess, and the American dollar, the United States played a dominant role in the postwar international economic system" (Q.Wang, *Hegemonic Cooperation* 60-61).

From a political science standpoint, when state A claims it is protecting the security of state B, it subsequently secures for itself the upper hand in dealing with bilateral security issues as well as economic and trade contentions. Thus,

---

[8] The Smoot-Hawley Tariff Act of June 1930 raised U.S. tariffs to historically high levels. The original intention behind the legislation was to increase the protection afforded domestic farmers against foreign agricultural imports. Massive expansion in the agricultural production sector outside of Europe during World War I led, with the postwar recovery of European producers, to massive agricultural overproduction during the 1920s. This in turn led to declining farm prices during the second half of the decade. During the 1928 election campaign, Republican Presidential candidate Herbert Hoover pledged to help the beleaguered farmer by, among other things, raising tariff levels on agricultural products. But once the tariff schedule revision process got started, it proved impossible to stop. Calls for increased protection flooded in from industrial sector special interest groups and soon a bill meant to provide relief for farmers became a means to raise tariffs in all sectors of the economy. When the dust had settled, Congress had agreed to tariff levels that exceeded the already high rates established by the 1922 Fordney-McCumber Act and was up to that time among the most protectionist tariffs in U.S. history. Available at: <http://www.state.gov/r/pa/ho/time/id/17606.htm>

Japan's acquiescence to the U.S. dictates in economic and trade contests was always a natural consequence of the dominant U.S. role in security matters. "The persistent attempts by American policy makers to gain the compliance of Tokyo, either by demanding access to Japanese markets or by restricting access to U.S. markets, related directly to the existence of the bilateral security alliance that gave Washington the privilege to act authoritatively and chiefly with America's unilateral interests in mind" (DiFilippo 59-60).

Therefore, the alliance not only provided less security to Japan but also offered the U.S. more leverage on Tokyo in economic and trade disputes. "Japan remain[ed] the target of continuing pressure from the United States, often to the point that Washington demanded structural reform, in bilateral trade and deregulation issues" (DiFilippo 59), ignoring Japan's economic sovereignty to run its own economy. American interference in Japan's economic affairs became clear during the 1990s, for example, after the United States' share of the gross world products and trade had started declining sharply in the mid-80s because of Japanese competition, mainly in the electronics and car industries. But this does not necessarily lead to the argument that the Japanese economy surpassed the American one during this period because "while the productivity growth slowed down slightly in the second half of the 1980s and the first half of the 1990s, [America's economy] still surpassed the Japanese productivity growth rate in the same period" (Q. Wang, *Hegemonic Cooperation* 67).

The ascendancy of the Japanese economy, however, in the late '80s and early '90s pushed the United States to try to slow down Japan's "usurpation" of America's world economic preponderance, as "Japan had become the world's largest creditor nation, with the United States as the largest debtor nation" (Q. Wang, *Hegemonic Cooperation* 70). But this did not decrease Japan's economic dependence on the United States, which continued well into the 1990s, nor did it soften American continuing pressure on Japan to restructure its economy, especially in the aftermath of the serious 1997 financial crisis in Asia.

Thus, the U.S.-Japan economic relationship was not very different from their security one– it was an unequal interdependence, a special but unequal interaction based on the power asymmetries between Washington and Tokyo, which resulted from the asymmetrical security alliance that, as this chapter has tried to demonstrate, offered the United States more power and Japan less security. Qingxin K.Wang substantiates this view. He said: "Japan's continued economic dependence on the United States since 1945 might have become an important structural power resource which the United States could employ to maintain a degree of American hegemony in Japan" (*Hegemonic Cooperation* 74).

The alleged U.S. infringement on Japan's economic sovereignty was demonstrated in a 1996 supercomputer dispute between American's first producer of vector supercomputers Cray Research and its Japanese counterpart NEC (Q. Wang, *Hegemonic Cooperation* 55). Cray Research complained to the U.S. Department of Commerce that NEC was dumping supercomputers on the American market, which in turn handed over the controversial case to the U.S. International Trade Commission (ITC) (Ibid). The ITC processing of the case and the outcome of this trade dispute revealed a great deal about the economic and trade asymmetries in the U.S.-Japan relationship, and clearly showed how Japan's security dependence on the U.S. led to Tokyo's acquiescence in bilateral trade contests. In September 1997, the ITC ruled that America's "domestic industry producing vector supercomputers was threatened with material injury by reason of LTFV [less than fair value] imports from Japan (qtd in DiFilippo 60), which was characterized by the Japanese as a "blatant fabrication" (*Associated Press*, September 26, 1997).

The Japanese government expressed its deep dissatisfaction with the ITC's ruling, and said it was surprised at what it called an "opaque and questionable" interference of the U.S. Commerce Department in the case even before the investigation started. Tokyo denounced American "trade harassment", and complained that "anti-dumping legislation is perhaps the largest source of hidden protectionism in the United States, and many countries have complained about its shortcomings" (Japanese Subcommittee on Unfair Trade Policies and Measures, 1998 Report on the WTO Consistency of Trade Policies by Major Trading Partners). Although the U.S. Court of International Trade (CIT) overturned the ITC 1997 ruling, and asked the latter to redo the investigation, the Cray Research vs. NEC case showed a concerted U.S. policy to insulate the American market from Japanese competition by fair means or foul, thus exploiting its preponderant security position in the U.S.-Japan alliance to achieve economic objectives. The United States seemed to be determined to safeguard its domestic market against competitive foreign producers, including the producers of an allied country that had been dependent on American security guaranties and harassed in other areas such as trade and commerce. Anthony DiFilippo said that "there was hardly any doubt that the new 'equal partnership' was really not equal, since America's dominance of the security alliance and its role as the ultimate protector of Japan ramified the entire bilateral relationship, from trade and other economic matters to science and technology" (28).

Japan's sense of both security and economic vulnerability was largely behind Tokyo's inability to deal fully with the paradox of being the world's second-largest economy and its second-rate world political status. Japan's dependence on U.S. security guarantees put Tokyo in a weak position militarily and economically. Preserving the nation's security in the troubled waters of post-Cold War East Asia was Tokyo's priority in view of the changing balance of power in post-Cold War East Asia. As the United States made the power/security relations in the region like a "hub and spoke" structure, Japan served as the hub for the series of American regional spokes, which it maintained throughout the region to face unspecified threats potentially from North Korea, but strategically from the rise of China as a likely competitor for regional ascendancy.

Though crucial to Japan's security, at least for the time being, the U.S.-Japan alliance was a mixed blessing for the Japanese because it was paradoxically marketed by Washington to Japan's neighbors as a reassurance that Tokyo would not rearm, instead of as a security umbrella for Japan. Those neighbors -particularly China and the two Koreas, which were largely victimized by Japan's behavior throughout the first half of the twentieth century- prefer that Japan stayed militarily neutral (See Chapter Three). Washington marketed the alliance in East Asia as essential to curb the development of an independent Japanese military policy. An American disengagement from Japan would increase Japan's sense of vulnerability, and subsequently could awaken its quest to go nuclear in order to be taken seriously, and accorded its proper role in Asia and in the world at large. "The U.S. nuclear guarantee and U.S. forces stationed in Japan reassured the rest of Asia that Japan would not rearm in a major way" (Fukuyama 76), and an abrogation of the U.S.-Japan alliance was not worth an arms race and a security standoff that would result from a nuclear Japan cutting loose from the United States.

Paradoxically, Washington tacitly hinted to the Chinese that America's alliance with the Japanese was a security guarantee against Japanese right-wing militaristic tendencies that favored a more independent Japanese foreign policy, a more assertive military strategy, and a more confrontational Japanese approach to relations with China (Calder 129-35). After all, right-wing, anti-China and pro-Taiwan forces in Japan became increasingly influential in Japanese domestic politics (Walker 21). It was this right-wing Taiwan lobby in the Diet that was seeking to use the separation of Taiwan from the mainland to increase Japan's security role in the Northeast Asia.

It seemed like "the United States and Japan lost sight of their relationship's overarching purpose" of being a stabilizing and a positive security factor in East

Asia (Fukuyama 76). One can go further to "suspect that the United States enhanced its security ties with Japan in 1996 expressly to strengthen its negotiating position with China" in matters relating to bilateral and strategic issues like the Taiwan problem and the superpower rivalry over regional and world ascendancy (Funabashi 26-36).

But this was all politics. The U.S. alliance with Japan served to minimize the cost of the U.S. forward military presence in the Western Pacific. It also provided a basis for America to be a major, if not the major, player in the region because it extended American power into the region, and has allowed the U.S. to claim that it is an "Asian Power". Washington always considered its alliance with Japan as "the linchpin of the United States security policy in Asia" (See Department of Defense Reports, 1995, 1996, 2001). Moreover, the alliance for the U.S. was not only for security considerations but also for economic and trade reasons, given the promising economic importance of the region. DiFilippo says that "the economic significance of the East Asia-Pacific area, and particularly Japan, require[d] a strong U.S. security presence" (28) in the region, which was differently perceived by major actors that had their own power and security calculations in supporting or condemning the American military presence in East Asia.

Despite the asymmetrical nature of the U.S.-Japan relationship, including their economic tensions, however, the United States relied heavily on Japan for burden-sharing as a major regional actor and a preferred partner in the Sino-American-Japanese triangle. This alliance at least theoretically provided security both against and for Japan. It had been a security umbrella in the region and a linkage to other nations that still remembered too well Japan's behavior in the 1930s and 1940s. For the United States, the alliance with Japan was a key to the overall power equilibrium in East Asia. Washington and Tokyo, for almost five decades, have:

> Viewed the maintenance of good relations as vital. The Japanese have become aware that their extraordinary economic success in part rests on their relatively open access to the American market and American military forces as their ultimate protectors. Americans have come to realize that Japan not only plays a key role in regional security and is the major economic force in East Asia, but also is vital to the health of the entire international economic system (Jordan 366).

The call to have U.S.-Japan relations strengthened came from the Japanese ex-Prime Minister Ryutore Hashimoto, who was a staunch supporter of strong and lasting U.S.-Japan cooperation in Asia, and who expressed Japan's determination to work with the United States to deal with the rising economic and military power of China, besides other unresolved regional issues. He said in June 1997:

> In the new chapter of our new century, Japan and the United States will be bound with even stronger ties and will further learn to live together and prosper together. This is essential for peace and prosperity in the World (*Presidents and Prime Ministers*, May- June 1997, Vo.6, No.3, 6).

Finally, the expansion of the Japan's bilateral alliance with the United States ostensibly provoked more tension and suspicion in East Asia, which threatened Japan's security because the alliance's new guidelines left almost no chance for a post-Cold War regional security arrangement based on a multilateral approach. Japan's neighbors believe that the U.S.-Japan alliance paradoxically provided America with more power, and put Japan's security in jeopardy in view of the negative security role the alliance was playing by creating, maintaining, and exaggerating a regional threat environment (*Japan Times Online*, September 18, 1997). DiFilippo substantiated the claim of this chapter that the post-Cold War U.S.-Japan alliance and especially the 1997 Defense Guidelines provided less security for Japan, saying that "a concern surfaced that the new guidelines would make Japan a target, should the United States become involved in a military dispute in the Asia-Pacific region" (DiFilippo 34).

Notwithstanding the counterproductive value of the U.S.-Japan post-Cold War alliance, the China factor complicated the task of this alliance. The impact of a rising China had its deep implications on the rationale and the doctrine of the American-Japanese military arrangement, for the failure to come to grips with this new and decisive driver in East Asia might reshape the regional order in East Asia in particular and in Asia and the world at large. Was it likely that a more powerful China would be more peaceful and more accepting of the international and regional status quo? Or would it result in a China that was more committed to revising the regional status quo, even through power politics, if necessary?

As the end of the Cold War did not end the U.S.-Japan security alliance, China perceived the consolidation of this alliance with a great deal of suspicion, and not as a positive security factor in the region, leading to the assumption that the alliance under study had negative security implications on the Sino-Japanese relationship, as the research hypothesis of this work argues. After the 1996 Clinton-Hashimoto Summit, the 1997 revised Defense Guidelines, and the 1998 U.S.-Japan agreement to cooperate on Missile Defense research, Beijing came to see the intensifying security cooperation between Washington and Tokyo as seeking to contain China's aspirations to rise to a great power status in East Asia's future balance of power.

3.3. The China Factor: Implications for the Triangle

3.3.1. China's Rising Power

China was of strategic importance to both Japan and the United States; its evolution was one of the post-Cold War defining events. Given its size, economic dynamism, and military potential, the way China would interact with the United States and Japan would shape the geopolitical landscape of East Asia and the international order of the twenty-first century. The U.S. was an already predominant power in Asia and was keen to prevent other power competitors from challenging its regional ascendancy (Mandelbaum 56). Japan was a nation that was torn between its security vulnerability and its strategic interest not to antagonize a rising China simply to please the United States. Therefore, the security and economic implications of China's emerging power on the U.S.-Japan connection were perceived as the post-Cold War major threat both to U.S. interests and to America's allies in the region, particularly Japan, whose security depended heavily on U.S. protection (Preble 2-19). From an American perspective, China's 'assertive' behavior in recent years and the perceived danger of North Korea's missile and nuclear programs were the most likely immediate causes of tension in East Asia (Suskind 81). Washington and Tokyo agreed that China's post-Cold War behavior, such as the 1995 move in the Mischief Reef and the 1996 and 2000 missile exercises across the Strait of Taiwan, were representative of China's intentions and aspirations.

Equally important, whether or not the rise of a great power poses a challenge to international security is also a question that ought to be tackled from a political science standpoint. It seems that *any* change in the balance of power in the international system is likely to cause a certain degree of instability, as states usually seek to adjust themselves to the new order. Great power transition theories suggest that changes in the balance of power have the potential to disrupt the existing order (Singer 390-400, 404-406). The demise of the Soviet Union and the consequent collapse of the bipolar international system contributed to rising Sino-Japanese rivalry over regional predominance and their respective perception of the U.S. military presence in East Asia. As any rising state in the international arena, China would seek to secure a central place in the post-Cold War order, and would not be passive in the process of the metamorphosis of Asian politics, and, like any great power, would seek to shape the pace and the terms of this process in its favor (S. Burton et al. 52).

Beijing and Tokyo had now come to view the U.S. presence in the region in a very different way. After the end of the Cold War, Japan sought to ensure military ties with the U.S. and thereby increase its national security. The Chinese, by contrast, hoped that the U.S. would help contain the growth of Japanese power, and not to seek to contain China. China's defense modernization programs and foreign policy objectives can realistically pose a challenge to U.S. interests in the Asia-Pacific region[9]. Steady improvements in China's economic and military capabilities could lead Beijing to become more assertive, thereby producing political tensions and perhaps even armed conflicts. A number of recent actions by the Chinese caused concern in America as to Beijing's true future intentions. China's territorial aspirations in the South China Sea and its "threats" against Taiwan cast some doubts as to whether China was really interested in "constructive engagement" with the United States. Would China be a cooperative or a competitive actor, or was Beijing willing to take whatever measures it saw necessary to gain a global recognition that was commensurate with its rising power attributes, be they economic or military?

Over the first five years after the fall of the Berlin Wall, the bulk of American strategic activity was devoted to three major issues, all of them in Europe. First, the United States focused on dealing with the transformation of the Soviet Union into a Russia that did not pose a threat to post-Cold War U.S. world ascendancy. Second, Washington was for a long time preoccupied with the reunification of Germany and the associated task of forging a new NATO, that turned for the first time in its history from a purely defensive alliance to an offensive one during the 1994 and 1999 air raids against Serbian forces in Bosnia, and against the now defunct Milosovich's forces in the Kosovo enclave.

---

[9] For more on the perceived strategic and security threats of China's military modernization program and its attendant rise in Beijing's political leverage on the world stage, see Bill Gertz, *The China Threat: How the People's Republic Targets America.* Washington, D.C. Regnery publishing, Inc., 2005. See also Kul B Rai. *America in the 21st Century: Challenges and Opportunities in Foreign Policy.* Upper Saddle River, N.J: Prentice Hall, 1997.

By the late 1990s, however, there was a perceptible shift in American focus away from Europe and towards Asia, where major security challenges and power competition were likely to happen. Nothing new; over the previous century, the essence of Washington's strategy toward the Asia-Pacific region had been to ensure that no single power, or group of powers – Russia, Japan, China, and even a United Korea– would dominate East Asia (Suskind 81). Today, this purpose remained unchanged even after the end of the Cold War. The United States sought to ensure that no other power shares with it the domination of the region under study (Johnson 67-96). From an American perspective, since the end of the Soviet-American bipolar contest, it became a Sino-American power struggle over preponderance in Asia, which the United States could not afford to lose at a time of an alleged Chinese pursuit of power that could threaten the current preponderant U.S. status in the region[10].

China was now the most serious American foreign policy challenge of the twenty-first century. A 2000 Congressional hearings session stated that "the ingrained belief of Chinese elites was that the United States was a declining power that could not maintain its position, allies, interests and power in Asia."[11] American decision-makers suggested that China's economic might, combined with its rising military prowess, would probably lead the Chinese to try to challenge America's preferred order in Asia. As Michael Vickers, a military analyst at the Center for Strategic and Budgetary Assessments in Washington D.C., argued, "getting into war with China is easy. You can see many scenarios, not just Taiwan- especially as the Chinese develop a submarine and missile capability throughout the Pacific. But the dilemma was, how [would] you end a war with China?" (Qtd in *The Atlantic*, June 2005, 54). According to the same source, China appeared to be increasingly dissatisfied with the status quo in East Asia. It appeared to be so disenchanted with the East Asian political status quo, especially regarding Taiwan, that it may use force to alter the existing

---

[10] Hearings of the Committee On National Security of the House of Representatives of the One Hundred Fourth Congress, March 20, 1996, p.1, 2, 35. Also, Hearings Before the Committee on Armed Services House of Representatives, One Hundred Sixth Congress, July 19, 2000, p.103.

[11] Hearing Before The Committee On Armed Services House of Representatives of the One Hundred Sixth Congress. 2nd Session. July 19, 2000, "Military Capabilities of the Peoples Republic of China". Washington: U.S. Government Printing Office, 2001

order, as the March 2005 Chinese anti-secession law, which primarily forbade Taiwan from declaring independence, clearly indicated.

During the early post-Cold War decades, the United States dealt with China as a strategic challenge (Suskind 179-80, 188). Washington's concern centered primarily on the strategic cost of the implications of China's emergence as a great power on the future of America's preponderant position in East Asia, which corroborates one of the basic arguments of this thesis, that the U.S was worried more about its power than about its security in dealing with Japan and China. A D. Mclennan said: "China was expected to become the dominant power in East Asia. It probably aspired as well to replace the United States at the top of the world hierarchy of power. It was already the second most powerful country and believes that in due course it w[ould] surpass the U.S. economy in absolute size" (52). Being closer to China, Japan, however, was concerned about this long-term trend, but for the near-term Tokyo was more concerned with the implications of the success or failure of Beijing's economic reforms on China's internal stability and Japan's national interests.

With the rising power of China and its potential ascendancy in Asia, Japan faced a serious security dilemma. China's claims to the sovereignty of Taiwan, the Spratly and the Senkaku Islands posed a direct threat to Japan's sea lines of communication (SLCs) and to its economic well-being, given the enormous oil and gas reserves in the Senkaku Islands (See Chapter One, Section Three). Unless the United States and Japan came to grips with China's significance to the future power and security equation of East Asia, Washington and Tokyo might soon have to acknowledge the impotence of their bilateral alliance in facing a potential Chinese takeover of Taiwan by force if Taipei, encouraged by the American-Japanese recent promises of protection, declared its independence. During the U.S.-Japan Security Consultative Committee (SCC) meeting in February 2005, Washington and Tokyo, for the first time, declared that Taiwan was "a common security issue" between the two allies, which invited a Chinese Parliament anti-secession Act on March 5, 2005, that denounced the 'unwarranted' American-Japanese interference in Chinese domestic affairs, and legally forbad Taipei from declaring independence.

Finally, the post-Cold War geopolitical developments in East Asia placed the People's Republic of China (PRC) in a prime position to play a major role in the complexities of Asia-Pacific politics. With the world's largest population, a rapidly growing economy, and a modernizing nuclear arsenal, Washington believed China was emerging as a serious challenge to the twenty-first century American foreign policy. The Soviet Union's collapse in 1991 and the subsequent end of the bipolar world gave China the opportunity to play a major role in the revision and development of the security structure in East Asia, which had been dominated so far by a Cold War alliance between the United States and Japan. Why did China want to have a say in Asian politics now? What changed in China after the geopolitical earthquake in the region at the end of the Cold War? To put it differently, what were China's new attributes of *Power*, assumed in this work as the driving dependent variable along with the *Security* one? Part of the answer was China's rocketing economic prowess and its miraculously consistent 9 percent growth rate for the previous decade.

3.3.2. China's Rising Economy and Its Prospects in the 21st Century

When we learn that in 2003 China "bought 7 percent of the world's oil, a quarter of all aluminum and steel, nearly a third of the world's iron ore and coal, and 40 percent of the world's cement", and was the world's leader in attracting direct foreign investment, pulling in $53 billion as compared to the United States $40 billion" (Fishman 223-86)[12], one can easily ascertain that indeed China already had the qualifications to be the next superpower after the United States. But, China's developmental and social problems could have impeded the chances of a rapid Chinese transformation into a real superpower. As the focus of this book, however, is the security implications of China's rising economic power and not its economic evolution per se, this section will only provide a brief overview of China's economic transformation and trade power from historical and post-Cold War perspectives as well during the first two decades that followed the end of the Cold War.

As China's industrial output rocketed in November 2003, factories made 17.9% more goods compared with the same month in 2002. Computer

---

[12] Ted C. Fishman. *China, Inc.: How the Rise of the Next Superpower Challenges America and the World*, Scribner, 2005. For more on China's economic potential in terms of analysis or figures, see also Rosenberg, David. "The Rise of China in Asia: Security Implications." Ed. Carolyn W. Pumphrey. Strategic Studies Institute, U.S. Army War College. January 2002: 229-262. For China's developmental problems, see Zhang Jun, Editor-in-chief of *World Economic Forum*, an authoritative Chinese economic journal issued by the Fudan University, Shanghai, China. In one of his prominent articles "Structural Imbalances", Professor Zhang depicts the implications of Chinese economic expansion for the world economy and for China. China's tremendous export industry, Zhang argues, "suggests a need for the global trading system to make more room for rising China...But at the same time we must bear in mind that China has enormous inner structural issues to overcome before making such export-led growth really sustainable".

production, for instance, jumped 75%, automobile output increased by 33%, and steel output was 23% higher. It was believed that economic reforms, low wage costs, and a massive domestic market helped turn China into the world's fastest-expanding major economy[13].

As a matter of fact, China's economic success could be traced to the structural reforms it had undertaken in the late-1970s. These reforms brought about the development of a free market and substantial levels of privatization of national economic sectors. China's decision to open its economy in large measure to the world resulted in increasingly lucrative economic relations with the outside world since the late 1980s. A lively trade developed between China and its East Asian neighbors, the countries of Western Europe, Japan, and especially the United States.

In 1978, China was among the world's poorest countries, with 80 percent of the population having incomes of less than U.S. $1 a day, and only a third of all adults able to read or write. By 1998, the proportion of the population with incomes less than U.S. $1 a day had declined to about 12 percent, life expectancy was 70 years, and illiteracy among 15- to 25-year-olds was about 7 percent[14]. The Chinese population enjoyed a spectacular improvement in its standard of living since the end of the 1970s, that is, since China began to integrate into the world economy. As the World Bank noted, over the previous 20 years, China achieved both an extraordinary decline in poverty and high levels of education and health status (Ibid). Furthermore, China has become one of the great economic growth models of recent times (Fishman 223-86). From the mid-1980s through the mid-1990s, for example, China's real gross domestic product (GDP) per capita grew at a rate of 6.9 percent per year, a growth experience exceeded only by Thailand and the Republic of Korea during the same period. China's overall growth remained robust even in the face of the terrible economic crisis that swept through East and Southeast Asia during 1997 and 1998 (Rosenberg 229-62). China's annual rate of growth in gross national product from 1997 through 1999, according to the World Bank, was about 7.9 percent per year (See the footnote on the previous page). By 1999, China had the seventh-largest economy in the world, surpassed only by the United States, Japan, Germany, France, the United Kingdom, and Italy. The

---

[13] "China's output surges in November 2003", http://www.centurychina.com/plaboard/).
[14] "WORLD ECONOMIC SITUATION AND PROSPECTS 2007", Department of Economic and Social Affairs (DESA), The United Nations. January 2007, Full Text available at: http://www.un.org/esa/policy/wess/wesp2007files/wesp2007.pdf.

World Bank, which based its estimates on purchasing power parity estimates, projected that by the year 2020, China might have the second-largest economy in the world, which has become a reality today (Ibid).

China's trade with the United States was then particularly fruitful, but incrementally uneven. By 1999, according to Chinese figures provided to the International Monetary Fund, China enjoyed a trade surplus with the United States in the range of $22 billion[15]; now, the surplus stands at almost $100 billion. These figures suggested that China was then one of the biggest beneficiaries of the trade opportunities that were provided by the World Trade Organization (WTO) regime, which it had joined in 2001. China was also a major beneficiary of the international regimes for money and finance, the International Monetary Fund and the World Bank. It is a member of both organizations. Moreover, as of June 2000, China was the second largest recipient of total World Bank loans made since the Bank began its lending activities in the late-1940s (Ibid). Given its tremendously successful economic performance, and the important link between that performance and its external economic relations, one might expect that China would be essentially satisfied with the contemporary East Asian status quo. China would also do everything it could to ensure continued participation in the international economic system so as to maximize its prospects for future growth and probably greater world power.

If China's economic reforms succeeded and its economy continued to grow strongly, it was highly likely that China would carry much economic weight in the world, which would have deep implications for U.S. economic and strategic interests in East Asia and on Japan's second-largest economy then (Bottelier, "China's Economic Rise", lecture 2005). As David Zweig, the Director of the Center on China's transnational relations at the Hong Kong University of Science and Technology, put it, "a big test of the U.S.-China relationship may come if China's current economic growth and need for resources push[ed] it to expand its military influence-a prospect that makes people nervous" (Zweig and Jianbai 33). The pursuit of economic success, however, would drive China to become more economically dependent on international trade. By 2020-25, one may assume that Beijing will be relying heavily on imported oil and other energy resources, probably from Central Asia, the Middle East, and Sub-Saharan Africa, which provides 8 percent of the world's daily oil consumption,

---

[15] World Economic Situation and Prospects 2007, Department of Economic and Social Affairs (DESA), The United Nations, January 2007)

and has almost 12 percent of the world's oil reserves then (Pan, "China, Africa, and Oil", lecture 2007). In this case, the Chinese were already more dependent on trade and imported energy, which required a strong military to secure the sea lanes through Southeast and Southwest Asia open to Chinese trade and energy imports, and China would have the enhanced economic resources that should enable it to increase its military capabilities[16].

As a result, the Chinese would likely increase their air and naval capabilities for power projection so as to ensure that China's economic security would not be disrupted by other major powers, particularly Japan and the United States. This would be essentially vital, should conflict break out in the Taiwan Strait. If the Taiwan issue was not resolved peacefully, which seemed to be a farfetched probability, at least for the foreseeable future, China would need to ensure that the United States, in cooperation with Japan, would not cut off China's economic lifeline. China would want insurance against the possibility that it might become economically choked to death as a result of any military or political contention in the region. It would, therefore, develop the air and naval capabilities that would allow it to maintain the sea routes open to Chinese trade and energy imports.

Conversely, these same capabilities might also enable the Chinese to threaten to close these same routes to other East Asian trading states, such as Japan, South Korea, and Taiwan, thereby threatening the security of these neighbors. Consequently, those nations might seek to enhance their own military capabilities as those of China increase dramatically, leading East Asia down the path of a regional arms race that would aggravate tensions between the regional main actors and deepen misperceptions among each other. The crux of the matter is that the continued rise of China was likely to create new interests and new capabilities, which could be perceived, rightly or wrongly, as a threat to the interests and security of other East Asian actors, especially the United States and Japan.

3.3.3. The China Security Threat in East Asia: Perception and Reality

Historically, whenever regional or world powers emerge, like Germany and Japan in the early decades of the twentieth century, they usually tend to

---

[16] For more on the security and strategic implications of China's rising economic competitivity, see China Security Review Commission, Report to Congress of the US-China Review Commission- The National security Implications of the Economic Relationship between the United States and China, July 2002, Chapter 8, 5)

question the status quo and become increasingly assertive. China was to be no exception. However, Chinese efforts to modernize militarily in an attempt to bridge the technological, operational, and logistic gap between the United States and nations as small as the island of Taiwan, were looked at from opposite standpoints. Beijing's efforts to remedy its military weaknesses could be executed in a purely defensive spirit but could also be a clue about the intentions of a rising power. Therefore, as the China-threat thesis was more a subjective than an objective argument, it seemed that China's "defensive" measures were perceived by both the United States and Japan as "assertive". "U.S. military planners defined as a threat Beijing's efforts to remedy its own weak position in the face of the overwhelming superiority that they acknowledged the United States held right up to the edge of the Asian mainland" (Schwarz 28). In conclusion, Beijing's "security" precautions, manifested in investing more to shorten the military gap with Tokyo and Washington, were construed as "power"-building efforts with the intention to dominate and not to defend.

According to a statement made by one Chinese official then, China's external security environment was "never more satisfactory since the founding of the Republic" in 1949 (S. Burton et al. 52). Did this imply that China felt less threatened in the new unipolar international system than it did during the Cold War, leading us to assume that China did not have a security problem anymore?[17] Such an assumption went unsubstantiated in view of China's suspicion of the security implications of the 1997 expansion of the U.S.-Japan alliance and the suspicious power/security calculations of Tokyo and Washington. The Chinese viewed that the post-Cold War alliance aimed at negating China's military modernization, and thus containing Beijing's alleged hegemonic aspirations in Asia, which did not lead to the conclusion that China was satisfied with the regional security environment.

China's sense of national humiliation, as long as Taiwan did not join Hong Kong and Macao in returning to the "embrace of the motherland", was on the rise. Unification since the days of modern China's father, Sun Yat-Sen, was always a priority of almost all successive Chinese leaders because it was perceived as a completion of national honor and dignity (Spence 294-98, 667-74). Moreover, Samuel S. Kim, a senior research scholar at the East Asian Institute of Columbia University, said that China's strategic analysts

---

[17] For more on this, see Tyler, Patrick M. "China's Military Regards U.S. as Main Enemy in the Future." *The New York Times* 23 June. 1999: A 8-9

rationalized that "without sufficient military power, it w[ould] not be possible to successfully enact China's national identity as a world power or to play a decisive role in global politics" (30).

Though China saw itself as a major regional power during the early decades of the post-Cold War decades, its expectations to be treated accordingly were growing as China's power kept rising. Whether or not China would pose a threat to its Asian neighbors had been an ongoing debate for the previous fifteen years or so. Regarding China's relations with its East Asian neighbors, Beijing sought to foster a regional environment that took China's interests into account and recognized the nation's new status as a key or rather the key regional actor in the post-Cold War era. Examples of deference to Chinese interests were quite numerous. Recently, Beijing tried to prevent an international conference on Falun Gong from being held in Thailand, and the Thai government acceded to China's demand, pressuring the local Falun Gong adherents to call off the conference (Martinkus, "Thailand's Quiet Crackdown." *South China Morning Post* 8 Mar. 2001.) Similarly, the ASEAN Regional Forum (ARF) was hesitant to move faster than China in progressing from mere discussion of security issues to becoming a forum for conflict prevention (Guoxing, "SLOC Security in the Asia Pacific." *Occasional Paper Series*, February 2000.)

As a matter of fact, the PRC's potential security threat in East Asia was felt from Beijing's behavior in the South China Sea regarding China's series of territorial disputes with a dozen of its neighbors. The standing dispute concerning the Spratly and the Paracel Islands with more than ten nations in Southeast Asia, China's occupation of Mischief Reef in early 1995[18], the 1996 and 2000 military exercises in the Strait of Taiwan, and last but not least, the Sino-Japanese contest over the oil-rich Senkaku Islands, all these incidents had set off alarms in the region as to China's future intentions. On the ground, China took several of the islands and reefs. In 1988, Beijing seized seven islands from Vietnam after a brief naval clash. In 1995, China occupied Mischief Reef, which had been claimed by the Philippines, and placed markers on several other reefs in the area claimed by Manila. A few stand-offs between Chinese and Philippine vessels occurred since

---

[18] For more on China's territorial disputes with a dozen of its neighbors, see Mark J. Valentian, "China and the South China Sea Disputes, Conflicting claims and potential solutions in the South China Sea", *Adelphi Papers* no. 298, International Institute of Strategic Studies, London.

[2] For more on China's National Defense in 2004, issued on December 12, 2004, and available at www.chinaview.cn.

then. Moreover, the Chinese continued to build on Mischief Reef (*South China Morning Post*, online version, February 16, 2001). The concerns about what China would do with too much power mainly emanated from the assumption that China's rapidly developing economy and increasing budgets for its military modernization programs could lead to a Chinese animus dominandi and even hegemony in the region. These concerns were further reinforced in the Spring of 2001 when Beijing announced that it was increasing the People's Liberation Army (PLA) official budget by almost 18 percent to reach approximately $17.2 billion (*The Military Balance*, 2000-2001, 183).

Furthermore, impressions of a more militarily assertive China were strengthened in the United States by the mid-air collision of a Chinese F-8 fighter jet and a U.S. EP-3 surveillance plane on April 1, 2001, and the 11-day standoff over the detained American crew in China. While these incidents and their subsequent developments played well into the fears of some of the China-threat thesis, these fears may be exaggerated, at least for now. The debate about the perceived China threat was dominated by hardliners and moderates in the United States; those who see China as a hegemon on the horizon, and those who advocated more caution in pre-judging China at this stage, when China's armed forces were "still debilitated by pervasive corruption and are organizationally and technologically far behind not only America's but also Japan's and South Korea's" (Schwarz 27). "China's navy would lose a battle in the home waters of Singapore or Malaysia", for example (Ibid).

But China had been investing more and more in modernizing its armed forces selectively and impressively, and "the Chinese were investing in both diesel-powered and nuclear-powered submarines; a clear signal that they intended not only to protect their coasts but also to expand their influence far out into the Pacific" (R. Kaplan 50). Hence, alarmists were gaining ground in inflating China's security threat to the U.S.-led status quo in East Asia, as China's economic dynamism could translate into military disparity with its neighbors, but not with the United States, as Washington "had such a jump on Beijing in its command, control, communications, computer, and intelligence capabilities-by far the most vital elements of a modern military's effectiveness, and by far the most difficult to develop-that American strategic supremacy in East Asia would grow, not diminish, in the coming years" (Schwarz 28).

Militarily, the most highly likely scenario of a U.S.-Japan military showdown with China would be naval, in the South, East, and Yellow Seas. Most of the contentious issues in these seas between the three corners of East Asia's twenty-first-century triangle were still unsolved, including the Taiwan problem, the oil-rich islands, maritime choke points such as the Straits of Taiwan and Malacca, and strategic unsinkable aircraft carriers- Guam and Okinawa. The former "represents the future of U.S. strategy in the Pacific [because] it was the most potent platform anywhere in the world for the projection of American military power" (R. Kaplan 58). The latter, however, paradoxically stood for the strength of the U.S.-Japan alliance because 70 percent of U.S. defense facilities in Japan were located there, notwithstanding the political and popular discontent of the Okinawans; it was also a reminder for the Japanese of the price they would pay should there be a military confrontation between the United States and China or North Korea. For a naval war scenario in Northeast Asia, China, having just one refurbished aircraft carrier at that time, whereas the United States has more than a dozen carriers deployed, would do a great deal of damage to China's standing in the whole Pacific Rim (R. Kaplan 58).

In a January 2004 article by Wen Wei Po, a Beijing-controlled Hong Kong newspaper, a Chinese military expert summed up China's post-Cold War military doctrine, which was a blend of defensive and offensive strategy. He said:

> One [option] is making quick reactions, including military reaction, when a crisis occurs… to display the strength for safeguarding the country's interests. The other is the capability of reciprocal deterrence. This means if you can threaten my international shipping route, I can also threaten your security in various fields, including your international shipping route security (Zweig and Jianbai 34).

Within the context of China's military modernization program, Beijing focused on missiles and especially submarines, which would be the backbone of any potential Chinese power projection plans. By the end of the 1990s, China had almost 70 diesel submarines of Russian design, which could be used to create mobile minefields in one of the flash points mentioned above, but it was estimated that it would be able to deploy at least 17 new stealthy diesel-submarines and 3 nuclear ones by the end of this decade (Ibid). Furthermore, China deployed scores of its submarines and frigates, 1,200 fighter aircraft, some 800 short-range missiles, and tens of thousands of troops along the Strait of Taiwan, which could be interpreted as a demonstration of strength, and not necessarily as a sign of an imminent attack on Taiwan (the Taiwan case will be discussed later in the next Chapter) (Calder 131). The Chinese nuclear submarine intrusion into Japanese territorial waters In November 2004 brought the positive Japanese public sentiment from 75 percent in the 1980s to almost 32 percent, as Japan's sentiment hardened in the face of a perceived Chinese security threat (Ibid).

China's nuclear weapons, which had some global reach, were another significant variable in the making of a China threat in the United States and Japan. Today, the "Chinese were investing in both diesel-powered and nuclear-powered submarines–a clear signal that they intended not only to protect their coasts but also to expand their influence far out into the Pacific" (R. Kaplan 50). The post-Cold War era saw a shift in Chinese nuclear doctrine away from purely strategic weapons to those of a more tactical nature. Robert G. Sutter, a senior specialist in International Politics in Washington, D.C., pointed out that "current Chinese actions assure that Chinese nuclear weapons were better designed and safer to handle than they might otherwise be. They also precluded a possibly more expensive and potentially more destabilizing buildup of conventional military forces China might undertake if [it] was no longer able to rely on [its] nuclear arsenal" (Sutter 20). China's strategic shift revealed a Chinese belief "that a small number of warheads sufficient to inflict unacceptable damage on a handful of enemy cities, constitute[d] a credible deterrent" (Johnston 9).

The decrease in the U.S. and Russian arsenals, in accordance with the two Strategic Arms Reduction Treaties- START I and II, paradoxically increased China's nuclear power. Though the U.S. and Russia were running behind the 2003 schedule to meet the START II limitations of 3,000 to 3,500 strategic nuclear warheads each, China benefited a great deal from this nuclear zero-sum game: the fewer nuclear warheads Washington and Moscow had, the narrower the strategic gap became between them and Beijing (Arbatov 213-15). The subsequent increase in China's relative nuclear strength brought about by the START reductions, combined with the increase in actual nuclear strength resulting from Beijing's modernization programs, all made China a force to be reckoned with. China's long-range security concerns, including primarily the Taiwan problem, sovereignty claims over strategic islands in the South China Sea and the East China Sea, might lead Beijing to reconsider its security calculus and seek a redistribution of power relations in East Asia.

In the same context of reforms in China's military doctrines, "Chinese strategists developed a concept of 'limited deterrence' [which] required sufficient counterforce and counter value tactical, theater, and strategic nuclear forces to deter the escalation of conventional or nuclear war" (Johnston 5). Although this shift to a shorter-range tactical doctrine could cause concern among China's immediate neighbors like Taiwan and Japan, it should be noted that it was still based on the doctrine of deterrence. China was pursuing impressive military modernization programs, but without proof to the contrary, they continued to be based on attempts to improve its world status and provide a viable defense of its own security. Efforts to modernize militarily could simply be indicative of China's desire to keep pace with other potential and known world powers.

In late 1992, the 14th Chinese Communist Party (CCP) Congress adopted unilateral "comprehensive national strength" as the official party line for China's national security strategy, a strategy that was a direct result of the end of the Cold War. With increasing global competition due to a larger number of international actors, China believed the road to world power status was becoming increasingly dependent on a strong military. Samuel Kim said that "the proposition that sufficient military power buys both deterrence and status reflects why China needed more and better high-tech weapons systems including nuclear weapons" (49). With China essentially surrounded by a threatening U.S.-Japan alliance, nuclear Russia, and India, and with no major allies, its strategy of comprehensive national strength emphasizing self-reliance and unilateral security came to substantiate the interplay between the need for security and the quest for power. In short, frightened by an ostensibly threatening U.S.-Japan security arrangement, China started seeking to reform and renovate its non-conventional second-strike capabilities.

On another note, China's sale of missiles and nuclear technology to countries like Pakistan, was viewed by the U.S. as "irresponsible". According to a *New York Times* article of August 1997, "American intelligence reported repeatedly that the Chinese were building a factory in Pakistan to turn out missiles, capable of carrying nuclear warheads that could reach India" (Rosenthal, sec. A). Beijing, however, insisted that the arms sold were for defensive uses, invoking the U.S. argument regarding Washington's arms sales to Taiwan. As China's economic modernization program required huge funding resources, the Chinese military was forced "to sell many of its advanced weapons and technologies in order to fund [its] own development programs" (Kim iii). Moreover, "China's missile sales... earned not only hard currency but also a much-sought diplomatic switch from Taipei to Beijing" (Ibid).

Beijing's relentless effort to be recognized as the "official China" and its desire to establish diplomatic relations with countries that were recognizing Taiwan, were paying off. Furthermore, "Chinese leadership found the arms sales, especially in the nuclear and missile field, as another way of demonstrating its status as a global power, and that regional conflicts in the Third World could not be resolved without China's participation" (Kim 30). Thus, the need for hard currency, the desire to gain diplomatic recognition, and the drive to become a global power, as well as the defensive motivations discussed above, generally motivated major China's arms sales.

Though some aspects of China's foreign policy were questionable by Western standards, researching the Chinese motivations for such actions showed that they were not totally "adventuristic." China's disputed territorial claims and arms sales can actually be traced back to its defensive needs, and not for offensive purposes as the United States and Japan advanced, which showed the antithetical power and security calculations between the United States and Japan, on the one hand, and China, on the other hand. Both sides were competing in Asia, though not necessarily openly, but for different reasons; Washington was working with Japan and other regional allies such as South Korea to prevent China from becoming a competitive hegemon. Beijing, however, understandably sought to pursue its own interests as a state operating within a competitive security environment, instead of seeking to dominate others.

China viewed Japan as an extension of a perceived U.S. hegemonic power in Asia (*Beijing Review*, no.21, May 24, 2001). The Chinese had a deep-rooted fear of a Japan that would be playing a fiddle role in an unequal security arrangement with the U.S., and becoming an American tool to cover up Washington's intent to dominate the region. The level of mistrust between China on the one hand and Japan and the U.S. on the other was a hurdle, that was not easy to overcome, for East Asia stability. "Despite recent efforts among Washington, Tokyo, and Beijing to improve bilateral and even trilateral relations, the fact that the United States and Japan were on one side of the security wall while China was on the other was fundamentally problematic" to the U.S.-Japan regional security calculations (DiFilippo 68).

Furthermore, the Chinese worried about the character and scope of the U.S.-Japan alliance and its implications for the future of the Taiwan problem, which had a deep impact on the effectiveness of the U.S.-Japan link in playing a positive security role in East Asia (Shambaugh 52-79). As Beijing saw it, Washington and Tokyo together presented a far more formidable challenge to Chinese regional security interests than China did to those of the United States and Japan[19]. China was highly sensitive to anything pertaining to Japan and its

---

[19] For more on this subject, See Shambaugh, David. "China's Military Views the World." *International Security* 24, no.3, Winter 1999/2000, 52-79.

changing international role because a future broadening of Japan's regional role would open the door to probable Japanese involvement in Taiwan, the South China Sea, the Spratly Islands, and the Strait of Malacca. The April 1996 Clinton Hashimoto Joint Declaration, which came only one month after the March 1996 Taiwan crisis reached its climax, exacerbated Chinese fears. The declaration made it clear that Japan would play new roles in maintaining stability in the "Asia Pacific" region, which was construed in Beijing as a reference to the widening scope of the U.S.-Japan alliance.

On another note, the PRC was wary of the U.S. proposal to establish a theater missile defense (TMD) system that would shield Japan and South Korea, allegedly from a missile attack from North Korea. The Chinese opposed TMD in part because they were concerned that Taiwan would be included in the system, but also because it would undermine their primary means of pressure over Tokyo and Taipei, that is, Chinese missiles. TMD would also closely integrate defense relations between the United States and these two regional American allies at a time when China was trying to weaken the U.S. influence in the area.

In the post-Cold War era, China and Japan were bound to diverge on the political, security, and trade levels. They particularly differed because of their constant and peculiar quest for a mixture of security and power. In their attempts to seek as much power as possible at the expense of each other, Japan and China were on a collision course because they did not trust each other. Their different approaches to the security of East Asia, together with their opposite view of the U.S.-Japan alliance, had a negative effect on the China-Japan relationship. Furthermore, the future of Taiwan would heavily depend on the state of the Sino-Japanese relationship because Japan's pro-Taiwan stand would complicate China's attempts to convince Taipei of the value of a peaceful reunification.

For Tokyo, the essence of Japan's Cold War China problem was defined by China's weakness, its potential for political instability and the implications of such instability for Japan's security and economic interests on the mainland, given the huge amounts of Japanese investments in and the volume of trade exchange with China. By the dawn of this millennium, and in the years ahead, it was China's growing strength that was to redefine Japan's China problem, in view of China's growing military might and Beijing's dissatisfaction with Japan's alleged accomplice role in supporting America consolidating its hegemonic position in the Asia-Pacific region. Geography was certainly an important factor. For Japan, China was a next-door problem, much like Mexico would be for the United States but with different aspects, and stability in China was important as much to Beijing as to Tokyo. This was true for Japan's commercial and economic interests as well as its national security.

Though China sought to develop good relations with Japan, there were still significant points of friction. Conflicting Chinese and Japanese claims about the Senkaku/Diaoyu Islands remained a security issue that ought to be considered within the context of the U.S.-Japan security alliance. China continued to send maritime research and even military vessels into Japan's maritime exclusive economic zone (EEZ) near the Senkakus and other areas, while the Japanese government turned down a Chinese proposal in March-April 2000 that some of their Coast Guard vessels be included in a multilateral force seeking to combat piracy in the South China Sea (Pryzstup, "China and the U.S.-Japan Alliance", Lecture 2000). Furthermore, the level of mutual distrust between Tokyo and Beijing made it difficult to fully implement a February 2001 accord to establish a mechanism for prior notification of maritime research activities in the disputed waters (Ibid).

In relation to the U.S.-China equation, it is worth pointing out that Tokyo was deeply uneasy about the "constructive strategic partnership" that evolved between the United States and China during the Clinton presidency of the 1990s (Funabashi 26-36). Then, despite American assurances to the contrary, China was perceived to be trying to outflank Japan while U.S.-Japan relations were particularly shaky over Japan's economic mismanagement and its impotence to help with the 1997 Asian financial crisis. China, in turn, tried to drive a wedge in the U.S.-Japan connection, even symbolically. The Chinese President Jiang Zemin's October 1997 visit to Pearl Harbor, for instance, which came at his request, was construed in Japan as a Chinese attempt to remind the Americans that it was not China that attacked the United States without a declaration of war, and therefore, China could not be America's enemy in East Asia. Moreover, China lobbied for Clinton's visit to Nanking in June 1998, the scene of the infamous massacre by the Japanese imperial army in 1937, which was a message to remind the Japanese of their WWII conduct in the region.

At the same time, Japan paradoxically feared a U.S.-China enmity. Should the vociferous anti-China rhetoric emanating from Congress impact policy-making in Washington D.C., warnings of Chinese antagonism may become self-fulfilling. This might considerably undermine the U.S.-Japan alliance. Though the United States and Japan sought to fathom the implications of China's emerging power on their respective interests, it was necessary to allude to the fact that Washington and Tokyo did not have identical views and calculations regarding China's geopolitical ascendancy to a major power status in Asia. It was true that the two allies converged on most security and economic issues relating to the rise of China as a potential superpower and probably a regional hegemon, but this did not necessarily mean that they had an overlapping or identical calculus about how to deal with a strong China.

The United States sought to broaden the alliance to maintain Tokyo's confidence in the U.S. commitment to Japan's security, and, at the same time, to secure Japanese cooperation about a host of regional issues, including mutual concerns about China's rising power and allegedly assertive behavior. Beijing, in turn, calculated that under the 1997 revised terms of the U.S. Asia policy, including the consolidation of Washington's alliance with Tokyo, Japan was likely to provide logistical and intelligence support to U.S. forces in the event of an American military intervention in a China-Taiwan conflict (J. Wang). While the 1997 U.S.-Japan defense guidelines cited sources of persisting instability and uncertainty in the Asia-Pacific region, including unresolved territorial disputes and potential regional conflicts referring to the problem of Taiwan, they also pointed to the heavy concentrations of conventional and nuclear forces in the region, clearly pointing at Chinese potential military aspirations. In short, that the United States was wary of Chinese military development and intentions was a justification for a continued American military presence in the Asia-Pacific region (Nye, "China's Re-emergence and the Future of the Asia Pacific").

So, in the absence of a clear and common enemy binding the U.S. and Japan together as the ex-Soviet Union did, it was difficult to imagine how the Chinese would believe that this alliance was not meant to contain China. Though the United States and Japan did not state explicitly that they were seeking to contain China, the Chinese looked for other indicators to evaluate the direction of the U.S.-Japan alliance. From a Chinese perspective, the alliance, for instance, failed to restrain the buildup of Japanese military power, and enabled Tokyo to establish the basis of an independent military capability, manifested by a series of regionally and domestically controversial measures and plans.

The series of events included Japan's new role-sharing activities, such as its sending of four warships to Afghanistan in November 2001 and to Iraq in 2003 to back up America's war efforts in Southwest Asia. Also, the list went on to include Tokyo's intent to upgrade its Self Defense Force to a ministry of defense, which took place in December 2006, and, most seriously, the late Prime Minister Shinzo Abe's pledge in September 2006 to review Article 9 in order to allow more room for future Japanese military interventions. All these assertive

Japanese measures took place with U.S. public backing. Therefore, the negative Chinese perception of the U.S.-Japan association made the American-Japan equation a negative security factor, particularly in East Asia, instead of one that was reassuring to Japan and China.

In short, besides the U.S. pattern of maintaining a threatening environment in East Asia by playing China and Japan off against each other, Tokyo and Beijing, in their turn, did not work in a way to make the triangle with the United States a genuine trialogue. One which could benefit the three parties concerned, and bring stability to a region that had the highest number of territorial disputes in the world. However, there was still a leeway for a Sino-Japanese cooperative relationship, given the significant implications that the Sino-Japanese equation carried for East Asia's future. Japanese policymakers hoped to influence and sustain China's market economy reforms as an incentive to increase the Chinese stake in open and free trade. On the one hand, like their American counterparts, the Japanese believed that the promotion of China's economic reforms would encourage the development of a native-born and stable democracy.

But in a clear departure from their American allies, the Japanese expected that a policy of engaging China would enable Japan to consolidate a position of political and economic strength in East Asia. When the U.S., for instance, deployed its aircraft carriers in the Strait of Taiwan in response to China's March 1996 military exercises, Japan expressed only "understanding" for such a move. Some analysts went even further to opine that U.S.-Japan relations might weaken considerably if Washington appeared to be forcing Tokyo to "choose" between its ties with the U.S. and China, because Japan was apparently seeking to avoid supporting one relationship at the expense of the other. Therefore, should there be a constructive three-way relationship between Beijing, Tokyo, and Washington, "Japan, the U.S., and China should construct a triangular relationship and maintain an equal distance from each other", as Kato Koichi, former secretary-general of the Pro-America Japanese Liberal Democratic Party put it (*Mainichi Daily News*, June 1998, 14). But this triangular relationship would be unreachable unless the United States and Japan stopped exaggerating China's rising power, and marketing the China-threat thesis in the Asia-Pacific region.

After all, China still lacked the capabilities to seriously threaten the security of its neighbors, and its intentions were probably more inclined toward maintaining the regional status quo, at least for the time being. Then, China still lacked the necessary inventories of power to project its influence regionally or globally, and it did not seem likely to develop such capabilities in the immediate future. Former U.S. Deputy Secretary of Defense Joseph Nye believed that "if Chinese military "modernization" continue[d] at its current rate, in twenty years it w[ould] have the capabilities of a mid-level U.S. NATO ally of forty years ago" (Gerson, "Fresh Look: Re-examining the role and impact of U.S. bases in Asia-Pacific", Lecture June 26-27, 1999).

The Chinese military was postured primarily toward defending the Chinese mainland from attack, dating back to the "people's war strategy" of the Mao era. "To bid for mastery of East Asia, China would have to fundamentally transform the doctrine, training, and structure of its military, which traditionally focused on defending home territory" (Schwarz 27). Though China's military modernization program over the last several years sought to develop and acquire new naval and air weapons systems, such as SU-27 and SU-30 fighter aircraft and two *Sovremennyy* class destroyers from Russia, these weapons did not necessarily bring Beijing longer-range power projection capabilities (*The Military Balance*, 2000-2001, 183, 186-187, 194-197). The People's Liberation Army's (PLA) Navy had no aircraft carriers up till the mid-2000s to project sea power, and its air force was still rather rudimentary, lacking long-range capabilities[20].

According to Michael Swaine and James Mulvenon of the conservative and even hawkish RAND[21] foreign policy think tank, only by 2010 to 2015 at the earliest would China be able to project one or two divisions, with almost 15,000 troops each, by air, land, and sea over 100 miles across the Strait of Taiwan, for instance. Swaine and Mulvenon also predicted that only by the year 2025 would China be able to project three or four divisions slightly further than the Strait of Taiwan ("Taiwan's Foreign and Defense policies: Features and Determinants", 2001, 113-14). One can go further to argue that China's navy was not even able to mount an amphibious assault on the tiny island of Taiwan, let alone to

---

[20] U.S. Department of Defense (DoD), Annual Report on the Military Power of the People's Republic of China: Report to Congress Pursuant to the 2000 National Defense Authorization Act, 2002, 49. Hereafter cited as DoD, Military Power of the PRC.

[21] The RAND Corporation is a conservative think tank group having a mixture of business and political interests in Washington D.C. It is funded by the Pentagon particularly the U.S. Air Force, and was formerly chaired by Donald Rumsfeld, the ex-Secretary of Defense, with Zalmay Khalilzad, the current US ambassador in Baghdad. RAND is usually taken as an example of the link between the military and the industrial sectors in the United States, that is the "Military-Industrial Complex", President Eisenhower warned the Americans against in his 1960 Farewell Address.

project Chinese sea power in the Asia-Pacific rim. It was then estimated that as late as 2025, China would still be unable to enforce a complete naval blockade on the island, as China still did not have any naval or air supremacy over any of its immediate neighbors because the Chinese military services were still largely rudimentary and poorly trained up until the end of the first decade of the twenty-first century. China's

> ships and naval aircraft occasionally train together, [and] ground and naval forces rarely exercised in tandem. In addition, China's military forces lacked the command, control, and communications and the centralized system needed" to project Chinese power in the South China Sea for example (Eland 3).

Furthermore, the reality of China's air projection capabilities testified to the dubious U.S.-Japan perception of what was called the China threat. The 2002 DoD report on China's military power predicted that China was a long way off from being able to project its power in the region or coerce its neighbors. The report indicated that the Chinese Air Force was hampered by inadequate electronic warfare and, air-to-air refueling capabilities, and pilot training. The U.S. Department of Defense estimated that only by 2010 will China have all the elements-operational concepts and training- of an integrated, modern air force (Department of Defense (DoD), "Military Power of the PRC", 18). "In addition, China's lack of an integrated air defense system for the foreseeable future - probably the next two decades- could leave its homeland open to retaliatory attacks" by more sophisticated air forces in the region, such as that of Japan, Australia, and even Taiwan (Eland 3). China's structural deficiency of an integrated air defense system was to take a while to repair. It would take more investment into buying more than the handful of Russian-made SA-10 and SA-15 surface-to-air missiles, and by further coordinating between and integration of its military services. Also, it would need to focus more on acquiring better amphibious power capabilities and less reliance on its army, as the future wars in the Asia-Pacific region would be more naval than ground confrontations.

While China wanted to have its interests taken into account by the countries in East Asia, it did not necessarily mean that China would automatically seek to dominate its neighbors the way the Soviet Union did in Eastern Europe, for example. Without power projection capabilities, the PRC lacked the means to coerce its neighbors; in fact, China developed cordial, cooperative relations with nearly most of them. After all, Beijing concluded long-term political, economic, and security cooperative agreements with all ten of the Association of Southeast Asian Nations (ASEAN) during 1999 and 2000 (Thayer 13). Beijing also entered into a Partnership of Friendship and Cooperation for Peace and Development with Japan in 1998 and a full-scale cooperative partnership with South Korea in October 2000 (Ibid). While it may be true that China originally joined regional organizations such as the Asia-Pacific Economic Cooperation (APEC) forum and the ASEAN Regional Forum (ARF) so as to ensure that they would not be used to harm Chinese interests, it is only fair to say that China was a useful and cooperative participant (Bob 6-9). It participated in the inauguration of the ASEAN Plus Three summit in December 1997, which brought China, Japan, and South Korea into strategic discussions with members of ASEAN (Ibid).

China also sought to resolve many of its outstanding territorial disputes with its neighbors. In the previous two years, Beijing signed agreements and protocols with Russia and Vietnam, resolving almost all of their remaining land border disputes. Indeed, China sought to reach an agreement with its neighbors to shelve the issues and to move forward cooperatively on other fronts. Examples here included the Senkaku/Diaoyu Islands dispute with Japan, and the Spratly Islands dispute with Brunei, Malaysia, the Philippines, and Vietnam (Thayer 11). It transpired that China and the Southeast Asian claimants were relatively close to agreement on a code of conduct to govern their behavior in the Spratlys, with one of the major stumbling blocks being Vietnamese insistence that the code also covered the Paracel Islands in the northern part of the South China Sea, which China had seized from South Vietnam in 1974 (*The China Quarterly*, No. 132, December 1992, 999-1028).

Moreover, the perceived China threat ought to be kept in proportion. In the first place, the Spratlys did not form part of the core territories of any of the claimant states, which meant that they were not an imminent security problem to the region; they were of peripheral, not core interest. In the second place, China no longer posed a political challenge to the claimant states. In the 1950s and 1960s, by contrast, China sought to undermine the political regimes of many of these states with its support of communist insurgencies. The most prominent case was the 1962 Indonesian aborted coup instigated by the Indonesian Communist Party sanctioned by Beijing. In the third place, as already mentioned in this chapter, Beijing had done its utmost not to let the Spratlys dispute preclude the pursuit of cooperative relations with these neighbors in other areas.

Following the final settlement of the Cambodia conflict with the conclusion of the Paris Agreements in 1991, China built a somewhat positive interaction with ASEAN, and worked to maintain the political status quo in Southeast Asia, with the exception of the dispute over the Spratly Islands. Moreover, Beijing entered into various dialogues and joined regional organizations with its neighbors to the south, such as the ASEAN Regional Forum (ARF) and the ASEAN-China dialogue (Thayer 11). Over the two years of 1999-2000, China concluded long-term individual cooperation agreements with the ten ASEAN member states, covering economic, political, and even military cooperation. It also acted as a good neighbor during some of the crises that plagued the region over the last decade.

China played a very constructive role during the 1997 economic crisis in Southeast Asia, contributing to the International Monetary Fund (IMF)-led bailout of Thailand and Indonesia. Beijing also promised not to devalue its currency, despite its declining exports, which could have undermined the ability of some of the Southeast Asian countries to use exports to regain their economic recovery from the crisis, and to realize the growth rates they had enjoyed up to the mid-1990s. Therefore, whether one looks at bilateral or multilateral relations, at economic or security issues, the evidence points in the same direction; China was up to then pursuing a non-aggressive foreign policy toward its neighbors and, to a large extent, was attempting to maintain the status quo in East Asia, except for the U.S.-Japan connection, which viewed China and was perceived by China as a threat to the region's stability.

Therefore, whether focusing on China's military capabilities or a combination of its intentions and capabilities, China was still a conservative, middle power that might not really matter to the degree that the coming-conflict-with-China camp was trying to advance (Bernstein and Munro 25), leading the discussion to argue that one ought to be aware of the dichotomy between perceptions of a China threat and the reality of a developing nation that would strive to feed hundreds of millions of its 1.3 billion population for a long time to come. Was a rising China a real threat to its East Asian neighbors as the United States and, subsequently, Japan attempted to market China's image on the regional scene during the first two decades after the end of the Cold War?

Though the American-Japanese September 1997 new defense guidelines emphasized that the alliance was not directed at China, Beijing understood that the Americans believed that the absence of an American security presence in East Asia would mean an unrestrained Chinese regional hegemony. The United States and Japan argued that their alliance was serving to reassure Asia-Pacific states that were nervous about rising Chinese power, a power which was very much exaggerated beyond reality in order to frighten those nervous nations into acquiescing to a U.S.-led security apparatus.

Finally, China's future intentions could impact U.S. regional and global interests. Its military modernization programs and arms control policies may lead to increased tension between the two countries since China's effort to modernize its military, regardless of its intentions, whether defensive or offensive, was interpreted in the U.S. and Japan as preparing for future hegemony in Asia. This fits into the theoretical framework of this book that if state A tries to seek more power to maximize its security, it almost automatically provokes suspicion from its neighbors, which could lead to an arms race or a vicious circle of action and reaction that generally results in armed conflicts based on a pre-emption ideology. As for the issue of arms sales, China said then that it was copying America in selling purely "defensive" weapons to weak countries or countries under threat, such as the controversial American sale of highly sophisticated weapons to Taiwan, which Washington perceived as under Chinese threat.

3.4. Summary

This chapter has looked at the two main security drivers in East Asia which were the controversial U.S.-Japan security alliance and the rise of China as a potential competitor with the United States for alleged regional hegemony. In the decades that followed the Cold War, the US-Japan alliance was controversial, and, to a large extent paradoxical, as it provided Japan with less security but offered a strategic advantage for the United States to perpetuate its preponderant position in the Asia Pacific region. As the first part of this chapter tried to show, this was an alliance that drew much criticism and skepticism from Japan's neighbors, especially China, North Korea, and Russia[22]. China perceived the U.S.-Japan alliance as a threat because Beijing suspected that the United States was using this alliance to contain the growing impact of China's rise as a superpower with increasingly growing interests, and thus to prevent the emergence of a serious competitor that might challenge the current status quo of world unipolarity. The alliance was a security challenge for China, since it was perceived as a further obstacle to a peaceful reunification with Taiwan,

---

[22] See Russian President Vladimir Putin's Interview with AlJazeera Arabic Channel on February 10, 2007.

given the February 2005 U.S.-Japan SCC declaration that the Taiwan problem was now a "common security problem" for Tokyo and Washington.

As for the North Korea factor regarding the relevance and the security value of the U.S.-Japan security alliance in East Asia, it would suffice to mention the 1993 and 1998 North Korean missile tests over the Sea of Japan, which also crossed Japanese air space and sent a wave of security panic into Japan. Regardless of the alleged U.S. exaggeration of the threat emanating from those missiles, the episode itself showed that Japan's association with an alliance largely perceived by regional actors as threatening made Japan less secure. Moreover, the repeated North Korean threats that in case the United States, in collaboration with Japan, carried out its secret "Operation Plan 5027" to invade North Korea, Japan would be the primary target of North Korean missiles.

Given the geographical proximity of the Japanese archipelago to North Korea and the political complexities of Tokyo's association with an alliance largely perceived as predatory rather than stabilizing, Japan, instead of the United States, would be the first loser in case of an American-North Korean conflict. North Korea's threats included even South Korea, perceived as another accomplice of the United States, which supported one of the arguments of this work that East Asia's security problems were inextricably linked and, therefore, needed a comprehensive approach that should take into account the trilateral aspect of the region's security nature.

For the North Korean or Taiwanese issues to be solved diplomatically, the U.S.-Japan-China commitment to a multilateral approach to the region's security requirements was a prerequisite to a better security environment and a more constructive interaction among the three corners of the triangle, a triangle which this work is seeking to explore in order to meet its overall objective of studying the U.S. claim that the American military presence in East Asia was still a positive security factor even after the demise of the Soviet Union and the end of the Cold War. But stability was not felt from the 1950-53 Korean War up till the end of the 2000s. Regional security continued to be not only an obstacle to sustainable economic and social development, but also was even exacerbated by the mere U.S. military presence, which most regional actors took as threatening rather than stabilizing.

The paradoxical nature of the U.S.-Japan security alliance, however, ought not to veil the deeply rooted asymmetrical aspect of this connection, bringing about less security to Japan in view of Tokyo's association with a country that was perceived as dominating and even hegemonic. Moreover, the United States even went further to take advantage of its privileged position regarding the security relationship with Japan to pressure the Japanese into acquiescing on economic and trade contentions with some American corporations such as the car and the computer industries. Japan's dependence on American security guarantees placed Tokyo in a weak position with respect to issues that went beyond security and stability in East Asia.

The Japanese became so acquiescent to American pressure that they went along with U.S. propositions to expand their bilateral alliance in order to widen Japan's prerogatives into "areas surrounding Japan". A move that not only elicited negative feedback from Japan's neighbors, but also infringed upon Article 9 of Japan's peace Constitution, which was overstretched to allow for Japan to send its troops to far away combat zones for the first time since WWII. But one of the reasons why Japan preferred a bilateral instead of multilateral approach to its security was the U.S. policy to wave the flag of the coming China threat and the implications of the rise of China on regional security, which needed, from a U.S. perspective, a sustainable American military presence in association with Japan.

The rise of the China factor and its implications on regional security was the second major driver in post-Cold War East Asia. As China was rising economically and becoming more demanding in terms of raw material and energy resources, the United States, using the Japan card, was increasingly becoming more suspicious of what China would do with its growing economic and probably military power, not only in East Asia but also in the world at large. The last part of this chapter has shed light on the dichotomy between the perception and the reality of China's security threat. It demonstrated how China's military modernization programs, combined with the latent Taiwan problem and Beijing's territorial disputes with its neighbors over a number of Islands in the South China Sea and the East China Sea, invited suspicion about China's increasingly assertive and even hegemonic post-Cold War tendencies.

But at the same time, the U.S. had a strategy to exaggerate the China-threat thesis in Japanese and South Korean eyes in order to market the claim that the American military presence in the region was a security requirement for America's allies' well-being. A presence that served as a deterrent for the Chinese not to try to dominate or coerce these allies in the absence of a strong American military presence. This takes the discussion back to the decisive role of the dependent variables of power and security in shaping states' calculations and determining the outcome of their interactions. As this chapter has demonstrated, Washington took advantage of its power preponderance not only to encircle China with a chain of military alliances and bilateral accords to prevent the rise of a challenging China, but also to extract economic and trade, besides political, bonuses even from its closest ally in the region –Japan.

Therefore, the interplay of a series of variables regarding the impact of the United States' alliance with Japan on the security situation in the region, and the strategic implications of the rise of China on America's dominant role in East Asia, did require the need to further explore what the U.S. wanted to do in the region and how it intended to deal with perceived threats to its preponderant position. The mutual Sino-American-Japanese allegations of being hegemonic would be studied through some American government documents, TMD armament programs, the U.S. "hub and spoke" approach, and China's disputes with some of its neighbors, in addition to Beijing's threats against Taiwan, which will be dealt with later in this book as a case study of hegemony.

Chapter 4

Hegemony in East Asia's Power and Security Calculations

4.1. How Hegemonic was post-Cold War America?

4.1.1. Hegemony and the "New American Century"

> Our armies do not come into your cities and lands as conquerors or enemies, but as liberators. ... It is [not] the wish of [our] government to impose upon you alien institutions. ... [It is our wish] that you should prosper even as in the past, when your lands were fertile, when your ancestors gave to the world literature, science, and art, and when Baghdad city was one of the wonders of the world. -General F. S. Maude to the People of Mesopotamia, March 19, 1917- (Ferguson, *Hegemony or Empire?* 154).

As the focus of this book is the interplay of the power and security variables in the post-Cold War U.S.-Japan-China triangle, the central objective of this work is to get to the answer whether the US military presence in Northeast Asia during the first two decades of the post-Cold War era was a positive or negative security factor. This chapter seeks to explore the reality of the U.S. hegemonic allegations from nations that viewed the US military presence in the region as negative and even destabilizing for the Northeast. The real issue here is how the three major actors in the triangle– the United States, Japan, and China– perceived each other through the prism of hegemony, as the term itself did not necessarily mean the same thing for each of them. This chapter also deals with both benign and malign hegemony from a political science realist point of view, and tries to apply its findings to the American military presence in East Asia. The purpose is to show that if American hegemony in the region was benign, it should be a positive security factor, and thus supporting the null hypothesis of this work; but if it was malign, it could only be a negative security variable in the region's security equation, which should substantiate the research hypothesis of this book.

This chapter, however, does not seek to analyze hegemony per se because it is beyond the scope and the focus of this book; rather, it intends to look at hegemony from an international relations viewpoint, as the theoretical framework of this work is a political science realist standpoint. It also takes the Taiwan issue as a case study of hegemony exercised by the United States and Japan, from a Chinese perspective, in an attempt to prevent a peaceful reunification between the island and the motherland. China's assertive posture regarding Taipei's increasingly "separatist" trends, however, and the 2005 anti-secession law passed by the Chinese parliament in February 2005, which made it imperative for the Chinese government to prevent a Taiwanese separation even by force, were perceived by Washington and Tokyo as hegemonic and assertive at that time. This chapter ends with a section that sums up the whole problem of this work and tries to answer the major question about the reality of the U.S. military presence in East Asia. Finally, this chapter will end with a retrospective recapitulation of the post-Cold War U.S. security role in East Asia, especially during the post-Cold War early decades.

Two major milestone documents revealed the U.S. post-Cold War strategy of how to take advantage of the post-Soviet era of American hegemonic unipolarity and, thus, how to perpetuate the alleged U.S. hegemony for as long as possible. These documents were the 1992 Defense Policy Guidance (DPG) and the 1997 Project for a New American Century (PNAC) (Sands 29). Both documents aimed to perpetuate Pax Americana through the twenty-first century through hard military power. The post-Cold War perceived American hegemony in East Asia, however, was not maintained only by its military forward presence, but also by a consistent and concerted effort to dominate the region's economic life in the region. This was attained by exerting political pressure and violating some countries' economic sovereignty by disregarding the basic principles of free and unfettered trade, which the United States itself demanded as early as the 1944 Bretton Woods Accords[1]. Though partially

---

[1] The Bretton Woods Accords are the outcome of a post-WWII international conference at Bretton Woods, New Hampshire, aimed at establishing an international monetary system that would prevent the repeat of the 1929 Great Depression. The new Bretton Woods System was based on a series of new economic and monetary rules which the signatories engaged to abide by. These rules included an exchange Rate System, Balance-of-Payments adjustments, and supplies of Reserve Assets. The Bretton Woods conference also established the International Monetary Fund (IMF), and the International Bank for Reconstruction and Development (IBRD). Though the Bretton Woods Accords were perceived by the then Eastern Bloc, and even by France's Charles DeGaulle, as an

abandoned in 1973 by President Richard Nixon, the fallouts of these accords, such as the domination of the U.S. dollar as the key international currency and the intrusive conduct of the IMF when bailing out nations in liquidity crises, further deepened the perception of the United States as a self-interested economic hegemon. A brief examination of the state of the U.S. economy and its current status should provide a hint as to where American economic hegemony was heading then.

From a scholarly point of view, regardless of its euphemistic and political manipulation or linguistic gymnastics, hegemony in general is a term that originally comes from a Greek political context when Spartans tried to dominate their Greek neighbors like the Athenians, the Chios, and the Lesbos, during the time of the Peloponnesian War[2] and after. Later, the term hegemony acquired a wider dimension to extend to international relations, and has come to depict a dominant behavior of a country or an alliance of nations that possesses the necessary economic, military, political, and probably cultural attributes to project its power regionally and globally. In international politics, a hegemon is a state that is able to impose its set of rules on the interstate system, and subsequently creates a certain political and military order. It generally provides certain advantages for states, or sometimes called satellites located within its orbit or protected by it. Advantages include security, economic and political privileges, which are meant to be like carrots that induce acquiescence. With the advent of the ideology of communism, however, the meaning of hegemony was expanded to include the domination of one social class over another class, thus describing an internal economic and social, but not necessarily political, situation. The champion of the last kind of hegemony was Antonio Gramsci, who argued in his *Prison Notebooks* that the hegemony of dominant social and economic groups stemmed in large part from the ability to impose their values, beliefs, and culture on those they would subordinate.

Consequently, it would be necessary to engage in a "battle of ideas" in order to transform the consciousness of the masses, which is essential if a successful

---

American design of monetary hegemony, the accords collapsed when the United States decided to suspend the convertibility of the dollar into gold. Eventually, in April 1973 a new international system of floating exchange rates was instituted, and the Bretton Woods Accords were officially dead.

[2] For more on the history of Greek wars, see *History of the Peloponnesian War*, Thucydes, Rex Warner, tans. Baltimore, Maryland: Penguin Books, 1903, 13, 22-23, 25, 358-366.

revolution were to take place (Williams et al. *The Dictionary of the 20th-Century Politics* 309-310). Gramsci's views regarding hegemony and its maintenance were applied to international relations to mean that hegemonic powers could partly retain their dominance by using the soft power of their ideas to attract the public. Overall, hegemony is usually the result of an excess of power that goes unchecked either by a rival superpower, by international law, or by domestic law in the case of class hegemony. Lord Acton, in a letter to Bishop Mandell Creighton, warned more than one century ago that "power tends to corrupt, and absolute power corrupts absolutely,... there is no worse heresy than that the office sanctifies the holder of it" (Letter to Bishop Mandell Creighton, April 5, 1887, reprinted in *Life and Letters of Mandell Creighton*, 1904).

Talking about hegemony, we can identify two kinds of hegemony that apply to the two Asian legs of the triangle- Japan and China in their respective relations with the third leg of the triangle- the United States. Hegemony could be structural, referring to the kind of unconscious and internalized acquiescence that the hegemon receives from others, and a surface one achieved through economic and military coercion. This could be achieved through a long-term exercise of coercive power, be it military, political, economic, and even cultural. Japan was a good example of structural hegemony, as the Japanese culture had internalized many of the American cultural characteristics. The increasing trend among Japanese youth to imitate American rock and roll music and hair cut styles could be a case study by itself[3]. Nial Ferguson, a supporter of a U.S. benign hegemony, argued that "the spread of America's language, ideas, and culture invites comparison to Rome at its zenith" (Ikenberry, "Illusions of Empire" 148). But the spread of America's language, ideas, and culture through the use of American "soft power", that is, the power of influencing others through persuasion and example- was considerably damaged by U.S unilateralism, and the abuses in Abu Graib and Guantànamo (Hoffmann 60).

Surface hegemony, however, is based on situational hegemonic activity, projects, and practices that are implemented through coercion and conscious transformation of the other (Gerson "Fresh Look: Re-examining the role and impact of U.S. bases in Asia-Pacific", Lecture June 26-27, 1999). China could fit

---

[3] See John G. Ikenberry. "Illusions of Empire: Defining the New American Order". *Foreign Affairs*, March/April 2004, Vol. 83, Iss. 2, p. 144-154). Also see for instance the film *Tokyo Pop*, 1988 by Carrie Hamilton and Yutaka Tadokoro. International Spectra Film Distribution Inc, 4000 Warner Blvd, Burbank, CA.

this definition of hegemony; this country was under enormous pressure from the United States to be a "responsible and peaceful" rising power. The term "responsible itself can infer a hierarchical U.S. view of the Sino-American relationship, and imply that the United States appointed itself in a higher position to set the rules of responsibility. A "responsible" China, from a US perspective, was a China that would not challenge the United States in East Asia, which revealed a U.S. hegemonic perception of the region's security and political equation. As the Japanese structural hegemony was combined with the concerted policy of the hegemon itself in order to internalize China's surface hegemony so as to make it a structural one, there were strong indications that Washington and Tokyo would work to corner China into developing as a "responsible" rising power, and "should China fail to move in that direction, it would be confronted by a reinvigorated [U.S.-Japan] alliance" (Przystup and Saunders 2).

After the end of the Cold War, the United States clearly became the sole superpower. Among today's major powers in the world arena, "only the United States retained the full array of great power attributes- military, [and] economic…"(Ikenberry, "Illusions of Empire" 145-46). The United States became an example of geopolitical hegemony that was manifested primarily through the highest U.S. defense budget in the world, which reached 396.1 billion dollars as of 2004, and through what Chalmers Johnson called an "empire of bases" (151-86). In contrast, Russia's defense budget during the first decade of the twenty-first century was the world's second-largest, but it was only 14 percent of that of the United States (Ch. Johnson 306). The Pentagon's budget was also more than the next 27 highest world defense budgets combined. As for the empire of bases that the United States had developed, there were now more than 725 American foreign bases in 154 countries (154). Chalmers Johnson saw five main missions for those bases:

> maintaining absolute military preponderance over the rest of the world, a task that includes imperial policing to ensure that no part of the empire slips the leash; eavesdropping on the communications of citizens, allies, and enemies alike…; attempting to control as many sources of petroleum as possible, both to serve America's insatiable demand for fossil fuels…; providing work and income for the military-industrial complex…; and insuring that members of the military and their families live comfortably.. (151-52).

The United States thus became a de facto militaristic nation after it emerged from the Cold War as the self-proclaimed winner and, therefore, the only superpower on earth. Consequently, the U.S. sought to dominate the world, as if vindicating Reinhold Niebuhr's 1952 prediction that the 'winner' of the Cold War would almost inevitably "face the imperial problem of using power in global terms but from one particular center of authority, so preponderant and unchallenged that its world rule would almost certainly violate basic standards of justice" (qtd by Hough, "President's Newsletter", Seminary 2003).

Indeed, since the disappearance of the Soviet Asia-Pacific fleet after the demise of the Soviet Union in December 1991, the American empire-like[4] or hegemonic behavior went a long way in alienating more and more nations that had openly opposed U.S. policies out of a survival concern, such as North Korea in East Asia, or more indirectly as China felt it could be the potential target of U.S. hegemony in the upcoming decades. "Most other countries were more affected and limited by U.S. policies than the U.S. is by anyone else's. Therefore, most countries were very uneasy about a world in which the U.S. was the single superpower" (Hoffman 60).

With no serious geopolitical or military rival, at least then, U.S. hegemony went astray without another superpower's restraint. John G. Ikenberry described the American monopoly of power, saying: "U.S. military bases and carrier battle groups ring the world ... For the first time in the modern era, the world's most powerful state could operate on the global stage without the constraints of other great powers. We entered the American unipolar age" ("Illusions of Empire" 147-8).

Unilateralism in dealing with regional and global security issues, insensitivity to the interests and concerns of others (Barber), contempt for international institutions, imperial pretensions (Ch. Johnson 73-78), and the recent unilateral impulses in U.S. foreign policy in particular were also further manifestations of hegemony. While Chalmers Johnson called such an attitude "a military juggernaut" (Ch. Johnson 4), Prestowitz argues it was "the hubris of a nation drunk on military power" (68) and a cultural arrogance that justified the use of force to make others like itself. In the post-Cold War decades, popular anti-Americanism in East Asia, even in some of America's strongest military

---

[4] For more on this subject, see Niall Ferguson. *Colossus: The Price of America's Empire.* New York: Penguin Press, 2004. Michael Mann. *Incoherent Empire.* New York: Verso, 2003. Emmanuel Todd. *After the Empire: The Breakdown of the American Order.* New York: Columbia University Press, 2003.

allies such as South Korea and Japan, was clearly on the rise (Tuazon, "Current U.S. Hegemony in Asia Pacific", Lecture March 1, 2003). There was a strong sense in East Asia that the United States was becoming too intrusive. Advocates of Asian anti-Americanism were prominent political figures like Mahathir Mohamed of Malaysia, Lee K. Yew of Singapore, and even former Japanese Prime Minister Morihiro Hosokawa, who said that what the Americans wanted Asians to do was "to become more like them... They wanted us to swallow an American culture of CNN and Hollywood, insisted that we welcome their rude and intrusive American media, while they lectured us on human rights" (Walker 19). The suspicion vis-à-vis the U.S. presence in East Asia became more visible in countries like China and North Korea, as the previous chapter showed. Indeed, American culture and ideals in the aftermath of the advent of the new world order held less appeal than they did in the past due to the negative perception of U.S. global behavior. Marketing these very 'ideals' in East Asia was increasingly viewed as an exercise of "cultural imperialism" and hegemony in the eyes of the region's public. It came down to John Ikenberry's point "that the nation's genuine idealism was subverted by the imperial pursuit of power and capitalist greed" ("Illusions of Empire" 145).

Therefore, the current debate about hegemony in this chapter is an attempt to make sense of the post-Cold War U.S. unipolar reality and its attendant dominant power politics. The argument that the United States was hegemonic was, of course, not new, as the United States and the Soviet Union used to trade allegations of hegemony during the Cold War, but what was new was the post-Cold War U.S. attempt to define the kind of American global and regional order; with East Asia and the Middle East being the focus of this hegemony. Domestically, Neoconservatives[5] celebrated the new American imperial age.

---

[5] Although the term "neoconservatives" was used as early as 1921 by James Bryce in his book *Modern Democracies* to describe those who wanted to combine progressive convictions and conservative maxims, the term has acquired new meanings as it has lost many of the original ones. Historically, neoconservatives believed that the 1960s counterculture aimed at undermining the authority of traditional values and moral norms. Neoconservatives' foreign policy approach emphasizes their domestic agenda. They have argued for an American power that can be used for "righteous" purposes such as exporting democracy, by force when necessary, and supported unilateralism, together with less reliance on international organizations and treaties which can distract from the U.S. will to conquer culturally, economically, politically, and militarily. During Clinton's years, neoconservatives joined the "Blue Team which argued for a confrontational posture toward China, and more military and diplomatic support of Taiwan. Today, neo-

"In neo-conservative thought, the idea of expanding hegemony was as important as that of encouraging democracy, [but] the neoconservatives [have] failed to understand the difficulties of both" (Hoffmann 61). Revisionists, however, saw that for over half a century now, the United States represented "the sole example of geopolitical hegemony since the fall of Rome" (Ikenberry, "Illusions of Empire" 149) and argued that the United States, at a time of concentration of power in one single pole[6], went astray and even became overstretched to a potentially breaking point, leading to the question that whether the sole superpower would "suffer the fate of great empires of the past: ravaging the world with its ambitions and excesses until overextension, miscalculation, and mounting opposition [would] hasten its collapse" (Ikenberry, "Illusions of Empire" 149).

The post-Cold War successive American administrations, Democratic and Republican alike, however, denied that the United States was a hegemonic or an empire-like country. Sandy Berger, President Clinton's national security adviser, declared in 1999 that the United States was the "first global power in history that was not an imperial power" (Ferguson, "Hegemony or Empire?" 155). A year later, George W. Bush, then the governor of Texas and a potential presidential candidate, echoed Berger's words. Bush said in 2000: "America has never been an empire......We may be the only great power in history that had the chance, and refused" (Ibid). "Refused" or not is the question that this section tries to explore. As this last chapter seeks to look at the post-Cold War U.S. demeanor in East Asia through the prism of hegemony, it fits with the main question of this book, that is, whether the American military presence in the region was a positive or a negative security factor in the post-Cold War Northeast Asia.

---

conservatism has shifted its focus from communism to what is called "islamofascism" which the 9/11 attacks provided with a raison d'être. They successfully urged the current Bush administration to use the United States means—economic, military, diplomatic— to realize America's expansive geopolitical purposes. Today, neoconservatives are supported by a panoply of foreign policy think tanks such as the American Enterprise Institute (AEI) and the Project for the New American Century (PNAC), and by some periodicals and magazines such as the *Commentary, Weekly Standard, Heritage foundation,* and *Policy Review.*

[6] For more on this, see Stanley Hoffman, *Gulliver's Troubles: Or, the Setting of American Foreign Policy.* McGraw-Hill, New York, 1968 and *Gulliver Unbound: The Imperial Temptation and the War in Iraq.* Rowman & Littlefield, 2004.

Post-Cold War America's effort, however, to define its commensurate political role with its economic and particularly military prowess characterized the legacy of the Clinton administration over the 1990s, and deeply affected George Bush's doctrine of unilateralism (Soderberg 285). However, during the Clinton years of the 1990s, the United States struggled to blend diplomacy and the use of force in a sequence of trouble spots, and played the role of a peace broker in the Middle East and Northern Ireland. The 1993 Israeli-Palestinian Oslo Accords and the 1998 Northern Ireland Good Friday Agreement substantiate the argument that Clinton's blend of realism and liberal activism was in sharp contrast "with Bush's hegemonic approach, which, built on a radical overestimation of U.S. capabilities, led to a failed adventure in Iraq and dangerous anti-Americanism around the world" (Soderberg 28).

As a matter of fact, the post-Cold War U.S. intent to preserve Pax Americana through the twenty-first century by hard military power was highlighted in the 1992 Defense Policy Guidance (DPG) and the 1997 Project for a New American Century (PNAC) (Sands 29), which revealed the new U.S. strategy of how to take advantage of the post-Soviet unipolar age. The engineers of these two blueprints held official positions in the Bush administration. They were, among others, Vice-President Dick Cheney; Donald Rumsfeld, the former Secretary of Defense; Paul Wolfowitz, former Deputy Defense Secretary; and Condoleeza Rice, the current Secretary of State. As George Bush came to power in 2001, the gist of these two documents was further developed into another four basic official public documents called the September 30, 2001, Quadrennial Defense Review, the January 2002 Nuclear Posture Review[7], the June 2002 Pre-emptive[8]

---

[7] The Nuclear Posture Review: In a 2001Memo entitled "Talking Points, FY01 and FY02-07", Donald Rumsfeld, the former U.S. Secretary of Defense talked about the need for a nuclear posture review to develop small tactical nuclear weapons to respond to threats which "can emerge rapidly and with little or no warning" (Suskind 77) from countries like China, North Korea, Russia, and Iran. As these nations are perceived to be "arming to deter" and even use WMD against the United States which "cannot prevent them from doing so" (81), the memo argues for an American disengagement from international nonproliferation mechanisms, and even from the "no-first-use" principle not only to be able to respond to potential non-conventional attacks against the United States, but also to use tactical U.S. nuclear weapons to prevent suspected countries from developing them in the first place. This is called nuclear pre-emption which is in line with Bush's overall post-9/11 doctrine of pre-emptive wars.

[8] Pre-emptive Doctrine: For more on pre-emption, which is an old concept that is based on a self-declared right of anticipatory "self-defense", see Chapter Two, Section 2.

Military Doctrine, and lastly the September 2002 National Security Strategy (Sands 29).

Although Iraq was just the beginning of a long-term and patient process to implement the DPG and the PNAC recommendations, the Committee for the Liberation of Iraq was one of the PNAC's offspring. Hence came the idea of the "American Century", a century when the United States, as a self-proclaimed righteous superpower, would go on a crusade after 'evil', to rid the world of people like Saddam Hussein, Kim Jong IL, the Ayatollahs of Iran, besides pre-empting potential competitors for regional and world hegemony such as China. Thus, it was clear that the DPG and the PNAC were meant to propel an American strategic vision of its unrivaled dominant place in the world arena, with more focus on what was perceived as a region of potential rivalry, like East Asia.

East Asia is a region of strategic geopolitical significance, and even before 9/11 took place, the Council on Foreign Relations[9], in a memo entitled "the U.S. and East Asia: A Policy Agenda for the New Administration", had recommended maintaining a forward American military presence in the region (Tuazon, "Current U.S. Hegemony in Asia Pacific", Lecture March 1, 2003). The United States, the memo reads, "should preserve a credible military presence and a viable regional training and support infrastructure" (Ibid) in Asia, officially to play the role of a pacifier or a stabilizer, that is a positive security factor, but strategically, as the DPG and the PNAC clearly specify (Ibid), to perpetuate America's dominant status.

In more practical terms, the PNAC recommended a substantial increase in troop levels in Asia, a region that hosts the bulk of the global 725 American military bases in 38 countries throughout the world (Ch. Johnson 154). Though this recommendation was made by the PNAC group in 1997, it only came to be implemented in 2001 with the advent to power of its founders, the neoconservatives, under the current Bush administration. But, as the 2003 invasion of Iraq went badly militarily and ideologically in view of the rising

---

[9] The Council on Foreign Relations has been an influential think tank on U.S. foreign policy since 1921. It limits its membership, which reached 2,670 in 1990, to actively involved, and high-profile specialists in American foreign policy. While it has its headquarters in New York, the Council is like a national club that holds meetings and has offices throughout the United States. Its major specialized journal is *Foreign Affairs* (Williams et al., *The Dictionary of 20th Century World Politics*. Henry Holt &Company, Inc, New York. 182).

numbers of U.S. casualties and the American failure to establish a democracy that would set an example to the rest of the Middle East, it was impossible to increase the 100,000 U.S. troops already deployed in and around Japan and South Korea. In fact, the United States had to draw down a number of its soldiers along the DMZ between North and South Korea because it needed them in Iraq, justifying that decision with the argument that the quantitative decrease of troops in Korea was compensated by a qualitative technological improvement in warfare and potential combat operations.

Equally interesting, the Project for the New American Century included the issue of weapons sales, which ignited much criticism from China, North Korea, and Russia. Part of the whole strategy was the concerted policy of continued arms sales to virtually all nations around China, starting from Pakistan and India in Southwest Asia, through Thailand, Indonesia, the Philippines in Southeast Asia, and up to Northeast Asia to Taiwan and South Korea. Besides, the PNAC envisions speeding up the process of deploying a highly controversial missile system called the National Missile Defense (NMD) system[10] , a 2000 Bush creation ostensibly meant to deter potential incoming missiles officially from North Korea; strategically, however, the NMD targeted China, which was most disturbing for the Chinese, since this missile program would include Taiwan and, of course, Japan (DiFilippo 95). If the United States was trying to play a constructive security role in Asia, both the weapons sales question and the problematic NMD system were counterproductive because they resulted in

---

[10] To prove the controversial nature of the U.S. National Missile Defense, this is a sample of some regional papers in the Asia-Pacific region. - "Flip Side of Pax Americana" An editorial in Melbourne's liberal Age held (7/18): "Internationally, this debate is proving disruptive and potentially dangerous. Washington appears to be alone in its enthusiasm for missile defenses. For this reason, Australia should treat with extreme caution Mr. Cohen's suggestion at the weekend that the Australia-U.S. joint facilities at Pine Gap could play a role.... There are powerful reasons for Australia to think twice before joining the Americans in embracing this vision".
- THE PHILIPPINES: "NMD's Destructive Force" Former Ambassador Armando Manalo wrote in the independent *Manila Times* (7/19): "The deployment of NMD is expected to revise all the ground rules in nuclear weapons management.... Deployment of NMD is likely to destroy all hopes of [future] agreements on nonproliferation. Its immediate effect is to encourage current nuclear powers to follow suit on a similar claim of security. As for potential nuclear powers, it is certain that NMD gives them the green light to proceed with their own nuclear plan. Worst of all, the U.S. action may start a new era of fear, which will cause the consequent destabilization". For more on this, See also Russian President Vladimir Putin's Interview with AlJazeera Arabic Channel on February 10, 2007.

more instability, more suspicion, and could have led to an open arms race in the volatile region of East Asia (*Far Eastern Economic Review*, February 4, 2000).

Furthermore, the U.S. Project for the American New Century explicitly linked the recommended increase in the U.S. military presence in East Asia to the rise of China. Accordingly, the United States would further expand and consolidate its already existing military alliances with nations like Japan and South Korea, and strengthen its military relationships with most countries in the region. Thus, creating such a network of alliances, bases, and docking privileges around China would provide the U.S. with a logistical privilege to further project its power in Asia, play the role of regional hegemon, and deter potential Chinese ambitions of any form of assertive or challenging behavior that could undermine the American status as Asia's pacifier, the role which the United States claimed it was playing especially in the post-Cold War era.

However, the American military presence in East Asia was too visible for the role of a pacifier and a stabilizer. Chalmers Johnson argued that "no single purpose can possibly explain the more than 725 American military bases spread around the world" (167). A quick review of what the United Sates had in the region under study in particular would clearly demonstrate that it was simply too hard to buy the positive security role or the pacifier argument. The U.S. maintained the largest military command outside America, called the U.S. Pacific Command (PACOM), which directly works with 14 out of the 45 nations in the Asia Pacific (Ibid). One hundred thousand troops were deployed in Japan (60,000), South Korea (around 30,000), Guam, Diego Garcia, and the rest on battle carriers patrolling the Pacific around the hour (Ch. Johnson 156-60). Tuazon, who worked at the Center for Anti-Imperialist Studies, argued that all these U.S. military deployments in East Asia served "the American Empire's strategic objectives to contain the rise of power competitors such as - but not limited to- China, and deterred the growth of other threats to its hegemony" ("Current U.S. Hegemony in Asia Pacific", Lecture March 1, 2003).

The United States, China, and most other nations in East Asia, including those that were complacent about the U.S. military presence in the region and those that were criticizing it, had to come to terms with the reality of American hegemony. At the dawn of the twenty-first century, the U.S. hegemony in East Asia was a term of at least tacit approval for Japan, South Korea, and Taiwan, but one of suspicion for others such as China, North Korea, and Russia. The U.S. political, military, and economic role in the region was "a term of approval and optimism for some and disparagement and danger for others....Critics who identified an emerging American empire, meanwhile, worry about ....the threat it posed to the institutions and alliances that secured U.S. national interests since World War II" (Ikenberry, "Illusions of Empire" 149-50). It was an already recognized reality by people in the Middle East and even in post-9/11 Europe (Wallace). In the United States, the recognition of the American empire was hardly in question (Ch. Johnson; Tuazon). In Europe as in Asia, "America bestrided the world like a colossus; neither Rome at the height of its power nor Great Britain in the period of economic supremacy enjoyed an influence so direct, so profound, or so pervasive" (Ikenberry, "Illusions of Empire" 151).

During the Cold War, the U.S. "security system of alliances and bases was built on manufactured threats and driven by an expansionary impulse" (Ch. Johnson 21). To put it bluntly, "the United States was not acting in its own defense; it was exploiting opportunities to build an empire" (22-23). In the post-Cold War era, however, the U.S. security mentality did not change dramatically, even after many of the perceived security threats had disappeared following the disintegration of the Soviet Union. This led to the assumption that Washington was now using the 'security' threat argument to cover up its strategic goal to perpetuate a current preponderant position as the post-Cold War sole superpower, in view of America's unrivaled military prowess and political leverage in the world. From the Sino-Japanese viewpoints, "the United States was [then] the only country with the capacity and the ambition to exercise global primacy, and it w[ould] remain so for a long time to come", (Jisi, "China's Search for Stability with America" 39).

Among the differences, however, between traditional forms of empires, such as the British, the Ottoman, and the Austro-Hungarian Empires, was that those fallen empires used to govern their satellites directly by military rule, and the so-called American 'empire' was less a nineteenth-century typical colonial empire than a new form of loose domination and indirect hegemony of all kinds (Ikenberry, "Illusions of Empire" 149). In Ikenberry's words, "if empire is defined loosely, as a hierarchical system of political relationships in which the most powerful state exercises decisive influence, then the United States [then] indeed qualifie[d]" (149). The second difference between the American 'empire' and those of the past was that post-9/11, America was trying to market the reality of its perceived hegemony under the guise of the crusade for "freedom" in order to give America's unilateralist and hegemonic conduct a benign veil.

The self-righteous concept of Pax Americana was marketed to the American people and the rest of the world through another self-complacent concept of an apocalyptic vision of "Good" against "Evil". For others, however, such as Peter Rodman, the Assistant Secretary of Defense, America was not "apologetic" about looking like an empire as long as it was a "benevolent" one, seeking the good of the world like helping with natural disasters such as the December 2004 Asian Tsunami and infectious diseases including the 2003/04 SARS (Rodman, Assistant Secretary of Defense, China Conference, Chicago Society, University of Chicago, April 28/29, 2006)[11]. But what about the excessive unilateral use of force, which had produced more "evil" than "good," not only to the world but also to the United States itself, which made the crusade argument a self-defeating strategy, to paraphrase Benjamin R. Barber, because it created hostile states bent on overturning the imperial order, not obedient junior partners (Ikenberry, "Illusions of Empire" 144-54).

In the post-9/11 era, the limits between security and power became further blurred. If the end of the Cold War put the United States in a dilemma about the moral and political justification of the continuation of the same Cold War security system, the 9/11 attacks saved the 2001 Bush administration from the embarrassment it would have faced. The pre-9/11 security system in East Asia, much like the Cold War system, basically hinged upon military bases, military forward deployments, airfields, and strategic "chokepoints" including the Strait of Taiwan, as Alfred Mahan put it more than one century ago. 9/11, however, provided the Bush administration, which was thirsty for power and determined to find an enemy to justify its crusade for hegemony, with a raison d'être. Suddenly, the United States had an excuse to justify the pre-emptive doctrine and the abrogation of most international agreements as well as moral restraints to go berserk and unleash American military power preemptively.

Although the 2003 war on Iraq came as the first manifestation of a post-9/11 imperial America, East Asia has was spared from the ramifications of the new U.S. hegemonic mentality. The U.S. government had clearly alienated much of the rest of the globe (Hoffmann 60). It heavily relied on the use or the threat of military force, which frustrated most nation-states, including traditional allies in NATO like France and Germany. As the United States became the center of international power, it simply turned into an international bully instead of an international example of humility. "Under Bush, the military-industrial complex[12] was no longer invisible– it became the most visible, most articulate

---

[11] See Bibliography/Primary Sources Section for full information on the Conference's date, venue, organizers and participants.

[12] The Industrial-Military Complex: In his farewell address on January 17, 1961, President Dwight D. Eisenhower warned that the "conjunction of an immense military establishment and a large arms industry is new in American experience…In the councils

and most aggressive driving force behind America's wars for world hegemony and domination today" (Tuazon, "Current U.S. Hegemony in Asia Pacific", Lecture March 1, 2003).

For almost four centuries, from the 1648 Westphalian world order and up to the post-Cold War emergence of the United States as the sole and unrivaled military superpower, international relations had been conducted on the basis of diffusion of power, that is, a multipolar order, but also on the assumption that sovereign states were interacting in an anarchic world where the use of force was always a reality of international relations. The pos-Cold War American unipolar world order turned the principle of the diffusion of power upside down (Ikenberry, "Illusions of Empire" 146). The world now had to deal with only one center of power, instead of a multilateral power structure. Also, the principle of sovereignty was put into question because of Bush's new pre-emptive and "contingent sovereignty"[13] doctrines.

But did this make the United States an empire? Certainly not, because the United States hardly had the profile of an empire. Traditional empires, such as the British and other nineteenth-century European ones, were able to directly run overseas colonies and to provide for their security, to have a central government, and also to tame them into internalizing the culture and adopting the political system dictated to them. With the exception of Japan, none of these

---

of government, we must guard against the acquisition of unwarranted influence, whether sought or unsought, by the military-industrial complex. The potential for the disastrous rise of misplaced power exists and will persist". During the Cold War, the military-industrial complex was known for its opposition to arms control and even to détente between the two superpowers. As the Soviet Union disintegrated, and by the advent of a neoconservative administration in the United States, the post-9/11 Bush's militarism has been seen through the prism of an alleged conspiracy between the arms industry and the Pentagon, together with officials like Dick Cheney and Donald Rumsfield, respectively the U.S. Vice-President and the ex-Secretary of Defense. The consequence is that the pentagon has taken over the responsibility of American foreign policy-making, resulting in a new penchant for military interventions before even exhausting diplomatic channels or trying to concoct forms of modus vivendi with the other.

[13] Contingent Sovereignty: it is almost the opposite of a longtime principle in international relations that the sovereignty of nation states would be mutually respected, and one of its basic attendant maxims is the nonintervention in the internal affairs of states. Contingent sovereignty is a Bush creation after 9/11, which was concocted to justify his 'war without borders', that is the self-proclaimed right to attack any perceived 'terrorist' target wherever it is, and in total disregard of the principle of states' sovereignty on their own territories.

criteria applied to the U.S. world position then. The United States was so overextended in its military deployments in Asia and Europe that it was not able to handle a short-term occupation of a small country like Iraq. The aftermath of the 2003 Iraq War revealed the limits of the U.S. power and dashed the immediate post-Cold War excessive U.S. ambitions to be able to fight two simultaneous wars, as the Clinton administration sought to achieve in the 1990s ("The Pentagon Quadrennial Defense Review", the *Brookings Policy Brief,* no.15, 1997).

The United States could, however, qualify as an "empire of the willing" or an "empire of invitation". It refrained from engaging in a direct rule of its satellite countries, and, instead, had very much engaged in power politics through coercive economic and political pressure, and even real use of military force in a way very much like a global imperial power that was either "intent on world domination" (Johnson 13). As a matter of fact, the United States, though it emerged as the sole superpower in the 1990s, was nervous about its world position in view of its chronic trade deficits with countries like Japan, China, South Korea, and even the small island of Taiwan. The declining competitivity of the American economy when facing the rising economic power of China and that of the European Union, besides that of the newly structured Japanese one, was a factor here. To put it succinctly, as the economic power of China and many other Asian nations was on the rise, the United States had to come to terms with the fact that its unrivaled global economic power was substantially on the wane, and as the U.S. economic dominance declined, American political and military hegemony could eventually extend to a coercive economic posture.

Michael Mann argued that four types of power could sustain or cause to fail nation-states and empires: military, political, economic, and ideological. Applying these categories to the United States, Mann described America's stand then as "a military giant, a back-seat economic driver, a political schizophrenic, and an ideological phantom" (86). Therefore, a weakened or declining America was highly likely to resort to more hegemonic actions to cling to its preponderant position. The United States might have unrivaled military power at least then, but its economic prowess was much less overwhelming[14]. Such

---

[14] For more on the declining U.S. share of the world GDP, the U.S. trade deficits with China and Japan, see David M. Lampton, "What Growing Chinese Power Means for America", HEARING ON: "The Emergence of China Throughout Asia: Security and Economic Consequences for the U.S.", The East Asian and Pacific Affairs Subcommittee June 7, 2005

imbalance pushed a nervous United States to overemphasize a policy of unrestrained militarism to make strategic economic gains, such as in the oil sector (Ch. Johnson 217-54). In practical terms, there was an awareness that the American economy could not sustain America's twenty-first century project, and therefore, agreements like Bretton Woods no longer balance American economic and strategic calculations. Hence, the examination of the current U.S. economic attributes should help our understanding of the reality as well as the prospects of the United States' political and military hegemony in East Asia and in the world at large in the early decades of the post-Cold War era.

4.1.2. U.S. Economic Hegemony

Historically, post-WWII American hegemony rested on a dominating U.S. economy that outstripped all of its competitors in Asia as well as in Europe for much of the past century. George Kennan, the then director of the State Department's Policy Planning Staff, said in 1948: "We have about 50 percent of the world's wealth, but only 6.3 percent of its population... Our real task in the coming period is to devise a pattern of relationships which will permit us to maintain this position of disparity" (Gerson, "Fresh Look", Lecture 1999)[15]. President Clinton, almost half a century later, echoed Kennan's words when he said: "We have 4 percent of the world's population, and we want to keep 22 percent of the world's wealth" (Ibid). By the end of the Cold War, as the American share of the world's wealth clearly fell almost by half, the United States still appeared to be pursuing the same strategy of economic expansionism through a panoply of mechanisms, such as the 1947 Bretton Woods Accords, the GATT and then the W.T.O, and doctrines including globalization and a world of no trade barriers (Ch. Johnson 255-81).

As the ability of a state to dominate the international system largely depends on its economic strength, the American hegemonic position worldwide is not only military but also multi-dimensional and considerably economic. The post-WWII American bid for a superpower status took the form of an American-controlled network of alliances, which was expanded to almost 725

Dirksen Senate Office Building, Room 419. The Nixon Center Prepared for: United States Senate Committee on Foreign Relations. Lampton is Dean of the Faculty and Director of China Studies, Johns Hopkins Nitze School of Advanced International Studies and Director of Chinese Studies.

[15] Available at: http://disarm.igc.org/jgasiakr.html>; www.globalissues.org/Geopolitics /Articles/Backing.asp.

military bases in 38 nations in the post-Cold War era, and the remote objective was always to consolidate the U.S. economic dominance (Tuazon; Gerson). It was the preponderant U.S. economic position, besides its attendant military power, which had allowed the United States for more than 50 years to be able to influence the outcome of its interaction with the rest of the world, namely with China and Japan. In the wake of WWII, "at home, economic might, cheap raw materials and a large internal market, produced a consumer boom. Abroad it financed the Marshall Aid injections into the European economies" (Gerson, "Fresh Look", Lecture 1999). Then, the United States was at a huge economic advantage because the war had caused no considerable damage to American industry or infrastructure.

In the 1990s, the "U.S. trade with Asia Pacific surpassed that with Europe, with more than $U.S. 500 billion in trade and investment of more than $U.S.150 billion" (Tuazon, "Current U.S. Hegemony in Asia Pacific", Lecture March 1, 2003), it is safe to propose a link between maintaining a substantial U.S. military presence in the region and post-Cold War America's economic calculations there, which was manifested in the presence of "about 400,000 U.S. non-military citizens [who] lived and conducted business in the region" (Ibid). Moreover, the claim of the link, which this book is trying to advance, between U.S. military and economic presence in East Asia is substantiated by a 2000 RAND Corporation report entitled "The Role of Southeast Asia in U.S. Strategy Toward China" wherein it warned against the geopolitical impact of the rise of China on America's economic prowess domestically and globally. The report also argued that America's economic interests in East Asia were indeed "important to the economic security of the U.S., [which] depended on preserving American presence and influence in the region and unrestricted access to sea lanes" (Ibid), which the United States was doing in the post-Cold War era.

Neil Ferguson, an advocate of a benign hegemony thesis, said: "The American order is hierarchical and ultimately sustained by *economic and military power*" (Ikenberry, "Illusions of Empire" 150-51) (Italics added). Despite the fact that most East Asian economies achieved much higher rates of GDP growth since the early 80s, the United States has not suffered any material diminution of its hegemonic position for the last 60 years. In the first five years after the fall of the Berlin Wall, the U.S. GDP grew by almost 30 percent from $5.2 trillion in 1989 to $7 trillion in 1995, compared to just 4 percent in Japan[16]. Moreover, in

---

[16] U.S. Bureau of Economic Analysis, "Survey of Current Business", National Income and Product Accounts of the United States, 1959-1988, vol.2, March 1996).

2005, the U.S. GDP grew by almost 4.4 percent, and the growth rate was estimated to be 3.5 percent in 2006, making the size of the U.S. economy as a proportion of the global economy likely to increase in the years to come (*Jisi*, "China's Search for Stability With America" 40). Therefore, the U.S. premium on the world arena over the past half-century was clearly the result of an inextricable link between American primacy and managing the world economy.

As a matter of fact, the U.S. geopolitical preponderance rested on a 'liberal' economic domination dating back to a series of post-war international financial arrangements that aimed at regulating the world economy and finance. Most of these arrangements were clearly meant to promote not only American economic interests, but also to serve U.S. geopolitical strategic calculations. In 1944, the United States imposed the Bretton Woods System of exchange convertibility on Western Europe and Japan to create a pattern of economic and financial dependence of the war-ravaged nations on the American economic as well as geopolitical goal of containing the perceived Soviet expansionism. But in its attempt to do so, the United States became much more expansionist even after the Soviet Union was gone and after the premises of the Cold War were by then moribund. Bruce Cumings said: "that the United States would be hegemonic was inevitable from Bretton Woods onward; that it might also become an empire was not" (355-360). The Open Door policy in the Asia-Pacific region, started by John Hay in 1894, was institutionalized by the 1944 Bretton Woods system, combined with other U.S dominated bodies of intervention and regulation such as the International Monetary Fund (IMF), the World Bank, and the GATT (Ch. Johnson 255-81).

Following WWII, the United States sought to build a 'liberal' international trading system that is beneficial to its economic interests over Asian and European economies in order to perpetuate U.S. geopolitical hegemony. For more than fifty years, "the postwar international economic order and the international security order became intimately joined to one another" (O'Brien and Clesse 165). This was in accordance with what Charles Kindleberger called in 1973 the three "tasks of the hegemon that include[d] the creation and maintenance of a liberal trade regime, the establishment of the international system, and playing the 'lender of the last resort' to prevent financial crises" that hurt its own exports (qtd in O'Brien and Clesse 166).

To achieve the first purpose, the United States pressured the war-ravaged nations in 1944 to find the Bretton Woods Accords, which have made the U.S. dollar the world financial lingua franca. As for the second task, America instigated the establishment of the GATT and later the W.T.O. to break down trade tariffs and get rid of practices of trade protectionism, which could hurt American exports all over the world. In return for the $ 13 billion Marshall Plan in 1947, for instance, which constituted only 1.5 percent of the then American GDP, the United States demanded an economic quid pro quo.

As a precondition for both the Marshall Plan and the American support for the movement towards European economic unification, the U.S. had the West Europeans extend what was called the principle of "national treatment" to American firms, which, accordingly, were to be treated as if they were European corporations benefiting from the enormous economic and trade potential of devastated European economies, together with the manipulation of the reconstruction opportunities in Europe (O'Brien and Clesse 168-69). "West-European governments were required to remove intra-European trade barriers and to cooperate and coordinate their economic plans through the Organization for European Economic Cooperation (OEEC)" (O'Brien and Clesse 172), which is again a U.S.-instigated forum.

In East Asia, U.S. economic hegemony easily took root because of the underdeveloped, pre-capitalist, and agrarian state of most, if not all, of the regional economies. It took two "revolutions" in China and Japan, respectively, in the 1970s and the late 1980s, to start the process of joining the U.S.-dominated international economic club. The former was political; it took place after the 1976 death of Mao Zedong, with the advent of a more liberal and pragmatic ruling elite in Beijing led by Deng Xiaoping, who triggered the on-going process of the "capitalization" of communism (Bottelier, "China's Economic Rise", Lecture 2005). Between the late 70s and the early 2000s, Communist China went a long way in liberalizing its economy, inviting huge foreign direct investment and offering enormous trade opportunities to the rest of the world, given its large market of more than one billion consumers.

The latter, however, was technological. In the early 80s, a major technological revolution in electronics and communications ushered Japan into a U.S.-dominated world economy, and gave Washington the opportunity to use its security clout to pressure Tokyo into accommodating most American-dictated provisions regarding international trade and finance. These two developments in East Asia seduced the United States into engaging Japan and China in the world economy by opening for them the prospects either of entering the GATT and later its successor, the W.T.O, or coming up with new regional economic organizations such as the Asia-Pacific Economic Council (APEC)[17] where China and Japan are now key members.

In the post-Cold War era, APEC, however, was used by the United States as a forum to promote its own economic interests in the region and to deepen the region's economic and financial dependence on U.S. support, by pushing member nations to further liberalize their respective trade policies in order to absorb more American products. Michael Mastandano supports this argument by stating that "United States officials ha[d] promoted trade liberalization bilaterally in negotiations especially with Japan, China, and South Korea, and multilaterally through the WTO. They ha[d] pushed financial liberalization in Asia under the auspices of the 'Washington Consensus' developed and implemented by the IMF and World Bank (IBRD)" (Ikenberry, ed. *America Unrivaled* 196).

Anything that came from a U.S. initiative, such as the Washington Consensus forum, and guaranteed an American upper hand in decision-making would be welcomed by the United States, but Washington would certainly veto all regional initiatives that were deemed as anti-U.S. hegemonic interests in East Asia. Malaysia, a country known for its "rebellious" demeanor regarding American hegemonic policies in the region, came up in the early 1990s with the idea of an East Asian Economic Group (EAEG) that would exclude United States membership. Deemed not only unacceptable but also 'unilateralist' by Washington, the EAEG failed because of U.S. pressure on Japan to oppose it (Wade 441-54). It was rather clear that the American push for wider regional economic reforms, which were consistent with the free and unhindered flow of goods between the two sides, benefited U.S. economic interests. As Mustanduno put it: "economic openness [in East Asia] plays into U.S. economic interests, particularly given U.S. competitiveness in the export of

---

[17] APEC stands for Asia Pacific Economic Cooperation. Officially founded in 1989-Canberra, Australia. APEC began as an informal Ministerial-level dialogue group with 12 members. Its declared goal is "free and open trade and investment in the Asia-Pacific by 2010 for developed economies and 2020 for developing economies". During its last annual meeting in 2006 which took place in- Hanoi, Viet Nam, APEC Economic Leaders issued a statement on the WTO Doha Development Agenda calling for ambitious and balanced outcomes. To prioritize its agenda, APEC takes a strategic approach to reform working groups and strengthen the Secretariat. Source: (http://www.apec.org/content/apec/about_apec/history.html).

services, agriculture and advanced technologies" (Ikenberry, ed. *America Unrivaled* 195).

Within the same vein of linking U.S. economic policies to its geopolitical strategies in the wake of WWII, the United Sates almost pursued the same policy of conditionality in helping to bring the devastated Japanese economy back on track. "Militarily, the U.S. was dominant and it c[ould] use this to ensure that no other state can politically attempt to restructure the international economy" (Gerson, "Fresh Look", Lecture 1999). The interaction between U.S. geopolitical hegemony and its military might clearly lead to the link between military power and economic hegemony. In order to guarantee Japanese security against perceived threats from both the Soviets and the Chinese, the United States extended its nuclear umbrella over Japan in 1956. The American-Japanese Mutual Security Treaty referred to the outbreak of hostilities in the entire Pacific region, which gave the United States the right to use air and naval bases in Japan to play the role of the hegemon in the Western Pacific. In return, the Japanese were given 'free' access to the American market in exchange for the right to anchor the American strategic position in Japan. As it was apparent from the endless trade wars between Washington and Tokyo regarding Japan's automobile and electronic products in the post-Cold War era (see Chapter Four, Section 5-2-2), this Japanese privilege ceased to exist with the demise of the Cold War. Thus, in an effort to contain the Soviet Union, and in the name of protecting Japan, the United States itself became a highly expansionist and hegemonic power in East Asia. A comprehensive estimate of the U.S. gains from economic hegemony over the past half-century was then around $1 trillion a year, roughly 9 percent of American GDP, with another 5-12 percent of its GDP that could be realized if the country drops its protectionist trade policies against Japanese cars, for instance (Q. Wang 63).

Moreover, the United States sought to take advantage of the dollar's role as a key international currency in a system of fixed exchange rates, as the 1944 Bretton Woods System stipulated, making the United States "far less restrained...than all other states by...foreign exchange constraints when it came to funding whatever foreign or strategic policies Washington decided to implement" (Ferguson, "Hegemony or Empire?" 159). The United States was a central hub of the world economy at that time, and the role of the dollar as the primary reserve currency conferred significant economic advantages. As the "lender of last resort", the U.S. secured the position of the global monetary hegemon. This was what Charles de Gaulle described as the "hegemony of the dollar" (Ibid) that gave the United States "extravagant privileges" to feel unrestrained by monetary obstacles to expanding not only its political and economic influence, but also its currency domination in East Asia (Ibid). This was manifested during the 1997/98 Asian financial crisis, when Washington bailed out the stricken countries, like Thailand, Malaysia, Singapore, and Indonesia, to pay the salaries of their respective government employees. Such a move showed the dollar as the savior of and the cure to most economic diseases. Thus, "the key role of the dollar in the international monetary system held the American alliance system and the world economy together, and the international role of the dollar as both a reserve and transaction currency actually [has] bec[o]me a cornerstone of America's global economic and political position" (O'Brien and Clesse 173-74) of a hegemon in Europe and Asia alike.

In East Asia, the U.S. dollar remained the global monetary standard during the post-Cold War decades, and the American economy continued to attract more Asian capital than all of the East Asian economies combined, including China and Japan, not to mention North Korea's economy, whose entire GDP was only one-twentieth the size of the U.S. defense budget. A large percentage of the $1.3 trillion in Asian governments' foreign exchange reserves was in U.S. assets. "With Asian capital markets still in their infancy, it would be a very long time before the pre-eminence of the dollar and U.S. capital markets are challenged" (O'Brien and Clesse 173). Moreover, while Japan's economic prowess received a deadly blow of credibility during the 1997/98 Asian financial crisis, Japan's model of developmental capitalism has elicited much criticism. Mustanduno said: "lifetime employment commitments and long-term relationships among firms ha[d] made the Japanese economy far less flexible than that of the United States in responding to economic downturns" (Ikenberry, ed. *America Unrivaled* 190). Therefore, it was obvious that an expensive military presence and an engaging political involvement in East Asia could not be achieved on the cheap. It needed resources for such an "indefinite' presence through a heavy economic presence and a liberal trade exchange with the region.

However, as Queen Victoria used naval and financial power to open markets well outside the British colonial jurisdiction, most of the tariff reductions achieved either under the GATT or the WTO apparatus were the result of American pressures (Ch. Johnson 255-281). Then, "America was not in the business of exporting free market democracy, it [wa]s in the business of freeing up markets and globalizing corporate capital and calling it democracy" (Barber 129). Paradoxically, such a system of free trade was even more beneficial to U.S.

potential economic rivals such as China and Japan, making the United States more and more a "global economic predator", since it lost the ability to match its own economic attributes to those of other societies. As Benjamin Schwarz put it, "the worldwide economic system that the United States protected and fostered has itself largely determined the country's economic decline; economic power diffused from the United States to new centers of growth; American hegemony, perforce, has been undermined" (qtd in Walker 18).

After the end of the Cold War, the Asia-Pacific region witnessed a shift in the structure and the balance of political and economic power; a shift that can pose a serious challenge to America's hegemonic status quo. Stephen W. Bosworth, the president of the United States-Japan Foundation and former U.S. Ambassador to the Philippines, said: "Less understood... was how substantially the balance of economic power within the Asian-Pacific region itself shifted away from the United States and how that inevitably changed the distribution of political influence in the area" (Bosworth 78).

Thus, America's own ability to maintain the existing forward military presence in East Asia was increasingly called into question, and a weaker American military presence in the Asian-Pacific region would consequently translate into less political influence. As the political leverage of military presence diminished, economic power would become more significant, and with American power projection capabilities overstretched, the United States was left with not too many options with regard to serious challenges to its position of controlling the outcome of endless East Asian conflicts. By analogy, Correlli Barnett argued that by the 1920s, "the British Empire was one of the most outstanding examples of strategic overextension in history" (Ferguson, "Hegemony or Empire?" 158), and that this overstretch had fatal economic consequences. This could very well apply to the post-Cold War United States in view of the heavy financial cost of the American military overstretch all over the world, especially in East Asia where it had most of its overseas troops stationed. In comparison to the British "military burden", for instance, between 1870 and 1913, which averaged almost 3.2 percent of Britain's GDP, the figure for the United States between 1950 and 1974 was 5 to 6 percent, and up to 9 percent in 2004 (Ibid).

Paradoxically, the continuing Japanese economic challenge and the rise of a giant Chinese economy, with potential military capabilities of power projection, were the main variables that shed clouds of doubt about the sustainability of the U.S. political and military preponderance in East Asia. Consequently, as U.S. economic hegemony was arguably waning, Washington's political leverage and military credibility were diminishing. By the first decade of the unipolarity era, the U.S. hegemonic position in East Asia, though still unrivaled, was no longer pivotal in setting the rules of the power and security game. Emmanuel Todd, from Colombia University, went further to suggest that the time came for the United States to deal with the new reality that it needed the world more than the world needs it. He said: "at the very moment when the rest of the world- [then] undergoing a process of stabilization thanks to improvements in education, demographics, and democracy- was on the verge of discovering that it could get along without America, America was realizing that it could not get along without the rest of the world" (qtd in Ikenberry, "Illusions of Empire" 152). So, in view of these signs of economic and attendant political decline, would the U.S. continue to honor its international commitments regarding economic as well as geopolitical and armament issues?

It is clear that post-9/11, America came to believe that restrictions on U.S. actions, be they economic, legal, political or moral, ought to be disregarded (Hoffmann 60), and the fundamental question was "how far and for how long the United States would remain committed to free trade once other economies- benefiting from precisely the liberal economic order made possible by U.S. hegemony- began to catch up with it?" (Ferguson, "Hegemony or Empire?" 156). One can also extend the question about how far the United States went in distancing itself not only from international trade and monetary regimes, but also from environment and arms treaties such as respectively the 1998 Kyoto Protocol and the 1972 Anti-Ballistic Missile Treaty (ABM) with the ex-Soviet Union. What is certain is that the post-Cold War neoconservative doctrine, as stipulated in their prominent roadmap of the Project for the New American Century (PNAC), called for a U.S. disregard of any international treaty that hindered the United States from going forward with its 'project.'[18]

4.1.3. Unilateralism: A Tool of Hegemony

As the United States championed a global order in the wake of WWII, built in part around multilateral rules and institutions, including the United Nations, the IMF, the World Bank, and the Bretton Woods Accords, the post-Cold War American enthusiasm about what was considered as "restrictive" international treaties seemed to be waning (Ch. Johnson 73-78). The American estrangement

---

[18] For more on this see also Charles Krauthammer, "The Bush Doctrine", *Time*, March 5, 2001; MaxBoot, "The Case for American Empire", *Weekly Standard*, October 15, 2001; and Richard Gwyn "Imperial Rome Lives in the U.S., *Toronto Star*, December 9, 2001.

from international law could be seen through the new perception that international rules were then viewed as constraints rather than opportunities, a posture which John Ikenberry, in his review of Sands' *Lawless World*, called "a return to an earlier era of national exceptionalism" (Ikenberry, Book Review in *Foreign Affairs*, November/December 2005, 78). There was a post-Cold War faulty premise of an imperial character that the United States was providing security for others, patrolling the seas and acting as a global leviathan or Goliath to check potential trouble makers, and expecting other countries' acquiescence in return (Mandelbaum, "David's Friend Goliath" 51-56).

Building on this self-complacent premise, the U.S. refused to play by the same rules it initiated, such as the ABM treaty, and maintained that this was the price the world must pay for the 'security' America claims it was providing. In short, the United States took the liberty "to remove the fig leaf of alliance partnership. Washington could now disentangle itself from international commitments, treaties, and law and launch direct imperial rule" (Bosworth 78). But an empire that had been built on hard military power alone was usually unsustainable and short-lived.

Regarding the U.S. grand strategy for global hegemony, which extended beyond the Asia-Pacific, the 1992 Defense Policy Guidance (DPG) and the 1997 Project for a New American Century (PNAC) provided graphic insights into the U.S. project that calls for the abrogation of "restrictive" international agreements to the U.S. twenty-first century project (Suskind 81-86). "The DPG particularly stressed that America would not be bound to its partners and to international laws and institutions while it stressed a more unilateral and pre-emptive role in attacking its perceived enemies" (Tuazon, "Current U.S. Hegemony in Asia Pacific", Lecture March 1, 2003)

Moreover, long before 9/11, the DPG had also recommended "that a war on terrorism must be launched. This war to be launched by the American Empire must be seen as a façade and just a part of a bigger strategy of projecting U.S. military power around the world, especially Eurasia, and cutting loose the multilateral bonds that constrained Washington's freedom of action and power" (Ibid). From George Bush's perspective, post-WWII international agreements and institutions by then became the very "bonds" which ought not to constrain America's freedom of action in its quest for modus dominandi (Ch. Johnson 67-73). In other words, since international treaties became a liability rather than an asset for U.S. hegemonic purposes, international institutions would have to complete, instead of obstructing, the U.S. global quest for more power. The selective approach which the United States adopted towards international agreements and institutions showed that the U.S. was seeking to re-mold some of these agreements to serve new American hegemonic calculations.

In the wake of WWII, American enthusiasm for an inclusive and comprehensive international order relating to topics such as the use of force, arms control, the International Court of Justice, and human rights, was not in question. The post-Cold War ambivalence, however, and even outright withdrawal from international treaties, added to the perception of the United States as hegemonic. This was apparently something to do with the impact of long-term shifts in the U.S. global position. As an example of self-righteousness, the United States viewed "that the American Empire could not exist under current international law, ethical concepts, multilateralism and global institutions like the United Nations because of the constraints and impediments that these pose on America's will and action" (Tuazon. "Current U.S. Hegemony in Asia Pacific", Lecture March 1, 2003). In short, the United States, under neoconservative influence, felt it was now the sole unrivaled superpower on earth, and American policymakers decided to go back on any international agreement which did not suit U.S. strategic interests (J. Murphy).

In cases when the United States showed preference for international institutions, however, they were overly dominated by Washington. "In times of crisis", Mustanduno explains, "[Americans] turned not to these regional institutions but preferred instead to rely on U.S.-led diplomatic efforts and institutional structures that the United States could more comfortably control" (qtd in Ikenberry, ed. *America Unrivaled* 195). To implement the now-failed 1994 Agreed Framework, for instance, with North Korea, which, in retrospect, was a palliative and not a cure to the vexed but broader question of the U.S.-North Korean relationship, Washington came up with a totally new entity called the Korean Peninsula Energy Development Organization (KEDO). Then, the United States did not trust the Chinese or even the South Koreans to oversee the implementation of the Agreed Framework; Washington decided to create a new structure wherein it would have the upper hand. Moreover, in dealing with the 1997/98 Asian financial crisis, the United States did not trust even its closest ally in the region -Japan- when Tokyo suggested "a regional financing facility" (Ibid). Instead, Washington went back to the International Monetary Fund (IMF), an institution it had created to maintain America's economic and political hegemony, but the U.S. unexpectedly turned to China for help and self-restraint not to devalue Chinese currency. This negative American attitude vis-à-vis multilateralism demonstrated that the United States always wanted to be Asia's principal source of economic and political order, an order that cannot be sustained without a forward military presence in the region, a post-Cold War presence which elicited controversial interpretations whether it brought about a positive or a negative security input in East Asia's volatile security environment.

But how could an 'American order', which the United States said was synonymous with the desired international order, be upheld by combining the embedded paradox of arbitrarily employing military power against enemies of the 'American order', and claiming respect for the rules of the international system? The answer lied within the term "paradox". The more the U.S. justified a unilateral exercise of power, the more it undermined the rules and institutions it argues it has a stake in maintaining. Michael Mann warns of a "new imperialism" that was driven by a radical vision in which unilateral military power enforced U.S. rule and overcame global disorder (Ikenberry, ed. *America Unrivaled* 196).

Moreover, the U.S. ambivalence about and contempt of international treaties regarding arms control, such as the Nuclear Nonproliferation Treaty, the Comprehensive Test Ban Treaty, the Anti-Ballistic Missile (ABM) treaty, and the Chemical Weapons Convention, had lately turned into outright withdrawal. In 2002, Washington even withdrew from the Anti-Ballistic Missile treaty (ABM), marking a new American attitude vis-à-vis international treaties. Nicole Deller said: "paradoxically, this ambivalence made the United States one of the greatest champions of cooperative security but also one of its great defectors" (86). Ex-President Jimmy Carter said in November 2005: "Our political leaders declared independence from the restraints of international organizations and disavowed long-standing agreements-including agreements on nuclear arms, control of biological weapons and the international system of justice" (Carter 16). Historically, one can assert, and with a great deal of certitude, that never in the history of U.S. domestic politics did an ex-president criticize a serving one in public and with such open condemnation.

The last issue that this section seeks to explore, as it needs to be further addressed, not necessarily from a theoretical point of view, since theories of political science have failed to predict how international relations would be conducted in an era of a sole superpower supremacy, is why there was very little resistance to the perceived post-Cold War U.S. hegemony. Characterizing the United States as fully evil or wholly good would fail to capture the nuances of the question of why there was no serious attempt to counter perceived American hegemony, no regional alliances in the making to stand against this U.S. hegemonic overture, and not even a bold verbal condemnation by the bulk of world governments of American behavior, especially in the post 9/11 era. Andrea Kathryn Talentino asked, "how can outside actors instilled and entrenched liberal norms in states governed by realist insecurities and divided by violence?" (33).

Indeed, the United States outstandingly managed to "instill and entrench" such "liberal norms" in Japan, for instance, whose physical security and political independence considerably depended on the U.S. military presence, not only in East Asia but also on Japanese territory despite Japan's domestic disenchantment about what was largely perceived as unnecessary and excessive (Preble 5). Therefore, the passivity of major players in the international arena whose interests were threatened by this American hegemony was a question that needs further inquiry. The question, on the opposite, concerning why there were attempts on the part of even major powers to ingratiate themselves with a perceived hegemon, instead of rallying to counter it, yielded different and sometimes opposite explanations. Not only did the difficulty of answering such challenging questions testify to the complexity of world politics, but it also transcended the outward simplicity of accounting for such a "voluntary" acquiescence on the part of most nations around the globe to the U.S. hegemonic posture.

Historically, perceived Goliaths are subject to checking of their power by other countries or alliances of countries. This was the case for Athens in the fourth century B.C., Carthage in the last two centuries B.C, Napoleonic France in the late eighteenth and nineteenth centuries, Germany during the first half of the twentieth century, and last but not least, the Soviet Union over the second half of the past century. This was not happening in the immediate decades of the post-Cold War era; however, it occurred against the backdrop of the United States as the sole superpower in the world, a status about which many nations had serious misgivings regarding its alleged hegemonic and arrogant exercise of power.

Hence came also the question of whether U.S. hegemony was benign or malign. If it were a malign hegemony, why didn't we see any states or alliances in the making to counterbalance the alleged U.S. hegemonic posture? The absence of potential alliances against America's post-Cold War perceived hegemony contravened both realist and neo-realist schools of thought, which have argued for almost a century now that the formation of alliances against rising hegemons is almost inevitable in an international system of anarchy and insecurity. But the "gap between what the world said about American power and what it failed to do about it was the single most striking feature of 21st century international relations" (Mandelbaum 53).

Despite widespread complaints about American hegemony in East Asia from China, North Korea, and even from America's closest allies, Japan and South Korea, these critics of this perceived malign American hegemonic conduct failed to organize into real military or even political or economic alliances against it. On the opposite, "Washington's close allies were now looking for ways to tame the United States' might. Many countries fear U.S. influence, and they have devised numerous strategies to manage and limit it" (Walt 130). So, one of the explanations for the absence of concrete anti-U.S. hegemony steps in East Asia may be that the United States was not threatening any nation in the region, and acted "benignly" and "responsibly" in dealing with East Asia's security problems, making the U.S. military presence in the region a positive security factor. But such an argument could easily be refuted by the fact that the half-century U.S. military presence and its attendant economic and political bullying of East Asian nations, such as North Korea over its nuclear programs and China regarding the pending Taiwan problem, was not benign or conducive to regional stability by any account, at least from the standpoint of the countries concerned.

Far from being a benign hegemon, the United States adopted a threatening posture in handling unresolved issues in East Asia, such as the North Korean nuclear standoff. As President Jimmy Carter put it, the United States "proclaimed a policy of 'pre-emptive war,' an unabridged right to attack other nations unilaterally to change an unsavory regime or for other purposes. When there were serious differences with other nations, we brand them as international pariahs and refuse direct discussions to resolve disputes" (Carter 29)

In East Asia, a volatile security environment where suspicion among neighbors prevails, it transpired that either a 'neutral' outsider or a preponderant power became necessary for producing stability and containing and deterring conflicts. This leads the discussion to the inference that since the East Asian neighborhood was filled with conflicts resulting from antithetical security and power calculations of the small as well as the major regional actors; the region may still need the United States' forward military presence and political engagement to maintain stability for the foreseeable future. Therefore, it is safe to argue that if most East Asian nations had to choose between the American preponderance and a potential Chinese regional domination, they would still choose the American one (Pomfret 6).

An Asian diplomat expressed the prevailing viewpoint among the region's countries. He said: "even with all its problems we would still need the United States. Basically, our choice was between a hegemony in Washington or a hegemony in Beijing. We were still choosing the United States" (Pomfret 7). This would contradict the opposite argument that major poles of power in Asia, namely China and Russia, were indeed preparing to counterbalance U.S. hegemony. On the contrary, Europe, Japan, Russia, and China sought to cooperate with, instead of challenging, the existing U.S.-dominated world order. "They were pursuing influence and accommodation within the existing order, not trying to overturn it" (Ikenberry, "illusions of Empire", 144-154).

From the perspective of those who either acquiesced to or even appreciated U.S. preponderance, it was hardly called "hegemony"; it was called the "enlightened exercise" of American power[19], which fitted the definition of a benign hegemon that provides security reassurances to vulnerable nations, which was in harmony with the positive security role which the United States claims it was playing in East Asia. Ferguson calls for the need for a "liberal" empire, or a world order that revolved around an American primacy and under the U.S. imperial supervision. Conversely, the U.S. exercise of power politics, the unilateral and arbitrary use of force against Third World nations to frighten potential adversaries, the careless disregard for international law, and last but not least, the messianic mission, which post-9/11 America adopted, were ironically what Ferguson called "an enlightened exercise of power".

Ferguson, however, who said that he was "fundamentally in favor of empire", had a vision that not only glorified but also legitimized colonial rule, since he favored an "adult" American supervision of a system based on "immature" minor actors. He argued that "the experiment with political independence– especially in Africa– had been a disaster for most poor countries", and therefore, these nations needed a return to colonialism, but this time a universal and a "benign" American one. This complacent view about a "benign", "liberal", "benevolent", and "helpful" hegemon supported the argument that the United States would probably enjoy being called a hegemon because it viewed hegemony as something inevitable for "a young, extremely well-endowed state, after just a century or more of relevant experience in

---

[19] The idea of "enlightened" exercise of U.S. power originally comes from Nial Ferguson in *Colossus: The Price of America's Empire*. New York: Penguin Press, 2004, and was later used by Michael Mandelbaum, *The Case for Goliath: How America Acts as the World's Government in the Twenty-First Century*. NY: Public affairs, 2006.

successfully managing the colonization of a largely uninhabited continent" (O'Brien & Clesse 286).

By analogy, describing the benign and benevolent role of the British Empire, Winston Churchill once said that the British mission was "to give peace to warring tribes, to administer justice where all was violence, to strike the chains of the slave, to draw the richness from the soil, to place the earliest seeds of commerce and learning, to increase in whole peoples their capacities for pleasure and diminish their chances of pain" (Glancey 8). Ironically, the same Churchill supported the use of poison gas, which he called a "scientific expedient', against the Iraqis in February 1920 when the latter started putting up resistance to the 1917 British occupation that followed the fall of the Ottoman Empire (Ibid). The British archives indicate that the gas bombing against Iraqi Kurds and Arabs took place in the Korak Mountains and the Kaniya Khoran area (Geoff 179-181). Even before the bombing, Churchill, then Secretary for War and Air, wrote to Sir Hugh Trenchard, "I do not understand this squeamishness about the use of gas. I am strongly in favor of using poison gas against uncivilized tribes," which contradicts the promise "to increase in whole peoples their capacities for pleasure and diminish their chances of pain" (Ibid). It was simply inflicting more pain on British colonies and diminishing their chances of pleasure.

Although the proponents of a "benign" America did not use the same terms in describing the post-Cold War U.S. interaction with the rest of the world, the analogy was so striking that America's new politico-religious discourse of the crusade for freedom and democracy almost echoed what Churchill had said about the 'noble' mission of the British Empire. At the dawn of the unipolarity era, even if the United States could hardly be called an empire in its traditional sense, it was indeed a hegemon. Despite its limitations to be primus inter pares, the US dealt with rising powers and potential competitors as the only primus following a pre-emptive strategy. "Luring" probable adversaries into revealing their intentions regarding the American-dominated status quo, and then dealing with them preemptively, was the US strategy. One basic principle of the post-Cold War U.S. policy in East Asia was to perpetuate the American hegemonic position in the region. Exaggerating China's capabilities, trying to predict China's intentions, and, in relation to others, selling the image that the United States military presence in East Asia was indeed a positive security factor, was the winning rallying cry.

China, North Korea, Russia, and most of the peoples of East Asia, however, didn't necessarily see the U.S. military presence in the region from the same positive premise. On the contrary, the U.S. image as an Asian hegemon had grown since the disappearance of the Soviet deterrent, and the U.S.-Japan alliance was one of the most important instruments of this hegemony. It was an image not only of a hegemon but also of an intrusive arrogance. Ironically, Japan's former Prime Minister Hosokawa said: "the cultural arrogance of a country with such problems of race and crime was breathtaking to people on our side of the Pacific. Frankly, there were times when rather more American isolation would be welcome" (Walker 19).

There is also the U.S. public opinion variable which played almost a nil role in curbing the post-Cold War United States hegemonic tendencies. A behavior that was usually associated with power supremacy and even an apocalyptic vision that the United States was "the greatest force for good in history", as George W. Bush put it in Texas on August 31, 2002, resulting in a situation where the U.S. made many more foes than friends, lost even its traditional key allies in Europe as in Asia, and therefore alienated much of the rest of the world (Hoffmann 60). In short, the current U.S. government "flaunted a level of military might that has been frustrating most other nation-states since the end of the Cold War. The Bush II United States turned into a schoolyard bully. Its goals were by no means reprehensible, but its hubris and unilateralism were. Sooner or later, the American public was likely to get embarrassed and have second thoughts" (Lewis 33).

So, to paraphrase Michael Mandelbaum, was this the American hegemony that people would not pay for, would continue to criticize, and would miss when it was gone (53)? Therefore, one can sum up by arguing that for a long time, we would miss the Cold War, the diffusion of power among at least two superpowers, and the balance of power and its attendant relative stability in international relations. We would also look forward to the future of a rising power, such as China, that could tip the balance back to normal, as the monopoly of power in international relations always resulted in more wars, instability and eventually less security.

Finally, as the stated American policies in East Asia were said to be based on the principle that no country should play the hegemon in the region, most Chinese attempts at reunification with Taiwan since Chiang Kai-shek fled to the Island in 1949, were marketed to China's neighbors as signs of potential Chinese hegemony which necessitates a strong American military presence. From a Chinese perspective, however, the U.S.-Japan common policies toward Taiwan were an unwarranted interference in China's domestic affairs, as Beijing believed that its problem with Taipei was purely internal. In this context of trading hegemonic allegations between the United States and Japan, on the one hand, and China, on the other hand, the next section will try to explore the validity of these mutual allegations by dealing with the Taiwan question as a case study of hegemony, rather than from historical or economic perspectives. China accused the United States and Japan of exercising hegemony by their unwarranted interference in what Beijing viewed as an internal matter; Washington and Tokyo, however, alleged that China was using the Taiwan problem to show an increasing assertiveness in East Asia and, therefore, becoming more and more hegemonic.

4.2. Taiwan: A Case Study of hegemony

Following the 1894-95 Sino-Japanese Pigtail War, victorious Japan forcibly seized Taiwan "in perpetuity" according to the April 1895 Shimoneseki Treaty, but the Island came under de facto U.S. "responsibility" in the wake of Japan's surrender to the United States in September 1945. Since then, China has perceived the eventual reunification with Taiwan as essential to China's recovery from a century of national weakness, vulnerability, and humiliation. China regards Taiwan not only as a security problem, but also as a question of national honor since Sun Yat-sen's 1919 pledge to return the island to the embrace of the motherland. "Chinese national leaders since Sun Yat-sen had all considered the loss [of Taiwan] a national humiliation and hence recovery of the island a sacred national mission" (Hsiao 28)[20]. During the 50 years of the Cold War, China failed to regain Taiwan because the island *suddenly*[21] became a structural element in the U.S. defense strategy of containing communism in Asia and isolating Communist China. Due to the U.S. Cold War geo-strategic calculations, Sun-Yat-sen's dream to end a century-long humiliation had never come true (Acheson 111-18).

In the post-Cold War context, "the Taiwan Strait is one of the world's most dangerous spots, because policy misjudgments or a mere accident could result

---

[20] See Rhaiem, Jalel. *The United States and China: Cooperation or Confrontation?* Presented in partial fulfillment of the requirements for the Degree of Diplôme d' Etude Approfondies, Manouba, September 29,1999), Chapter 3, Section 3.

[21] See also National Security Council Memos: No. 37/6, August, 4, 1949, "Memorandum by the Department of State to the Executive of the National security Council"; No.37/7, August 22, 1949, "Position of the United States with respect to Formosa"; No. 37/8, October 6,1949, "Report by the NSC on the Position of the United States with respect to Formosa"; No.37/9, December 27, 1949, "Possible United States Military Action Toward Taiwan Not Involving Major Military Forces".

in war" between China and the United States, possibly involving Japan either directly or indirectly (Pye 5). The problem and the future of Taiwan have transcended the domestic Chinese sovereignty issue and clearly became part of the power and security game within the triangle under study. The American Japanese Security Consultative Committee (SCC) on February 19, 2005, declared that Taiwan was now a *"common security concern"* between Washington and Tokyo (Ministry of Foreign Affairs of Japan, "Joint Statement: U.S.-Japan Security Consultative Committee", February 21, 2005).

The '2 + 2' statements set the foundation of a common future strategy between the United States and Japan, marking the Taiwan issue as a point of "convergence of bilateral, regional, and global interests" for both Washington and Tokyo (Przystup and Saunders 3); a convergence which went beyond their bilateral relationship to extend to a regional security environment that was characterized by the uncertain implications of the rise of China as a potential threat to the U.S.-dominated status quo in East Asia.

Taiwan, a case of U.S.-Japanese regional hegemony from a Chinese perspective, and a democratic "success story" for the United States and Japan, was not only a Civil War and a Cold War leftover, but also the hottest issue in the post-Cold War complex East Asian security environment. Given the sensitivity of this question for Beijing, which saw Taiwan as a "renegade province" and therefore a domestic issue, the U.S.-Japanese official stand that Taiwan had to be dealt with as a regional, rather than a domestic, issue was perceived by the Chinese as an American, with Japanese complicity, exercise of hegemony through unwarranted interference in China's domestic affairs. "China viewed the status of Taiwan as an internal matter. But only by coordinating its U.S. policy with its policy toward Taiwan could Beijing curb the separatist forces on the island" (Jisi, "China's Search for Stability with America" 46), testifying once again to the interrelatedness of the region's security package, as this book argues.

In addressing the Taiwan problem, the three nations' approaches were deeply impacted by their respective power and security calculations. Therefore, this section seeks to shed light on the Taiwan issue either as a case of hegemony or as a serious security problem in East Asia to which China would have to readjust its approach and accommodate others' calculations. Thus, within the U.S.-Japan-China triangle, the Taiwan case study constituted almost the entire population of the cases of how 'Power' and 'Security' interplay, as seen through the interactions of the units of analysis within a certain state system based on the core concepts of power and security.

The Taiwan Case study did fit into the triangular framework of this book in view of the involvement of the United States, Japan, and China in dealing with this case on the basis of the security and power equation. Each party approached the Taiwan problem from the standpoint of its own security calculations and its power position vis-à-vis the other two parties. Beijing viewed the recovery of Taiwan, besides being a security problem, as vital to China's emergence as a rising great power, making the Chinese attempt to regain Taiwan an exercise of animus dominandi in the eyes of the United States and Japan. Michael Swaine even goes further to suggest that regaining Taiwan was a matter of survival for the Chinese Communist Party. Swaine said: "Losing Taiwan against Beijing's will would deal a severe blow to Chinese prestige and self-confidence; Chinese leaders believe[d] that their government would likely collapse in such a scenario" (18).

The United States and Japan, however, were dealing with the Taiwan issue in the 1990s as well as the 2000s decades from a geo-strategic and even hegemonic standpoint. Since the 1969 Nixon-Sato Declaration that Taiwan's security was a U.S.-Japanese common concern, it was for the first time in February and again in September 2005 that the United States and Japan openly reiterated their common commitment to the security of Taiwan, which was an unwarranted intervention in China's domestic affairs, and therefore an exercise of hegemony, from the Chinese point of view. Beijing saw the February 2005 U.S.-Japan Security Consultative Committee declaration that Taiwan was "a common security concern" between the two countries as an American Japanese manifestation of their common intent to dominate East Asian affairs and dictate a regional order that suits their own security and geopolitical agenda.

In Beijing, there was some ambivalence. To the extent that the American military presence reduced the chances for Japan to re-militarize, it was welcome, but should this presence be used to reduce China's leverage on Taiwan, it became a case of U.S. hegemony. China maintained that the rationale of the U.S. military presence in East Asia, including the newly expanded U.S.-Japan alliance and the U.S. military presence along the demilitarized zone between the two Koreas, sought to contain rising Chinese military power, and to prevent a "peaceful" reunification with Taiwan, besides being a destabilizing factor in relation to the South-North Korean conflict (Tyler, "China's Military Regards U.S." A 5). In April 1996, Tokyo and Washington began to work out guidelines for Japanese support in times of need, which turned out to be one of the most important security developments for the region. The Japanese would support U.S. efforts to maintain 'security' in "areas surrounding Japan," and Taiwan is one of the nearest "areas" to the Japanese archipelago.

The potential U.S.-Japanese cooperation in the eventuality of security problems, that is, a Chinese military move against a potential Taiwanese bid for de jure independence, meant that China could not play a Japan card against the U.S. or try to dislodge the Americans from the region. Consequently, it was highly unlikely to see China becoming "a global challenger to the U.S., nor would it be able to exercise regional hegemony so long as the United States stayed involved in East Asia and maintains its alliance with Japan" (Nye, "'The Nye Report': Six Years Later" 100).

Therefore, one can argue that the American Japanese commitment to the security of Taiwan could be an exercise of hegemony, for it was perceived by the Chinese as an interference in China's internal affairs and an attempt to contain Beijing's rising power. It was therefore a policy which increased the chances of instability in East Asia, making the United States' regional role a negative security factor in the region, which supports the research hypothesis of this work that the United States Asia policy in the post-Cold War early decades had a negative security impact on East Asia's complex security situation.

This was a situation where the three actors almost reached the brink of war across the Strait of Taiwan in March 1996 and, to a lesser extent, in 2000. During Taiwan's 1996 presidential campaign, China declared most of the Strait of Taiwan a closed military zone, and started a series of military exercises across the Strait aimed at disrupting Taiwan's presidential elections. The Chinese fired M-11 mid-range missiles at targets close to Taiwan's two busiest ports. In accordance with the 1979 Taiwan Relations Act (TRA), the United States, using its military bases in Okinawa, Japan, dispatched two aircraft carriers-the Independence and the Nimitz-to sail to the Western Pacific region ostensibly to prevent a potential Chinese military move against Taiwan (Bernstein and Munro 149-53). The TRA considers even a blockade on Taiwan as a "threat to the peace and security of the Western Pacific area and of a grave concern to the United States" (The TRA, Section 2 (a) (4)).

During the 2000 presidential elections in Taiwan, almost the same scenario was repeated, except that China was less assertive than in 1996 because the balance of power was again not in China's favor, and the cost of a military confrontation was too high to handle for the Chinese, whose economy was in desperate need of the peaceful flow of foreign capital. Then, China escalated its anti-Taiwan rhetoric, but refrained from firing missiles or tampering with across Strait shipping. It was clear that the U.S. deployment of two major aircraft to Taiwanese waters represented "the clearest possible sign of U.S. determination to remain the prime security guarantor in the region" (Walker 20), or at least to show that the U.S. military presence in Northeast Asia was contributory to stability and security.

The 1996 and 2000 incidents across the Strait of Taiwan were among the most relevant cases when the two dependent variables of power and security were inter-played by the three actors. This was clear from their respective actions and reactions to each other, bringing to the fore the independent variable of interaction by which we can conceptualize and quantify the two criterion variables. Indeed, the two cases show that the core concepts of power and security were decisive variables in shaping the three nations' respective policies regarding the Taiwan problem. It turned out that the strongest controlled the outcome of the interaction, and the weakest had eventually to blink. The eventual Chinese withdrawal from the Strait of Taiwan, and the election of a pro-independence president, Chen Shu-Bian, in Taiwan, substantiates the argument that the outcome of the Sino-U.S.-Japanese interaction in this case was governed by the state of the balance of power, which was in America's favor because of the latter's overwhelming power that was buttressed by its strong alliance with Japan. The final resolution of the standoff also demonstrated the subjectivity of the terms "defensive" and "offensive", as China believed it was acting in self-defense, whereas the United States took it as an exercise of power politics on the part of the Chinese. From a U.S. perspective, however, the American military presence in East Asia succeeded in defusing tensions and crises between Taiwan and China, which could have brought the region to a military confrontation.

Both cases clearly show that the interaction between states is generally based on the distribution of power among them, since the eventual Chinese withdrawal from the Strait of Taiwan in 1996 and again in 2000 meant that Beijing concluded that a war with the United States was not winnable. Moreover, "given the substantial benefit Chinese development derives from the very large Taiwanese investment in China, along with the lucrative Taiwanese tourist trade, a major Chinese attack against Taiwan would be self-destructive and [also] threatened to make an "unthinkable" nuclear confrontation with the United States inevitable" (Gerson, "Fresh Look", Lecture June 26-27, 1999). That was why Beijing's military exercises were counterproductive and even self-defeating, given the Chinese failure to influence the outcome of the Taiwanese elections, and the opportunity China gave to the United States to show the relevance of the American military presence to East Asia's stability, and to add to the credibility of the China-threat thesis in the region.

This was also a triangle where one actor felt threatened by the concerted efforts of the other two, leading to the claim that the United States and Japan were exercising hegemony and cooperating to dominate the future of East Asia through a renewed security treaty officially called the U.S.-Japan Alliance for the twenty-first century (Mufson 16). Taiwan, from a Chinese perspective, was an internal matter between the motherland and a "renegade province", that is an issue of physical security (Hsiao 118). The United States and Japan, however, saw the question as a threat to regional stability. Washington described the Chinese behavior across the Strait of Taiwan in 1996 and 2000 as a show of force and an attempt to dominate the region by trying to play the role of the hegemon not only in Taiwan, but also in Japan and South Korea[22].

Theoretically, the exercise of power by states becomes tangible when state A tries to change the behavior or the policy of state B through economic pressure and by the threat or the use of force. China, for instance, tried to coerce Taiwan into a more conciliatory posture by threatening to invade the Island if Taipei declared independence. The United States, in line with the 1979 Taiwan Relations Act, argued that in case of a Chinese military move on Taiwan or even a blockade, America would not remain passive. In both exercises of power, we noticed that China had somewhat succeeded in moderating the behavior of the independentists in Taiwan, and America managed to deter a Chinese military take-over of the island. This is what P.A. Reynolds called "negative feedback", that is when State A succeeds in modifying state B's behavior (Reynolds 200). Therefore, it is safe to argue that the three-way post-Cold War interaction between the U.S., Japan, and China regarding the Taiwan question revolved around their competition for both security and power. This interaction was a mixture of quid pro quo[23] and tit for tat[24] politics, depending again on the

---

[22] Hearings of the Committee On National Security of the House of Representatives of the One Hundred Fourth Congress, March 20, 1996, 1, 2, 35, and the Hearings of the Committee on Armed Services of the House of Representatives, the One Hundred Sixth Congress, July 19, 2000, 65, 77, 79).

[23] Quid pro quo: Latin concept meaning "something for something". In politics, and negotiations it refers to actions taken because of some promised action in return for the first. It can also apply to gestures of good will from State A to State B as a confidence-building measure.

[24] Tit for Tat: It is the opposite of the quid pro quo politics. It depicts a situation where two states or groups of states reciprocate with an escalating action when they feel provoked by a similar action from their adversaries. It tends to exacerbate the conflict and usually leads to war.

distribution of power among the three main actors in the region as well as their respective calculations in either keeping Taiwan separate, or regaining the Island's sovereignty.

Strategically, Taiwan is of critical significance to the United States' regional and global objectives for a range of reasons. First, the future of Taiwan was considerably important to Washington's preponderant position on the East Asian chessboard because a separate, not independent, Taiwan was always, and was likely to continue to be, a tantalizing wild goose chase to induce a rising China into becoming "responsible and peaceful", that is complacent with the American hegemonic status quo in East Asia. Playing the Taiwan card if Beijing decided to challenge the United States for the domination of East Asia or question the need for the American military presence in the region, showed a great deal of success in neutralizing China's lack of cooperation regarding a wide range of regional and world issues. The list included China's opposition to imposing sanctions on North Korea because of its intransigence regarding its nuclear weapons programs, the gigantic U.S. economic interests in China[25], America's post-9/11 controversial crusade on terrorism, and last but not least, enforcing international nonproliferation regimes in the Middle East.

Second, from a legal point of view, the Taiwan Relations Act stipulates very clearly that the United States is committed to the security of Taiwan, and the failure to defend Taiwan in times of need would almost certainly affect the credibility of U.S. security reassurances to other nations in East Asia, especially Japan and South Korea. Third, U.S. support of Taiwan was closely tied to the U.S. long-term stand regarding the China-Taiwan conflict over the "one-China" policy, since a Chinese military takeover of Taiwan would contradict the three Sino-American Communiqués of 1972, 1979, 1982[26], and Section 2 (a) (4) of the Taiwan Relations Act. Taiwan is also strategically important not only to the United States, but also to Japan, the third pillar of the East Asian triangle.

---

[25] For more on the U.S. economic and trade interests in China, see Rhaiem, Jalel. *The United States and China: Cooperation or Confrontation?* Presented in partial fulfillment of the requirements for the Degree of Diplôme des Etudes Approfondies, Manouba, September 29,1999, Chapter Four.

[26] For more on these Communiqués, see Steve M. Goldstein, "Sino-American Relations after Normalization -Toward the Second Decade", Epharta, PA, Foreign policy association Headlines Series (FPA) no.276, 1986, 17. See also Harry Harding, *A Fragile Relationship: the United States and China since 1972*, The Brookings Institution, Washington, 1992.

Though Tokyo's stance regarding the Taiwan question was inextricably linked to that of Washington, Japan did have its own security and power calculations.

Politically, the fact that the United States was consumed by the Iraq quagmire and its controversial war on terror would lead to the assumption that the U.S. simply cannot afford a crisis over Taiwan, at least for the time being. So, the United States was actually putting great pressure on Taiwan not to provoke the Chinese and not to cause trouble in the region. Therefore, Washington could resort to a modus operandi with China regarding the vexed question of Taiwan in order to explore ways of keeping Taiwanese separatist forces under control lest they drag both countries toward a military confrontation neither side wants. But "the chances of a confrontation between Beijing and Washington, in other words, could be reduced further [only] if China's leaders believed that the option of ultimate reunification remained on the table for the foreseeable future" (Swaine 59-60).

However, as the United States was consumed by the 2003 Iraq invasion, "gamesmanship continued to plague cross-Strait affairs, as each side calculates how time may or may not be on its side, and acts accordingly" (Campbell and Mitchell 72-73). China could come to the belief that the U.S. was unlikely to drown itself in another war in East Asia, which it could win militarily but could not bear politically and economically. China could be encouraged by the fact that Taiwan matters far more to China than it did to the United States, and therefore, it was highly unlikely that the U.S. would go to war with China over Taiwan, especially with a U.S. government that had rebuked quite often Taiwan's independentist trends over the last couple of years.

China's military build-up in the Strait of Taiwan has continued and gained momentum, especially since the current Taiwanese president announced that he intended to hold a referendum in 2004. Indeed, since July 2002, "the cross-Strait military balance is shifting steadily in favor of China, and missile deployments and information operations in particular support an apparent strategy of coercion that might provide a credible political-military option to Chinese leaders in coming years" (Campbell and Mitchell 69-70). As Bill Gertz put it, "a nuclear war with China over its dispute with Taiwan was a real danger. And even though the Clinton administration went to great lengths to ignore it, that danger was growing" (*The China Threat* 72).

Japan, the third major actor in the post-Cold War Japan-U.S.-China triangle, was part and parcel of the problem as well as the solution to the Taiwan question in view of the historical context and the people-to- people connection. Historically, the island was under Japanese sovereignty from 1895 up to Japan's defeat in WWII. Despite the Japanese occupation of Taiwan during the Second World War, thousands of aboriginal Taiwanese fought and died for the Japanese Imperial Army not only on the island but also in Southeast Asia. Trying to honor the aboriginal service to Japan, a group of those 'veterans' tried in 2005 to erect a monument in a Taipei suburb (Faoila A.12). At the level of people-to-people interaction, there was strong evidence that there was a mutual sense of appreciation between the Japanese and the Taiwanese. Contrary to the Chinese and Koreans, there was a large group of Taiwanese who viewed Japan's imperial history in sympathetic terms. Some of them even delighted in speaking Japanese. Even "Imperial-era structures, including the elegant Presidential Office Building that was once the seat of the Japanese governor, was painstakingly preserved and declared a national treasure" (Ibid).

A 2001 Mainichi poll asked a group of Japanese to identify countries most friendly to Japan. Taiwan came third, just behind the United States and South Korea[27]. In Japan, then, the pro-Taiwan political forces were gaining more and more momentum. After the end of the Cold War, "Japanese right-wing forces no longer shrank from offending Beijing by making overtures to pro-separation forces in Taipei" (Jisi, "China's Search for Stability" 44), which was considered as part of the Japanese complicity in a U.S. hegemonic interference in China's domestic affairs.

In Taiwan, a national policy adviser to Taiwanese president Chen Shui-Bian (2000-2008) revealed in 2005 how strong the Taiwan-Japan connection was and how much the Japanese had invested in the island. He said: "The Japanese built universities, roads, and other infrastructure. They educated us, they turned us into a more modern society...we welcome Japan becoming more involved again in Taiwan" (Spaeth 13). As for Taiwan-Japan economic exchange, both nations were exchanging a record 2.3 million tourists each year, besides the fact that Japan was Taiwan's largest trading partner (Faoila A 12). A military conflict in the Strait of Taiwan could considerably disrupt the free flow of raw materials and goods to and from Japan, which makes Taiwan part of Japan's security calculus in view of the Sino-Japanese relationship of rivalry and power competition in East Asia.

Although it is difficult to understand the logic of Japan's own national security calculus, it is very clear that there was a tangible post-Cold War shift in

---

[27] Advertising Department of the Mainichi Newspapers, November 2001, http://web-japan.org/stat/stats/22OPN48.html.

Japan's perception and policy regarding the Taiwan problem, and this was happening with the full consent and counsel of the United States which was quite determined to use the Taiwan card politically and militarily in order to discourage any potential Chinese challenge of the security status quo in East Asia. Since the 1972 Sino-Japanese Communiqué, Tokyo kept a de facto embassy in Taipei, calling it the Interchange Association, an equivalent to the U.S. Taiwan Institute (Rhaiem 93-110). During the Cold War, and under American dictates, Japan abode by the "one China" policy, and tried to avoid being directly involved in the China-Taiwan controversy. After the end of the Cold War, however, both Washington and Tokyo took a series of political and military steps that not only angered the Chinese, but also almost changed the face of the region's security architecture, making another East Asia triangle- the United States, Japan and Taiwan. The Taiwanese president said during an interview in March 2006 that "peace and stability of the Taiwan Strait and security of the Asian Pacific region [we]re the common concerns for not only Taiwan, but also Japan and the United States...Japan ha[d] a requirement and an obligation to come to the defense of Taiwan" (Faoila A 12). President Chen went even further to call for a "quasi-military alliance" between the United States, Japan, and Taiwan (Ibid).

Furthermore, the recent series of new Japanese overtures toward Taiwan were expressed by the bilateral Japan-U.S. Security Consultative Committee on February 19, 2005, which called for "the peaceful resolution of issues concerning the Taiwan Strait through dialogue" (Ministry of Foreign Affairs of Japan, "Joint Statement: U.S.-Japan Security Consultative Committee", February 21, 2005). In reaction to what the Chinese perceived as an unwarranted interference in China's domestic affairs, and hegemonic behavior on the part of the United States and Japan, Beijing passed in March 2005 an anti-Secession Law whereby China asserted its authority to use "non-peaceful means" against Taiwan if the latter took any formal separatist measure. In a defiant gesture, however, the Japanese responded by sending their first military attaché to Japan's quasi-embassy in Taipei, leading Tadashi Ikeda, Japan's first-ranking diplomat in Taiwan, to shed light on how Tokyo would react to a Chinese military attack on Taiwan. He said: "there was always a question of what Japan would do. Now the Taiwanese could say that both the U.S. and Japan are on their side" (Preble 14). The fact that a Japanese diplomat was talking on behalf of both Japan and the United States consolidates this book thesis that the U.S.-Japan convergence regarding their common position towards the Taiwan issue was indeed conspiratorial against China, aiming at depriving Beijing of a potentially strategic card in a likely competition over the domination of East Asia.

From the Chinese perspective, Japan's most problematic and provocative overture regarding the Taiwan question was Japan's Foreign Minister Taro's calling of Taiwan a law-abiding "country" in March 2006 ("Japanese Foreign Ministry Again Calls Taiwan a 'Country'", *Agence France Presse*, March 9, 2006). Taro announced that "although I know there w[ould] be a problem with calling [Taiwan] a country, firm relations between Japan and Taiwan should be maintained" (Ibid). Though Taro did not explain whose "law" Taiwan was abiding by, one would argue that the Japanese diplomat must have been referring to the U.S. hegemonic order in the region, which was marketed to the Japanese as a "strategic partnership" between "two normal countries" (Preble 1). Former Prime Minister of Japan Koizumi was accused by the majority of the Japanese of poor neighborly relations in view of his blind support of U.S. hegemonic policies all over the world (Preble 12-13-14). Japan was perceived by China again as an accomplice of the United States in preventing the reunification of Taiwan with the mainland, not for Taiwan's sake but for the American Japanese hostile perception of a rising China, which they feared could replace the United States as the regional hegemon and thus endangered the security of America's key allies in the region, especially Japan. But Japan would have to deal with serious legal questions before it can actually come to "the defense of Taiwan", such as Article 9 of the Japanese Constitution.

Although Tokyo's ability to deploy its military abroad was very limited, due to Japan's pacifist constitution dictated to the Japanese by General Douglas MacArthur in the wake of Japan's defeat in WWII, there was already a controversial 1999 law that allowed Tokyo to respond to threats in nearby waters, which could provide a legal basis for Japan to intervene militarily in case of a Chinese move against Taiwan, as the Strait of Taiwan could fall within the parameter of "nearby waters." Though this law was a broad interpretation of the Japanese constitution, political leaders in Japan tried to go around it by arguing that Japan would not be involved in combat operations on the U.S.-Taiwanese side but could contribute rear-guard refueling, transportation and medical services inside Taiwan (Faoila A12). Japan could also use the United States to exchange military intelligence with Taiwan. Moreover, as the 1997 U.S.-Japan New Defense Guidelines expanded Japan's security "prerogatives" to "areas surrounding Japan", Tokyo defined those areas in functional rather than geographic terms. China, however, regarded this potential security cooperation as a proof of a U.S.-Japanese regional hegemony, since it anticipates, among other things, a Taiwan contingency.

Because of the geographical proximity of Taiwan to Japan, which was less than 175 miles west of Japan's southernmost island of Ishigaki, and in view of the strategic significance of the island, it was highly likely that Tokyo, in times of need, would stretch the interpretation of the phrase "surrounding Japan" or "nearby waters" to include Taiwan, since a military conflict there would threaten Japan's economic interests. Also, a "Chinese takeover of Taiwan would likely alter the strategic balance in East Asia," which would hardly be accepted by either Tokyo or Washington (Preble 14-15).

Furthermore, there was an ongoing process of constitutional reform in Japan, which started in the mid-1990s. The Japanese Diet, with its bicameral chambers, established a Research Commission on the Constitution in January 2000, which issued its final report in April 2005 (Kajimoto 5). It is worth emphasizing the fact that this parliamentary report found out that as much as 85 percent of the members of the Diet supported a revision of the notorious Article 9, which they saw as an impairment to Japan's sovereignty and an obstacle preventing Japan from playing a regional and a world military as well as political role that was commensurate with the country's economic prowess (Ibid). Therefore, it is safe to assume that if and when Article 9 was amended, we could see a radical overhaul in East Asia's security chessboard, including Taiwan's future either as "a *renegade province*" or as a "law-abiding '*country*'".

In reaction to Japan's new stance regarding the question of Taiwan and Japanese efforts to amend their pacifist constitution, China's *Chengdu Shangbao* newspaper wrote in November 2004 that "Japan's abandonment of its peace constitution c[ould] only intensify the mistrust that the countries and the peoples of Asia have towards Japan"[28]. Facing a comeback of Japan's militarism with an American accomplice, China's security calculus would also considerably change in the direction of an inevitable confrontation with a hegemonic America and a rearmed Japan.

As a matter of fact, the condemnation of Japan's desire to review its constitution came also from other Japanese neighbors, namely South Korea. *Chungang Ilbo*, a South Korean paper, predicted that "it was highly likely that a change and expansion of the role of the Self Defense Forces would aggravate

---

[28] "Japan's Defense Debate Stirs Concern", BBC News, November 19, 2004, http://news.bbc.co.uk/2/hi/asia-pacific/4025805.stm>.

the regional situation if the military situation in Northeast Asia turns bad" (Ibid). The security situation across the Taiwan Strait could indeed "turn bad" if the new Japanese stance towards Taiwan pushed Taiwan's president to take further adventuristic steps toward formal independence, thus inviting a Chinese last-resort military response. Paradoxically, a Sino-Taiwanese military showdown across the Strait of Taiwan was not in America's near-term interests due to the U.S. focus on the "war on terrorism" in the aftermath of the 9/11 terrorist attacks.

Indeed, the argument that the United States might not be very enthusiastic about Japan's calling Taiwan a "country" was based on the evidence that Washington "expressed concern that too sudden a shift could embolden" the Taiwanese president's quest for political support to move forward with his referendum plans (Faoila A12). On the one hand, the United States wanted Japan to support Washington's ambiguous and tantalizing policy towards the Taiwan issue, thus dragging Tokyo into a confrontational relationship with its giant neighbor, which precluded any possibility of a Chinese-Japanese rapprochement at the expense of the U.S.-Japan alliance.

On the other hand, the United States would not accept losing the "initiative" to Japan in playing the Taiwan card against Beijing, which would be useful if the latter decided to challenge America's hegemonic regional order, manifested primarily in its "empire of bases" (Ch. Johnson 151-86) in East Asia. This can lead to the conclusion that the U.S. was simply using Japan for America's strategic objectives to keep China under constant pressure by showing a strong and common American Japanese resolve regarding the Taiwan question, and at the same time, showing reluctance in supporting Tokyo's independently assertive stance with regard to this issue.

Taiwan, in its turn, had its own security and power calculations. Taipei understands rather well the China-U.S. zero-sum game over Taiwan as a case of hegemony rather than a security issue. Taipei also understood U.S. domestic politics quite well, and succeeded in playing the independence card, first to test America's resolve to defend the island in case of a Chinese backlash, and second to see how China would react to an American pledge to intervene militarily if Beijing attacked Taiwan. During the 1990s, the Taiwanese, and with them, the Japanese, could see Clinton's alleged tilt toward China, and therefore refrained from taking any provocative steps that would anger the United States before it angered China. Notwithstanding the 1996 American reaction to China's military maneuvers across the Strait of Taiwan, U.S.-Chinese relations during the decade of the 90s did transcend the Taiwan problem, which became a secondary issue in their bilateral relations, like the human rights one. In a 2006 the Armitage Group report, we read: "looking back on the 1990s, the study group expressed concern that China had become the principal focus of American policymakers… Implicit in this concern was the criticism that the attention paid to China had come at the expense of the U.S.-Japan" and the U.S.-Taiwan relationship, too (Przystup and Saunders 2).

The advent, however, of a neo-conservative Republican administration in the United States in 2001 coincided with the rise to power in Taiwan's presidential elections of an independentist president, Chen Shu-Bian, who run for and won the presidency in 2000 and 2004 on the basis of a pledge to organize a referendum that would normally open the door for an official declaration of independence. Since 2004, "Taiwan enjoyed the most supportive U.S. administration since 1979, and a distracted China….Chen took increasing, gradual steps over the past year to assert Taiwan's independent political identity, including recent statements concerning a potential referendum on Taiwan's status" (Campbell and Mitchell 62). Encouraged by George W. Bush's declaration in April 2001 that the United States would "do whatever it took" to come to the defense of Taiwan if the island was attacked by the Chinese (Bush's Interview by the ABC News Channel on April 18, 2001), Chen Shui-bian sought to organize a referendum on the future of Taiwan and write a new constitution that would negate the past source of Taiwanese sovereignty, and define the island's sovereignty as Taiwanese instead of Chinese, which was a break with the "one China" principle. Finally, such a "sense of a 'window of opportunity' might lead Chen to continue to test the boundaries of the possible, at best challenging China's forbearance, and at worst, endangering stability" in East Asia (Campbell and Mitchell 66).

The United States, however, did rebuke Taiwan's president over his plans for a referendum on relations with China in late 2004. In reaction to Chen's "separatist" or "independentist" posture, Bush, in a statement on 9 December 2003 during the visit of then China's premier Wen Jiabao to Washington, stated that "the comments and actions made by the leader of Taiwan indicate that he may be willing to make decisions unilaterally to change the status quo, which we opposed" (Taiwan Communiqué No. 106, January 2004). This contradicted Bush's 2001 commitment to defend Taiwan. This was in line with Washington's murky policy of "strategic ambiguity" which required convincing Beijing that the United States would defend Taiwan if China attacked while simultaneously alluding to Taipei that the United States would not defend it if the Taiwanese provoked a Chinese attack. Though this murkiness in the U.S. position regarding the China-Taiwan equation was deliberate, it survived the Cold War mentality and became even murkier.

As for China, though Beijing publicly stated time and again that the question of Taiwan is an internal matter, it knew very well that such a question could not be resolved domestically. Also, the Chinese were aware that the stakes were high and the economic and political cost of a military invasion of Taiwan would be too much to bear. Moreover, the Chinese leaders were under few illusions about the repercussions of a military showdown with the United States, which was under legislative obligation to defend Taiwan even in case of a Chinese blockade on the island, let alone an outright military attack on Taipei. But at the same time, Beijing could not afford to see Taiwan go independent because, once again, the cost of losing sovereignty over Taiwan would lead to the potential to see provinces like Tibet, Xinjiang, and Inner Mongolia asking for self-determination as they had already done. And "the damage to China's political and social stability in being seen to lose territory, in other words, would be even greater than the diplomatic and economic damage resulting from a conflict with the United States" (Swaine 55).

Therefore, in dealing with the highly sensitive issue of Taiwan, China was in a rather delicate situation of a loser in all cases. Weighing losses and opting for the least damaging one would be Beijing's best posture vis-à-vis the dilemma of either losing Taiwan together with its negative political and national repercussions, or fighting a lost war with an American-Japanese alliance that was militarily superior and strategically determined to prevent Taiwan's reunification with a rising and threatening Communist China. This was, besides the potential economic losses a war over Taiwan could inflict on the Chinese economy that was largely dependent on foreign investment and increasingly linked to the flow of oil from the Middle East and elsewhere, which passes through the Straits of Malacca and that of Taiwan.

A situation as such could very well push the Chinese to alter their calculus of power and security in relation to the United States and Japan. In order to be able to change Washington's stance and behavior regarding the Taiwan problem, China could resort to the same strategy used by the United States itself, that is the carrot and stick policy. As the Chinese recognized the reality of the American-dominated post-Cold War world order, it was highly likely that Beijing would conclude that in view of the military balance of power, the chances that China could prevail in such a conflict were really low. Therefore, China was though to think of a kind of a negotiated modus vivendi with Taiwan, and thus acquiesced to the U.S. wish.

To put it succinctly, it is safe to assume that "China's deployment of military forces along the Taiwan Strait was [simply] intended to deter Taiwan and the United States from closing off the option of eventual reunification" (Gerson, "Fresh Look", Lecture June 26-27, 1999). Moreover, "WTO accession and leadership change in China would likely serve as a constraint on its external behavior in the near term, including over Taiwan" (Campbell and Mitchell 68). Eventually, China might very soon realize that only by accommodating the U.S. hegemonic interests not only in East Asia but also in the world at large could Beijing curb the separatist forces on the Island.

Yet separatists in Taiwan, supported by parts of the U.S. defense establishment and certain members of the U.S. Congress, had pushed for independence, making Taiwan China's Achilles heel and thus serving the U.S. hegemonic agenda in the region. Basing their stand on the unsubstantiated assumption that China, given a choice, "would ultimately permit Taiwan's independence rather than confront the United States" (Swaine 58), Taiwan's supporters in the U.S. Congress, liberals and conservatives alike, went even further to advocate a U.S. abrogation of the "one China" policy and support of Taiwan's bid for self-determination.

I asked **Interviewee 1**, who believed that for good strategic reasons, the Americans and the Japanese would not want Taiwan to go back to China because Taiwan is strategically a giant aircraft carrier, why China would not take advantage of the U.S. weakness in East Asia, and become more assertive with Taiwan's growing separatist trends. **Interviewee 1** argued that there were two main reasons why China refrained from taking advantage of the U.S.'s lack of focus on East Asia.

By military standards, "the Chinese could not win a war at this point in time with the United States over Taiwan. So, it would not be wise for them to cause trouble. It would be much smarter for them to continue to grow their economy."[29] Second, China was becoming more and more powerful because it was accumulating more and more wealth every year, and it was not in China's interest to start a war in Asia that would jeopardize the Chinese economy. Therefore, both Washington and Beijing were aware that war between them over Taiwan would be in nobody's interest, and subsequently both sides tried hard to avoid such an eventuality. From an American perspective, the U.S.

---

[29] Personal Communication: My Interview with **Interviewee 1** at the University of Chicago, April 28, 2006, University of Chicago.

political and strategic interests were "best served by a policy that s[ought] not only to deter the use of military force but also to ensure that reunification between Taiwan and China remains an option" (Bush 186).

As this section has shown, the case of Taiwan was one of the most complicated security issues in post-Cold War East Asia, because China dealt with the issue as a purely domestic one and perceived the United States-Japan stance towards Taiwan as an exercise of hegemony. The fact that China was seeing Taiwan as a domestic issue while the United States and Japan internationalized the Taiwan question, may lead to the conclusion that the chances of resolving this problem peacefully were getting slimmer. When states do not agree on what is domestic and what is not, it means that there is a serious problem of communication among them, which could increase the probability of confrontation.

As Beijing irrevocably stated that it would not allow Taiwan to go independent and adopted the March 2005 Anti-secession law, which pledged a Chinese military response in such an eventuality, the U.S. and Japan moved from the "one-China" policy to considering the Taiwan issue a regional and "common security challenge" between them, and even calling a Taiwan a 'country.' Also, as China said it could not wait indefinitely for a reunification with Taiwan, the United States and Japan repeatedly stated that they together would not allow a non-peaceful resolution of the Taiwan problem. This set the stage for a highly likely security problem in Northeast Asia, leading one to ask about the nature of the U.S. military role in the region, whether it was a positive security one, or a negative and destabilizing factor. China viewed the U.S.-Japan stance towards Taiwan as hegemonic, and as having nothing to do with the Washington-Tokyo commitment to 'regional peace.'

Finally, while China got increasingly powerful, the United States and Japan sought to balance against it. As China became more powerful, incentives for the United States and Japan to keep Taiwan on the other side of the ledger would increase. At the same time, there would be no decrease in China's interest in getting Taiwan back. Taiwan is of tremendous symbolic importance to the Chinese, and it angered the Chinese considerably to see that the United States and Japan were, in effect, protecting Taiwan and making it practically impossible for China to get it back. Therefore, the resolution of the Taiwan question was not to be a bilateral agreement, but it was going to be a China-Japan-U.S. trilateral problem to solve, keeping the post-Cold War East Asian security architecture a triangle, instead of a square or a pentagon, because the Taiwan issue, like the North Korean one, cannot be solved bilaterally.

4.3. The New Century's U.S. Security Role in East Asia: Reality and Prospects

To the peoples of the Asia Pacific, however, the threat to their independence and security is and will always be U.S. imperialism. So much blood has been spilled because of U.S. imperialism, which has been asserting itself here for more than a century" (Tuazon, "Current U.S. Hegemony in Asia Pacific", Lecture March 1, 2003).

As the United States had finished with a Cold War adversary about which it knew much regarding its capabilities and intentions, Washington was then facing the spectrum of another cold war with an unpredictable contender in East Asia- China. The U.S.'s growing concern about the ramifications of China's rising power challenged American military and geopolitical strategists for almost two decades now. In the United States and Japan, the question was not about whether to contain China, but how to do so. "The issue, specifically, was that China would eventually emerge as what Pentagon planners call a 'peer competitor' to the United States in East Asia- that is a great power with the economic and military muscle to challenge America's preponderant position in a region which was sure to be the economic pivot of the new century" (Schwarz 36). Compared to the ex-Soviet threat, the China threat was perceived to be more "formidable" because the United States thinks it knew little about China's capabilities and intentions in view of the secretive nature of the Chinese (R. Kaplan 49). As a matter of fact, the China threat thesis in the American policy-making apparatus was already gaining momentum, which was in line with the premise of the realist school that a rising power was usually construed as a potential challenger to the status quo.

At the dawn of the twenty-first century, the pro-confrontation proponents in the United States argued that since China was likely to be the only challenger to the then-American hegemonic position in East Asia[30], the need to prepare to fight this challenge was becoming more urgent than ever (R. Kaplan 49-64). In April 2001, George W. Bush declared in an ABC interview that the United States would defend Taiwan if China attacked the island, thus touching the most delicate nerve of the Sino-American relationship (Eland, "The China-Taiwan Military balance" 2).

---

[30] For more on U.S. domestic friction as to what policy the United States should opt for towards the rising power of China, See among others Jia Qingguo. "One Administration, Two Voices", School of International Studies, Beijing University, Beijing, China.

Moreover, in April 2001, a Chinese pilot collided with an American EP-3 spy plane over the South China Sea and forced it to land on the Island of Hainan; the U.S. crew was detained for almost two weeks before it was released on an American pledge not to sell Taiwan the controversial Aegis missile system. Five years later, Washington did not tell the world whether the collision had taken place above international waters or above Chinese territorial waters, because both sides refused to release recordings of the conversations between the two pilots concerned and ground controllers, or even the data that showed the precise positions and headings of both the Chinese and the American aircraft. That would have clarified serious points of contention like the intents and actions of both pilots, and the distance maintained between the two planes (Crampton, "Neither China nor U.S. is Telling All About Spy Plane", *International Herald Tribune* 8). Though the U.S. crew was released in return for Washington's promise to 'delay' the sale of the Aegis missile system to Taiwan, the EP-3 incident showed how fragile the Sino-American relationship was in the post-Cold War era, and how quickly it could spiral down to a real military showdown (Ibid).

In September 2005, the Committee of Defense Review (CDR) of the United States House Armed Services Committee, which ran parallel to the Pentagon's Quadrennial Defense Review, and aimed at identifying "threats' to U.S. national security and reviewing the American force structure, issued its report. The statutory document urged attention to "China's military modernization, which included a 13 percent increase in its defense budget and the development of a growing defense industry that would be capable of producing sophisticated weaponry such as submarines, destroyers and strategic bombers within the next 10 years to 15 years" (Bullock, "Asia Most likely to shape U.S. Defense Policy", September 2005). Moreover, this report indicated that a "one-size military or defense policy was certainly not going to fit all of the defense and security challenges that the United States faces in Asia over the coming decades" (Ibid). But what the report failed to do is to name those "security challenges" which the U.S. has to confront in the region under study.

Furthermore, the 1992 Defense Policy Guidance (DPG) and the 1997 Project for a New American Century (PNAC) advocated "a world dominated by the unilateral use of U.S. military power to ensure Pax Americana; to assert the U.S. national interest; and prevent the rise of any possible power competitor for the future" (*World Tibet Network News* 12). According to official statements, however, the United States continued to focus on maintaining a stable balance of power and sought to play the role of a pacifier in post-Cold War East Asia

(Department of Defense, Quadrennial Defense Review Report, Washington, D.C., September 30, 2001, 1). The former Assistant Defense Secretary in 2006, told me at the "China and the Future of the World" Conference in April 2006 at the University of Chicago, that the United States "welcomes the rise of a peaceful and a responsible China."[31]

I asked Secretary Hill what he meant by a "peaceful and responsible" China. Would that mean that the Chinese ought not to challenge the "reality of power politics in East Asia, based on the premise of the US primacy, while China should follow?" Secretary Hill told me, "We are not looking for China to be subservient to the U.S. by no means at all. China is going to emerge in a way that it has global interest". Two weeks later, Deputy Secretary of State Robert Zoellick echoed the same discourse regarding what the United States "expected" from a rising and powerful China. Zoellick's September 2005 speech before the U.S. House of Representatives International Committee contained the often-cited invitation to China to become a "responsible stakeholder"[32] that would refrain from challenging the existing regional and international system dominated by the United States and its key allies, such as Japan in Asia, the United Kingdom in Europe, and Israel in the Middle East. This was in line with the "hub and spoke" policy that the United States has adopted for decades now.

So, despite the realistic recognition of China's "global interests", the fact that the United States saw potential Chinese attempts to challenge the existing geopolitical and security system in East Asia as an alarming signal about China's future intentions shows that the U.S. premised the expectation that China ought to be "peaceful and responsible" on the self-complacent belief that "America's political, diplomatic, and economic leadership contributes directly to global peace, freedom, and prosperity" in East Asia (Quadrennial Defense Review Report 1).

Therefore, the United States built its post-Cold War policy in East Asia around the claim that the region needed an American forward military presence to ensure peace and stability[33] among unfriendly neighbors such as North Korea and South Korea, China and Japan, and China on the one hand and the rest of

---

[31] Chicago Society: *China and the Future of the World.* The University of Chicago, April 28–29, 2006. Opening Keynote by a former U.S. defense official.

[32] Zoellick, "Whither China: From Membership to Responsibility?" Remarks to National Committee on U.S.-China Relations, New York, NY, September 21, 2005. Also see Zoellick, Testimony before the House International Relations Committee, May 10, 2006).

[33] See the Press Conference held by U.S. Secretary of State Condoleeza Rice and her South Korean Counterpart Bon Ky Mon on October 16, 2006 in Seoul, South Korea.

East Asia on the other. But in reality, the U.S. aimed at preventing "hostile" powers that might disturb American dominion in the region (Ibid). In addition to East Asian historical animosities and territorial disputes, there was the rise of China and its potential impact on America's position on the Asian chessboard. So, the United States adopted a self-righteous policy that East Asia needed and welcomed the American presence, and subsequently built its own regional strategy on a self-serving excuse. In other words, the bottom line for this current U.S. policy was, as Leifer put it, "to educate an irredentist China in the canons of good regional citizenship and to sustain the active engagement of the United States in regional affairs" (18), leading to the inference that the United States was trying to tame China into entering the U.S. club.

The crux of the matter was how to read China's emergence as a regional power and potentially a world rival to an unrivaled United States so far. Was it going to be like hoping for the best but preparing for the worst? That was a combination of military and geopolitical preparations to prevent such an eventuality, and simultaneously welcoming the rise of a "peaceful and responsible China" on the world stage through a strategy of an Orwellian doublespeak about "strategic partnership", "constructive engagement", and a "Concert of Asia" strategy (Khoo and Smith 4).

As a matter of fact, the "Concert of Asia" idea was an analogy to the Concert of Europe, which was formed by Britain, Russia, Prussia and France in 1815 in the wake of the 1815 Waterloo defeat of Napoleon by the British, and the emergence of a European system of monarchical multipolarity that was fused with a relationship of kinship among most of those monarchies[34]. This concert was a coercive security alliance whose members tried to use it as a mechanism to collectively manage regional affairs. In 1849, Russia, for instance, intervened in Hungary to restore Austrian rule (Khoo and Smith 4). But given the different geopolitical history as well as the military and political culture between Europe and Asia, the idea of a Concert of Asia where Asian nations, weak and strong, would meet to manage their regional conflicts is far-fetched. Trying to copy a nineteenth-century European security model and apply it to twenty-first-century East Asia simply failed to capture the nuances of the situation in the post-Cold War Asia-Pacific. Unlike early nineteenth-century Europe, power was concentrated in one single pole in East Asia, which was seeking to prevent

---

[34] See Kissinger, H. *A World Restored: Metternich, Castelreagh, and the Problems of Peace1812-1922.* Grosset and Dunlap, NY, 1964. See also Bridge, F.R. and Bullen, Roger. *The Great Powers and the European State System.* Harlow, Longmans, 1980.

the emergence of another peer power, and refused to acknowledge the right of a rising actor that had its own security concerns and historical rationale to assert itself.

Achytari suggested that in the 1990s, there were four 'great powers' in Asia, the U.S., China, Japan, and Russia, that could converge to contain rivalry between other Asian nations and among themselves (84-101). Though the idea seemed quite plausible, it was first based on the assumption that Russia was a major power, which was highly debatable in view of Russia's socio-economic and political problems in the years after the ex-USSR crumbled. Russia was then barely a middle power, and without its rusting nuclear weapons, it could easily be degraded to a "moribund superpower" (Khoo and Smith). Second, considering Japan as a 'great' power was not really accurate, given the weakening Japanese economic and demographic variables. **Interviewee 1** told me that Japan was a "sinking power", not a 'great' one[35]. Japan had one of the most aging populations in the world and was expected to lose at least one-quarter of its population in the next four or five decades. Out of a population of 127,463,611 in 2006, the age structure was as follows: 0-14 years, 14.2%; 15-64 years, 65.7%; 65 years and over, 20%. As for the medium age total, it was 42.9 years.

So, who was left then? The United States and China, and, as mentioned before, given their positions on the Asian chessboard as respectively a de facto hegemon and a rising ambitious power, the idea of a concert between two antithetical actors was simply unrealistic. Indeed, we were ultimately left with a unipolar center of power and an emerging regional power seeking a redistribution of global power that would recognize China's changing security interests and power weight not only in East Asia, but also in the world at large. Reunification with Taiwan and fair and open access to oil, which China would definitely need for the next three to four decades for its continuing economic and industrial boom over the last decade or so, would be China's 21st century priorities. Conversely, those two Chinese objectives were two red lines for the

---

[35] Personal Communication: My Interview with **Interviewee 1** at the University of Chicago, is a founder of his own school of neo-realism called 'offensive realism' which borrows from Hans J. Morgenthau's realism and Kenneth N. Waltz' neo-realism, but is known for its own approach to international relations. Among his works are *The Tragedy of Great Power Politics*, New York: Norton, 2001, Translated into Chinese, Greek, Italian, Japanese, Korean, Portuguese, Romanian, and Serbian; *Liddell Hart and the Weight of History*, New York: Cornell University Press; London: Brassey's, 1988; *Conventional Deterrence*, New York: Cornell University Press, 1983. The interview took place on April 28, 2006.

United States, and mere talk about them would mean to Washington that China was not going to be "peaceful and responsible."

Moreover, for a "Concert" to succeed, it must be consensual instead of coercive. The post-Cold War East Asian security environment was very different from that of 19th century Europe, and, therefore very difficult to be resolved in the same way. One of the major obstacles was the suspicion among Asian nations, especially those between the United States and China. *People's Daily*, which was the quasi-official newspaper in China, rejected an official White House report that called for American "global leadership in the new century", arguing that 'leadership' here was simply synonymous with American "hegemony" ("China Accuses U.S.").

Therefore, there was strong evidence that China did see the United States as a threat instead of a strategic partner, thus, making the mere talk about an East Asian security community rather unrealistic. The lack of the necessary goodwill and the disingenuous intentions on all sides rendered the idea of a 'concert of Asia' realistically impracticable. Susan Shirk, Clinton's deputy Assistant Secretary of State for East Asia, did not have any false hoped about it; she said, "achieving a full-fledged Asia-Pacific Concert of powers will be difficult"; nevertheless, "an effort to forge a Concert should be undertaken even if it was unable to reach the ambitious standard of the nineteenth century Concert of Europe and achieves only ad hoc multilateralism or regular consultations among the powers" (qtd in Khoo and Smith 4).

As the idea of a "Concert" in Asia was arguably a failure, the United States, together with its traditional allies in the region, turned to the ways and means of discouraging Asia's "rising hegemon" from challenging the status quo in the region. To achieve this goal, Washington relied on what was usually called the "hub-and-spoke" strategy (Cossa), which was building a U.S. hub of military authority, political influence, and economic leverage and creating the spokes around it. Historically, the United States has built ANZUS³⁶, CENTO³⁷, and

---

³⁶ ANZUS: The 1951 Pacific Security Treaty binding Australia, New Zealand, and the United States. The alliance worked quite smoothly until the electoral victory of the New Zealand Labour Party in 1984, which decided to ban U.S. nuclear-powered and nuclear-capable ships from entering New Zealand Waters. A policy branded by Washington as a violation of Article 2 of the pact, deciding on August 12, 1986 to suspend all its security obligations to New Zealand. Since then, ANZUS has been practically suspended, though not formally dissolved.

³⁷ CENTO: A 1955 America-led alliance in the Middle East to deter the Soviet Union. Originally known as the Baghdad Pac; it later became CENTO after Iraq withdrew in 1959.

SEATO[38], helped found ASEAN[39], and supported ASEAN's Asian Regional Forum (ARF), whose aim was to serve as a club for member states to voice their individual or collective security concerns. Washington was also a member of the Northeast Asian Cooperation Dialogue (NEACD), which paradoxically includes North Korea but aimed at justifying the American bilateral alliances with Japan and South Korea. Both alliances were meant to contain and neutralize the perceived North Korean threat to the security of America's allies. Therefore, it seemed safe to assume that "the manner in which the United States treated multilateral security institutions in Asia clarifies further its hegemonic strategy" (Ikenberry, ed. *America Unrivaled* 194).

Japan, South Korea, Taiwan, and others were simply made to believe that they could not survive without the American military being stationed on their respective soils or in their territorial waters to stave off potential threats, which the United States either invented or magnified in order to create a tense atmosphere of fear and suspicion in the region (Ch. Johnson 115). Moreover, the United States sought to coerce vulnerable nations which mixed feelings about U.S. hegemony to open up their ports for docking privileges. Although "most Southeast Asian states were reluctant to grant the United States access to their bases to pre-position their military equipment; most also acknowledge and welcome the role that U.S. forward deployed forces play in maintaining regional stability" (Ikenberry, ed. *America Unrivaled* 198). By the end of the Clinton presidency in 2000, the United States had already secured long-term access accords for naval facilities with countries like Indonesia, Malaysia, Singapore, and Brunei[40]. In condemning terms, Chalmers Johnson described

---

It included The US, Britain, Turkey, Iran, Pakistan, and Iraq. CENTO died in 1979 after the Khomeini 1979 revolution in Iran.

[38] SEATO: created in 1954 in Manilla, it included the Philippines, Australia, France, New Zealand, Pakistan, Thailand, Britain, and the U.S. Like NATO, SEATO was part of the U.S. Cold War strategy of containment against the Soviet Union, but it was so loose that it died in 1977 after members started withdrawing unilaterally.

[39] ASEAN: (Association of Southeast Asian Nations) A non-Communist regional grouping in Southeast Asia formed on August 8, 1967 originally by Indonesia, Malaysia, the Philippines, Singapore, and Thailand, but later joined by Brunei in 1984. ASEAN's stated objective has been to safeguard the region against great power rivalry, and to act as a forum for the resolution of the intraregional differences.

[40] U.S. Department of defense, "United States Security Strategy for the East-Asia pacific Region", Report of Office of International Security Affairs, Washington, D.C.: Government Printing Office, 2000.

the U.S. post-Cold War posture as an "international protection racket: mutual defense treaties, military advisory groups, and military forces stationed in foreign countries to 'defend' against often poorly defined, overblown, or nonexistent threats" (85). It simply comes down to a policy of divide and rule.

As a matter of fact, the United States sought to play the hegemon not only through its forward military presence in the region and its security alliance with Japan, but also through a divide-and-rule policy. Washington had a history of playing the two major actors-Japan and China- in East Asia against each other in a tricky balance of power game. The fact that the perceived American hegemony in East Asia was maintained by the U.S. forward military presence in the region especially on Japanese and South Korean soils, East Asia was divided against itself between those who criticized and those who welcomed this American presence. The United States, though it drew down some of its forces from the Demilitarized Zone (DMZ) between North Korea and South Korea in 2003 prior to the Iraq invasion, and withdrew from its naval facilities in the Philippines, notwithstanding the 1998 status-of-forces agreement with Manila, still maintains some 37.605 soldiers and 2,875 defense civilians in the DMZ, and 46,648 troops in Japan[41]. But the overall number of U.S. troops in East Asia could easily reach 101,127 uniformed people, besides some 50,283 American dependents (Ibid).

Therefore, it would not be repetitive to further emphasize that the 1951 United States-Japan Security Treaty (MST) was always the hub of the American military presence and of the U.S. security architecture in general, not only in East Asia but also in the Asia-Pacific region at large. Revisiting the MST is, of course, from a different perspective. In Chapter Three, Section one, the MST is dealt with as a paradoxical security alliance that provided more power leverage in East Asia, but resulted in less security for Japan. Here, the U.S.-Japan alliance would be highlighted as a U.S. instrument of hegemony, since it was used by Washington to further its political and economic interests in the region.

The MST can also be one of the basic case studies where the power and security game was clearly manifested in the interaction between the United States, Japan, and China. As the February 1995 revision of the U.S.-Japan Alliance known as the "Nye Report" recommended, the new United States Security Strategy for the East Asia-Pacific Region, published by the U.S.

---

[41] U.S. Department of Defense, Washington Headquarters Services, Directorate of Information, Operations, and Reports, Worldwide Manpower Distribution by Geographical Area, September 30, 2000.

Department of Defense, expanded the coverage of the U.S.-Japan security pact to involve the Japanese military in future conflicts in East Asia and elsewhere (Dibb 26; Sasae 27)

In the wake of the end of the Cold War, some Asian scholars and military experts in Japan and the United States, such as Bruce A. Wright and Mark O. Hague[42], opined that the bilateral Cold War alliance became obsolete simply because its raison d'être was gone with the disappearance of the Soviet Union as the declared target of such a security structure (Wright and Hague 60-64). The early stages of Clinton's Asia policy were guided by economic and governmental agencies; little effort was invested in security issues (Nye, "'The Nye Report: Six Years Later' " 95). There was even some speculation that the U.S.-Japan relationship would take an adversarial turn. Some writers went further to describe Japan as America's new enemy (Friedman and Lebard). Some East Asian nations, except China, began to anticipate a dismantling of American security structures in the region, such as the U.S. largest military base outside the continental United States in Okinawa (Johnson 151-86). This argument, however, was not shared by the Chinese, who were attempting throughout the 90s a double track strategy which aimed first at driving a wedge between Japan and the United States, and ingratiating Beijing with Washington, and second at preparing for the worst-case scenario of a newly strengthened and expanded alliance between China's two major adversaries in East Asia (Nye 96-99).

As the bulk of an overall U.S. military presence of more than 100,000 soldiers in the Asia-Pacific region was based in Okinawa, Japan was almost like "an unsinkable aircraft carrier for the United States"[43] in the Asia-Pacific region at

---

[42] According to Bruce A. Wright and Mak O. Hague, in "The U.S.-Japan Alliance: Sustaining the Transformation". JFQ / issue 44, 1st quarter 2007, 60-64), the first time Tokyo deployed its Maritime SDF minesweepers to the Persian Gulf was at the end of the first Gulf War in 1991, paving the way for participation in support of United Nations (UN) peacekeeping efforts in Cambodia in 1992 which was the first time since World War II that Japanese ground troops operated outside the country. Since then, Japan has sent its SDF troops to Mozambique, the Golan Heights, Rwanda, East Timor, Honduras, Indonesia, and Pakistan under the UN flag, besides the Iraq deployments in 2003.

[43] "Military Situation in the Far East". Hearings before the Committee on Armed Services and the Committee on Foreign Relations, the United States Congress. The Senate Committee on Armed Services and the Senate Committee on Foreign Relations: Session 1, May 3-5, 7-12, 14, 1951; Session 2, May 15-17, 21-26, 28-31, 1951; Session 3, June 1-2, 4-9, 11-13, 1951; Session 4. June 14-15, 18-22, 25, 27, 1951; Session 5, August 17, 1951.

large. The declared objective of the U.S.-Japan alliance was always to maintain peace and security in East Asia, and the emphasis was usually on this alliance being an asset that contributed considerably to East Asian security, making the U.S. presence in East Asia again a positive security factor. In an attempt to demonstrate the positive aspect of the U.S. military presence in East Asia, which China saw as hegemonic and threatening, Madeleine Albright, Clinton's Secretary of State during his second term from 1996 to 2000, said in a press conference with the then Japan's Foreign Minister Obuchi that the U.S.-Japan alliance "was the foundation for the stability in the Asia-Pacific. It was the cornerstone of our strategic policy in Asia...thanks to our success in reinvigorating our security relationship during the last two years, that alliance was rock-solid for the 21st century" (Albright-Obuchi Press Conference, April 30, 1998)[44].

However, the U.S.-Japan Mutual Security Treaty could hardly be called an alliance or even a treaty because both terms legally mean that two or more parties entered voluntarily into an alliance, implicitly conveying the idea of consensus among the signatories. In no way did this apply to the MST. Japan was forced into signing a treaty of unconditional surrender in return for ending direct occupation by General Douglas Mac-Arthur after WWII, except for Okinawa, which was still the major American bastion of hegemony and the lynchpin of the U.S. military structure in the Asia-Pacific rim (Johnson 151- 86). The Japanese "peace constitution" was literally written by MacArthur, according to which Japan renounced one of the basic attributes of sovereignty, the right to raise an army. Moreover, the United States dictated most of the MST provisions, which practically transformed Japan into an American protectorate or a remote territory like Guam, wherein the U.S. has been able to maintain bases, station troops, and deploy nuclear weapons.

The 1994 and 1998 American efforts to include Japan in the missile shield called THAAD, and the efforts of the Bush administration to include post-Cold War Japan into an increasingly controversial National Missile Defense program (NMD) did not necessarily show, at least from a Chinese perspective, an American obsession with Japan's security. All it could show was a U.S.

---

[44] Albright-Obuchi Press Conference, April 30, 1998. The Press Conference was held in Tokyo, and was given by U.S. Secretary of State Madeleine Albright and Japanese Foreign Minister Keizo Obuchi. The conference followed bilateral meetings at which the United States and Japan signed an agreement aiming at expanding Japanese logistical support for U.S. troops in times of need.

determination to use Japan as a geopolitical card to pressure China into accommodating the U.S. hegemonic position in East Asia, or to face the consequences of confronting not only the United States but also Japan which, "despite [its] large share of the world market, continued to have to rely on U.S. military hegemony" in East Asia (Gerson, "Fresh Look", Lecture, June 26-27, 1999). By placing Japan under the U.S. nuclear umbrella and accepting to expand Japan's security "responsibilities" in the region, the U.S. probably opted to contain or modify potentially assertive Chinese behavior.

As a matter of fact, the clause that was missing in the United States-Japan security treaty and its recent revised versions, was whose security this treaty is protecting, especially after the end of the Cold War. With the Soviet Union gone, there was no credible and clear enemy in the Asia-Pacific rim, which the United States sought to face down, except Communist China as an already regional and potentially rising world power. Accordingly, the U.S. moved even more earnestly to consolidate its alliances with both Japan and South Korea. The February 27, 1995, Nye report recommended that the U.S.-Japan MST be the backbone to maintaining any future American hegemony in East Asia. Then, Nye called for the Clinton administration to try to "identify common security interests [with Japan] for the post-Cold War era" (Nye 78). The term "identify" itself was problematic here, because if it revealed anything, it simply revealed that the U.S.-Japanese "security common interests" which alluded to a common enemy, did not exist already, but the U.S. had to find them or even to create the. This leads the argument to the point where one should ask the question of who was there in Asia that could be identified as an enemy to both the United States and Japan. Historical and geopolitical evidence all pointed out to China. Zbigniew Brzezinski, Carter's national security advisor, called it a strategy of "Amerippon" order that is a process of integration of not only American-Japanese geopolitical interests but also elites from both countries (Itoh qtd in Miliband and Panitch, eds. 198-99).

The April 1996 Clinton-Hashimoto Summit described as the "most significant" one in the post-Cold War era by then Secretary of Defense William Perry, was the turning point as to the nature of the American military presence in East Asia in general. Clinton and Hashimoto did name their potential common enemies, which undoubtedly included China's aspirations of regional ascendancy, manifested through Beijing's military modernization programs and China's territorial disputes with its neighbors, in a clear hint to the Taiwan stalemate. In other words, the United States was not secretive about the post-Cold War rationale of its alliance with Japan, which Washington used to perpetuate a political, military, and economic order in East Asia that favored the American agenda. What was called the Armitage approach stated that "Today, [the alliance] st[ood] as a central element in the efforts of Washington and Tokyo to deal with the post-9/11 security challenges to international order posed by terrorism, the proliferation of weapons of mass destruction, and the future direction of states at the crossroads, notably China, India, and Russia" (Przystup and Saunders 3). But since Russia was not a strategic peer anymore during the first two decades after the fall of the ex-USSR, and India was an American nuclear ally now, in view of the U.S.-India nuclear deal of March 2006[45], it was China that was singled out as the potential U.S. "security challenge."

As for the Japanese position, Japan's commitment to further consolidate its alliance with the United States in a post-Cold War era when there was no clear threat to the security of the country, raised many suspicious Chinese eyebrows. Except for a couple of North Korean nuclear weapons which, if ever used, would first target American forces stationed across North-South Korea borders in the DMZ, Japan was ostensibly under no clear and significant threat that might warrant further allying itself with a United States that was viewed as playing the role of world hegemon and seeking to keep the region under constant tension and unrest (Catley 2-6). Adopting such a posture, combined with a WWII history of aggression against its neighbors, Japan risked alienating most of its

---

[45] The U.S.-India Nuclear Deal was signed by George Bush and Indian Prime Minister Manmohan Singh on March 2, 2006 in New Delhi. The agreement, if approved by Congress, would allow India acquire American technology for civilian nuclear power. In return, India agrees to split its nuclear program into civilian and military components, and put most of the civilian facilities under international inspection for the first time. But the deal has elicited much criticism and congressional scrutiny, as it is suspected to undercut the Nuclear Non-Proliferation Treaty by rewarding a country that refused to sign that treaty and cheated to build nuclear weapons by using supposedly civilian imported reactors. Proponents of the deal praise India for its excellent non-proliferation track record, that is India's refraining from exporting nuclear technology to other countries like Pakistan which allegedly, shedding serious doubts on the subjectivity of the terms like "proliferation". Besides the fact that the U.S.-India nuclear deal is said to be a "strategic security blog» by the Federation of American Scientists, more than thirty seven Nobel Prize winners from this federation signed a letter to the Congressional leadership opposing the agreement. Moreover, the U.S.-Indian bilateral agreement has provoked regional concerns from nations like China which sees the deal as aimed at containing its military modernization programs. Gary Thomas "U.S.-India Nuclear Deal Under Scrutiny by Congress" *Washington Post*. April 3, 2006.

immediate neighbors, and provoked more suspicions about its immediate as well as strategic power and security calculations to work within a regional multilateral security apparatus, which did not necessarily exclude the United States, but that accommodated the security interests of most parties in East Asia and assuaged the security concerns of some nations in the region such as North Korea, China, and to a lesser extent Russia.

On the contrary, Japan went even further in expanding the geographical areas within which Tokyo could have a strategic interest to work more closely with the United States through their alliance. Not only did the 1997 Defense Cooperation Guidelines version vaguely expand Japan's military "responsibilities" in "the areas surrounding Japan", but it also geopolitically extended Japan's potential "security threats" closer to China's mainland to "include turmoil on the Korean peninsula, military confrontations over Taiwan, or in the South China Sea, the Malacca Strait and the Middle East" (Gerson, "Fresh Look", Lecture June 26-27, 1999). Intentionally, these five geographical areas identified as sources of "threat" to Japan's security were major points of contention between China, on the one hand, and the United States and Japan, on the other hand, leaving little room for doubt that Japan was being used by the U.S. to maximize its gains at the expense of a rising China.

To put it bluntly, Japan was being dragged into an American game of encircling China not only militarily, but also economically and strategically. This was clear from the quiet but earnest race between the Chinese and the Americans over Middle Eastern oil. There was little doubt that the United States, notwithstanding Tokyo's supporting stance, would be willing to share with Japan the benefits of its hegemony in East Asia. China did not expect a 'Pax-Japamerica' to replace Pax-Americana, but it was indeed concerned that a Pax-Nipponica should not take hold of East Asia (Itoh qtd in Miliband and Panitch, eds. 199).

Furthermore, the Japanese were not secretive about how they perceived their position across the East Asian security chessboard. They had chosen to continue to work with the United States both militarily and politically, in view of Japan's dependence on Washington for its own security and even economic well-being. The U.S. is Japan's largest importer of Japanese products, so the continuity in the two countries' military cooperation would serve not only America's hegemonic position, which the Japanese themselves were not very hesitant to recognize publicly but was also in line with Japan's strategic economic and trade policies, at least for the inconceivable future.

Moreover, the military alliance with the United States served to kill two birds with one stone. First, it was a cheap security ride for the Japanese, since it relieved them of expending their own military budget to almost five times the 1 percent of Japan's GDP as prescribed by the country's so-called Peace constitution. Despite continuous calls from Washington since the Reagan administration to pay for its security share, Tokyo was paying much less than the Americans were expecting (DiFilippo). "Japan may be a subordinate security partner, but the U.S.-Japan alliance also allowed Tokyo to forgo a costly buildup of military capacity that would destabilize East Asia" (Ikenberry, "Illusions of Empire" 148). Second, in spite of the American failure to protect Japan from two Korean missiles in 1993 and 1998, the alliance did provide Tokyo with a sense of security against a perceived Chinese threat, North Korean direct missile threats, and Russian encroachment around the Kuril Islands (Cossa).

Thus, Washington almost secured an upper-hand position in East Asia. This was feasible by relying for this purpose on a military presence which it intended to maintain for an "indefinite duration" (Nye, "'The Nye Report': Six Years Later" 95-104). And such an overall objective was in line with the United States' intent to maintain a forward military presence that would ensure a preponderant American position in Northeast and Southeast Asia, using its military alliances, essentially with Japan and South Korea, together with its dominant maritime position in the region.

From the United States and Japan's viewpoints, the American security presence helped provide the 'oxygen' for East Asian development, that is security[46], as the latter was indispensable for the region's lifeline economic routes and energy import sea lanes. Hence, such argument substantiates the null hypothesis of this book that the U.S. role in East Asia since the end of the Cold War was a positive security factor in the interaction among the three-unit system of the U.S., Japan, and China, even though America's military presence in the region served the U.S. national interest to prevent, among other things, the rise of competitive hegemons (Baker 33). Japan, however, accepted to alienate its neighbors by allying itself with the United States, largely perceived by most East Asian nations as playing a negative security role in the region. In

---

[46] Briefing by Joseph Nye, Assistant Secretary of Defense for Internal Security Affairs, on February 27, 1995: Nye argues that the U.S. military presence of almost 100,000 U.S. troops in Asia is vital to the region's security and economic prosperity. Because trade with Asia accounts for so much of the world's economic activity, the prosperity of Asia is important to the US's and the world's security.

return, Japan would not bother facing on its own a vindictive China or an unpredictable North Korea.

With regard to the trilateral equation in East Asia, among the three actors in the U.S.-Japan-China post-Cold War triangle, Japan had the biggest effect on the Chinese-U.S. relationship. During the early decades after the end of the Cold War, the U.S.-Japanese security alliance was strengthened, not weakened. In sharp contrast, the Sino-Japanese equation did not keep abreast with the U.S.-Japan relationship. A series of recent issues exacerbated a relationship already strained by Japanese Prime Minister Junichiro Koizumi's controversial repeated visits to the Yasukuni Shrine, such as the one in August 2004. The series of Sino-Japanese differences also included the accidental intrusion of a Chinese submarine into Japanese territorial waters in November 2004, a visit by former Taiwanese leader and independence activist Lee Teng-hui to Japan in December 2004, Japan's ongoing publication of textbooks that whitewashed its World War II misbehavior, and the Spring of 2005 anti-Japan demonstrations in a number of major Chinese and South Korean cities. Therefore, as such cases show, the historical conflicts between Japan and its neighbors and the mutual antagonism between the peoples of East Asia could easily become political problems that could evolve into serious crises.

Thomas Christensen characterized the Sino-Japanese relationship as a rocky connection that was woven by terrible WWII memories and ethnic conflict. He said: "although Chinese analysts presently feared U.S. power much more than Japanese power, in terms of national intentions, Chinese analysts viewed Japan with much less trust and, in many cases, with a loathing rarely found in their attitudes about the United States" (Christensen 52). Though the Chinese were uncomfortable with the U.S.-Japan alliance in terms of its negative security implications, they were reluctant to admit that this very alliance did constrain as much as it protected Japan. A Japan, unconstrained, could reject the Chinese post-Cold War desire for a multilateral security structure. Makoto Iokibe, the president of Japan's Military Academy, said on March 27, 2007 in Tunis that it was the Chinese who were not enthusiastic about multilateral and direct dialogue in addressing East Asia's concerns. The Japanese might even go further to revenge their half-century-imposed dependency on the United States for their own security. Indeed, "a direct Japanese approach to China would only confirm Chinese fears of a revanchist Japan" (Ikenberry, "Illusions of Empire" 148-49). Tokyo governor Shintaro Ishihara went one step further in increasing China's concerns about Japan's future intentions. He suggested in April 2000 that Japan should be ready to put down "uprisings" in Korea or China. Ishihara also used racial terms in referring to potential Korean and Chinese rioters ("Militarism Brewing in Japan", *China Daily* September 25, 2000).

Moreover, taking advantage of the 1998 North Korea launching of a missile that flew over Japan, the right-wing Japanese conservatives worked to garner political support in the Japanese Diet to consider amending the so-called peace constitution. They even stretched their interpretation of the existing constitution to the point where it could allow "the use of nuclear weapons by Japan (Gerson, "Fresh Look", Lecture June 26-27, 1999). In short, as the "China threat" theory gained followers in Japan, Japanese right-wing forces were becoming more and more assertive, and here was where the U.S. military presence in East Asia could offer some stability in East Asia, since it not only protected Japan, it also muted Japan's alleged militaristic tendencies.

But this was a disguised blessing for the United States because it put Washington in the delicate situation of having to reconcile both ends of how to guarantee Japan's security and at the same time to allay China's security fears and dispel the Chinese suspicion of a hegemonic America in the region. So, if it were not a case of a Sino-Japanese security dilemma, it must have been a case of an American hegemonic dilemma wherein Washington failed to persuade both Beijing and Tokyo that "in the absence of a U.S. hegemonic role, the chances of Japanese-Chinese geopolitical competition would increase substantially" (Ikenberry, ed. *America Unrivaled* 197).

Not only was the United States the sole preponderant power in the region since WWII, but it also boasted the fact that it had historical legitimacy to be so. The fact that the United States felt it had a historical right to be involved in East Asia was more problematic because Washington looked at the history of its policy in the region as a source of a "legitimate" self-proclaimed right to play a dominant role among Japan, China, and other minor regional actors. American interests in East Asia dated back to the 1844 Sino-American Wangshia Treaty, the U.S. effort to open up Japan to international trade in the 1850s, the U.S. mediation of the end of the Japanese-Russian War in 1905, and last but not least, the reconstruction of Japan as a 'model of civilian democracy'. The United States, however, tended to ignore that history was not on the American side. In view of "the U.S. role in Britain's militarily enforced opium trade with China, Admiral Perry's terrorizing Black Ships which were essential to the forced opening of Japan, and the deal behind the 1905 Portsmouth Treaty". A treaty according to which the Japanese were forced to recognize the U.S. domination of the Philippines in exchange for an American recognition of Japanese colonization of Korea (Gerson, "Architecture of U.S. Asia-Pacific Hegemony" 6-8).

On this basis, the U.S., on the one hand, used its asymmetrical alliance with Japan to further coerce China into accepting the status quo of an American hegemonic position in the region, and on the other hand, hinted at the possibility of tipping the balance of power in favor of Beijing, if and when the Japanese started to contemplate challenging the U.S. dominating posture. "Ideally, the U.S. [was seeking] a hierarchical U.S.-Japanese-Chinese condominium, with Japan and China competing for the privilege of being the United States' "number one" regional partner" (Ibid). Thus, rather than playing a constructive role that was conducive to more security in East Asia, the United States pushed the region's two major actors further apart. Beijing feared that the consolidation of the U.S.-Japanese alliance came at China's expense, and that the growing closeness was motivated by their common concern about the increase of China's power.

Hence, power and security calculations in Asia, in general, shaped the contours of the post-Cold War U.S. strategy in the last decade of the 20th and well into the 21st centuries. And the basic question is all about the ways and means to preserve the current preponderant U.S. position in the world at large. To achieve this purpose, the first task was to identify potential challengers to the U.S. hegemonic posture, which was not that difficult, given that the Soviet Union was gone, and Russia was a quasi-third world country, but Communist China was then the only potential nation that was highly likely to assert itself as a regional superpower.

The very fact that China's power was rising did threaten the U.S. hegemonic position in East Asia. The nature of international politics in an environment of competition for power and suspicions about others' intentions precluded any room for trust or genuine cooperation between a well-established hegemon determined to prevent the rise of competitors and a rising and ambitious power seeking to change the status quo. "When power relationships are correctly calibrated, wars tend to be avoided. Only a similarly pragmatic approach would allow [the U.S.] to accommodate China's inevitable-and legitimate–re-emergence as a great power" (Gilpin 49). The crux of the matter was that the United States was and would be a hegemon in East Asia, at least for a while, and China was an emerging regional power that expected the U.S. to accommodate its security and geopolitical interests, which set the stage for a volatile interaction between the two countries for the coming decades, and opened the door for more U.S. military and political clashes with China in the years to come.

This eventually left the post-Cold War security situation in East Asia in a shambles, because of the combination of an unpopular U.S. military forward presence and the unrivaled American manipulation of geopolitics in the region. It also left little doubt in the mindset of Chinese military strategists that the United States post-Cold War policy regarding China was deeply affected by the advantageous American international standing as the sole hegemon in the world and the U.S. expectation that China would have to accommodate itself to U.S. dominance in the Asia-Pacific rim. This was clear through the relentless American effort to refashion the foundations of U.S. policies in the Asia-Pacific region. Washington sought to restructure irrelevant military alliances to coerce China into an East Asian U.S.-Japanese–dominated country instead of recognizing the reality of China as a regional power that would have a major role in shaping the security future of a region that the United States did its utmost to dominate. Erecting military alliances around China aimed at preventing the latter from ascending to the rank of a regional power that could one day contemplate challenging Pax Americana in the Asia-Pacific region, which would sooner or later happen.

However, because hegemony was in the eye of the beholder, the answer about who was hegemonic and who has not defied the simplicity of the question. The pos-Cold War East Asia was in a situation wherein China, on the one hand, and the United States and Japan, on the other, were trading allegations about their respective "hegemonic" approaches in addressing East Asia's security issues. Therefore, China's rising economy, its ongoing military modernization programs, China's perceived threats against Taiwan, and China's endless territorial disputes in both the South China Sea and the East China Sea all these grievances were used by the United States, Japan, and East Asia's small states to argue that Communist China was working on power projection capabilities in the region ("Global Intelligence Update", April 26, 2000). According to John Pomfret, "the modernization program pursued by the Chinese military was concentrating on missiles, warhead delivery systems and their accuracy, Western military experts say, China was also upgrading its nuclear forces; it possessed several dozen delivery systems" (A 01).

Driven by nationalist sentiment and an urge for power, small nations in East Asia suspected that China was seeking to replace the United States as the dominant power in Asia. Vulnerable states in Southeast Asia, such as Singapore, Malaysia, and Brunei, which were suspicious of China's strategic intentions, found at least psychological comfort in ASEAN as a forum where they could discuss their security concerns and coordinate their policies with the U.S. maritime presence in the area. In short, the states concerned in East Asia felt that they lived in a potentially dangerous neighborhood, and they therefore needed to take their own precautions against probable Chinese coercion.

Instead of facing their perceived common threat–China's rising power, most of the vulnerable nations in Southeast Asia, like Indonesia and the Philippines, preferred U.S. hegemony to the Chinese one. Besides the April 2001 incident with the American EP-reconnaissance plane, it was reported that Chinese ships and aircraft harassed two American naval vessels, which Beijing accused of spying, conducting research on oceans– the USNS Bowditch and the USNS Sumner were allegedly in international waters (Eckholm 13). Moreover, in February 2002, the Xinhua news agency reported that China would "expand its maritime surveillance and control rights from 50 nautical miles (nm) to 100 nm by the year 2010 and further expand its jurisdiction to the entire 200 nm exclusive economic zone by the year 2020" (Gertz, "China Enacts Law Extending its Control").

Though the Chinese clearly violated the 1982 United Nations Convention on the Law of the Sea, to which China acceded, the United States did not yet ratify this convention, as Washington considered military and non-commercial state-owned ships immune from foreign jurisdiction. There was no common view yet among the United States, Japan, and most of the small nations in the vicinity of China, on the one hand, and China, on the other hand, regarding Beijing's claims in the South China Sea, the Paracel Islands, the Spratly Islands, and especially Taiwan. This led to a series of frictions between China and its neighbors, to more suspicion of China's assertive maritime conduct, and therefore, to an increasing demand for a continued U.S. military presence in the region (Dillon et al. 18-19).

As for Northeast Asia, the U.S. individual alliances with Japan and South Korea have reassured Tokyo and Seoul that the chances of Chinese miscalculations would be dramatically less in the presence of strong American military bases. Regardless of America's strategic intentions in East Asia, the United States somehow succeeded in convincing vulnerable countries in the region that even if they didn't totally agree with U.S. policies, they still had to appreciate the U.S. military presence, which was successfully "sold" as more of a reassurance against potential Chinese hegemony than a threat to their respective security.

According to Hideaki Kaneda, retired Vice Admiral of Japan's Self-Defense Forces, Japan had to reconsider its national maritime strategy to keep abreast with recent Chinese modernization programs ("National Maritime Doctrines and Capabilities", Lecture 8th – 9th March 2005). Most of the nations concerned with East Asian security believed that the United States, since it did not have any territorial ambitions in East Asia, could better play the role of "honest broker' than any other state in the region, given overwhelming American power capabilities. For them, the American military presence in East Asia brought stability and, therefore, was a positive security factor, as stability in its abstract sense is measured by the absence of warts between member states.

Like the United States, China had two voices regarding its perception of the United States, whether hegemonic or just a military pacifier in East Asia. "Many Chinese still viewed the United States as a major threat to their nation's security and domestic stability" (*Jisi*, "China's Search for Stability with America" 39). The divergent views between the Chinese military and that of the political leadership mostly characterized China's dealing with the United States as a hegemonic power that needed to be confronted at some point in time, or a strategically needed country for technology transfer and for a stable security environment in East Asia, that was conducive to the economic well-being of the rising but fragile Chinese economy. China's third and sixth White Papers of 2000 and 2004, which were issued by the military every two years to highlight potential threats to China's security and interests, stated that the United States does not want to see China strong and powerful, which supports the thesis that the U.S. military presence in East Asia was perceived by the Chinese as a negative security factor, instead of a factor of stability. More recently, China's 2004 White Paper suggests that "complicated security factors in the Asia-Pacific region were on the increase. The United States was realigning and reinforcing its military presence in this region by buttressing military alliances and accelerating the deployment of missile defense systems. Japan was stepping up its constitutional overhaul, adjusting its military and security policies, and developing the missile defense system for future deployment."[47]

The Chinese view of the United States was changing incrementally from bad to worse. More frequently, the U.S. was painted not only as a negative security factor in East Asia, but also as an outright threat to Asian-Pacific security. Shen Dingli, a prominent arms control expert at Fudan University in Shanghai, echoed a quasi-official discourse when he stated that "we had never said it so bluntly before...I think China was more clearly preparing for a major clash with the United States" (Pomfret A1). Thus, while the Americans were weighing their options on whether to engage or contain China, the Chinese, however, were now talking about an inevitable confrontation with the United States. John Pomfret wrote, "while few in China, except for some strategists in the army, seem to think war was

---

[47] *China's National Defense in 2004*, Information Office of the State Council of the People's Republic of China, December 2004, Beijing.

inevitable, the fact that conflict with the United States was openly discussed is a significant development in China's security thinking" (A1).

Indeed, from a political science point of view, a Sino-American confrontation over immediate and latent issues or over long-term strategic geopolitical calculations was highly probable. We had a situation here where there was a sole hegemonic superpower that was trying to perpetuate its preponderant position versus a rising regional, at least for the moment, power that was seeking a fairer share of big power privileges, called a redistribution of the balance of power. In support of this book's main thesis that the post-Cold War U.S. military presence in East Asia was a negative security factor in the region, China's Defense White Paper said that "no fundamental change was made in the old, unfair and irrational international political and economic order...certain big powers were pursuing 'neo-interventionism', a 'neo-gunboat policy', neo-economic colonialism, which were seriously damaging the sovereignty, independence, and development interests of many countries, and threatening world peace and *security*" (Italics added)[48].

There was little doubt here that the "certain big powers", which the Chinese defense White Paper alluded to, was a clear reference to the United States, because the paper mentioned the U.S. almost 13 times, all but two in a negative way. Although the paper dealt with the series of misgivings China had against the United States, the reference to the post-Cold War U.S. East Asian policy as a "neo-gunboat policy" that has damaged the "sovereignty, independence" of "many countries", first referred to the Taiwan problem, which was seen as a purely domestic Chinese issue, and second, highlighted the Chinese perception of the American military presence as a destabilizing variable in the regional security equation. From a Chinese standpoint, "driven by its hegemonic ambitions, the United States was showing its force more and more. The United States had time and again created disturbances against China, and interfered in China's internal affairs" (Bernstein and Munro 30).

Even if the confrontational military view in China was not prevailing for the time being, the fact that conflict with the United States was incrementally gaining momentum among academia as well as among the military establishment was a reminder of the precarious and dangerously unstable Sino-American relationship, which wa viewed as an obstacle to China's major

---

[48] *China's National Defense in 2004*, Information Office of the State Council of the People's Republic of China, December 2004, Beijing.

two priority goals: the reunification with Taiwan and gaining control over the strategic shipping lanes in the South China Sea, especially the Strait of Malacca, through which more than 80 percent of China's oil shipments from the Middle East and elsewhere passed. How to achieve the first purpose–taking Taiwan back-was already discussed in the previous section, but in order to achieve the second strategic goal–securing its energy supplies for an economy that was expected to be the world's first consumer of oil by 2020–China sought to build a series of strategic military bases along the major sea lanes from the South China Sea to the oil-rich Middle East (Pomfret A 01). The Gwadar military port, for instance, currently under construction in southwest Pakistan, was strategically located so as to guard the throat of the Persian Gulf, with electronic eavesdropping posts to monitor ships – including warships– moving through the Strait of Hormuz and the Arabian Sea[49].

Also, China was building container port facilities at Chittagong in Bangladesh for its naval and merchant fleets, besides other naval bases and electronic intelligence gathering facilities on islands owned by Myanmar in the Gulf of Bengal. In Thailand, China was planning to build a $20 billion-worth canal across the Kra Isthmus to connect the Indian Ocean and the Gulf of Siam, which would provide an alternate oil import route that avoided the Strait of Malacca, which was the most strategic chokepoint for the sustainability of China's growing economy (Ibid). Moreover, China was developing the necessary infrastructure in the South China Sea to allow large-scale deployment of naval and air force units by fortifying bases on Hainan Island. As for the Spratly and Paracel islands, a matter of dispute between Beijing and at least another dozen neighbors, China was building runways large enough to handle long-range bombers (Ibid).

Although the Chinese recognized the preponderant U.S. position in East Asia as a de facto variable in regional security daily business, they rejected "serving" under the American hegemonic umbrella. China, therefore, was allegedly working "to reduce American influence in Asia, to prevent Japan and the United States from creating an obstacle to China's ascendancy to world power, to build up a military with force projection capability and to expand its presence in the South China and East China Seas so that it could control the region's essential sea-lanes" (Bernstein and Munro 19). Rapid expansion of the shipping industry

---

[49] India Discussion Forum – "Indian History, Culture, Politics, News, Strategic Security, Hinduism. Strategic Security of India-China: Relations and Developments", available at: http://www.indiaforum.com/forums/index.php?act=Print&client=printer&f=8&t=134.

was part of China's twenty-first-century strategy. China was already the world's third-largest trading nation and was rapidly developing its port capacities to manage an increasing volume of trade, and by 2010, China's shipbuilding capabilities were expected to surpass those of Japan and South Korea (Holt 1). Then, Analysts suggested that by 2010, China would have 70 of the most modern surface vessels, several modern strategic nuclear submarines, and several tens of modernized attack submarines, exceeding the modern forces of both Taiwan's navy and even Japan's Maritime Self-Defense Force combined. If the rapid growth of China's navy continues, it is expected to have the world's largest naval force by 2030[50].

Moreover, under cover of its conciliatory mood during the first two decades after the Cold War, China allegedly kept a low profile to buy more time in order to build the necessary power to back its aspirations regarding Taiwan and beyond. As mentioned before, America's end game in Asia, however, would be to derail China's quest to become a twenty-first-century power peer, which set the stage for a cold struggle, or even an outright cold war, as Avery Goldstein from Stanford University argued in his *Rising to the Challenge*. Between an already established world hegemon and a rising power with the potential of becoming a real competitor for East Asia's hegemony, if it chose to do so, power competition was almost inevitable.

Therefore, it could be just a matter of time before China became the East Asia hegemon, since it had the potential to do so. By the 2000s, Beijing's development pace, the United States and Japan would be in no position to achieve or at least to perpetuate their existing hegemony in Asia. There was only one country that could become a hegemon in Asia, and that was China, as the United States did not surely prevail anymore in every conflict, particularly regarding North Korea's nuclear weapons.

This was the reason why the United States and Japan would not let Taiwan, for example, fall back into the hands of China. As an outsider to East Asian regional affairs and in view of the official as well as the popular discontent with the U.S. military presence on the respective soils of the East Asian nations, the United States could be pushed in the future to move its military installations off-shore, leading to a diminution of its political leverage on the countries concerned. Japan, in its turn, seemed to be a sinking power in the 2000s. Its

---

[50] U.S. Department of Defense, Annual Report on the Military power of the People's Republic of China: Report to Congress, National authorization Act 2002.

population was shrinking, and it was likely to shrink drastically in the decades ahead. Japan would not be in a position to dominate Asia; there was only one country that might be in a position to dominate Asia in the years ahead–it was China.

Indeed, Washington failed to disarm North Korea or even to prevent it from detonating its first nuclear bomb on October 9, 2006. After Pyongyang tested its first nuclear bomb, the United States and Japan tried to opt for tough actions against North Korea, including strong U.N. sanctions, but China refused to go along. Choking sanctions, from a Chinese perspective, could bring the regime down. Such an eventuality would result in a flood of refugees across the Chinese-North Korean borders, leading to more tension across the whole region and less security for all parties, particularly South Korea and Japan, the two key U.S. allies that provided the post-Cold War U.S. military presence with a *raison d'étre*.

As China did not want another nuclear neighbor, in addition to India and Pakistan in Southwest Asia, Beijing was also unlikely to accept that the United States and Japan take over the initiative in its own backyard. Even after the U.N. Security Council adopted the 1718 Resolution to punish Pyongyang for testing a nuclear bomb, China refused a strict implementation of the resolution lest it became too weak in the eyes of the North Koreans, in view of the Chinese-North Korean ideological, political, and military special relationship, and consequently lost its leverage on Kim Jong Il. "Even the most unilateralist-minded U.S. administration would be unable to ignore China's interests on the Korean peninsula. [After all], China was Pyongyang's neighbor, had a permanent seat on the United Nations Security Council, and possessed its own nuclear weapons," which explained why Washington believed "that it would be far better for Beijing to act to rein in Pyongyang than risk leaving it to Washington to do so" (Robyn Lim, *The Wall Street Journal Online*, February 18, 2004).

As North Korea agreed to resume talks, ostensibly to dismantle its nuclear reactors, China took the credit for that, leading to more Chinese influence regarding the potential outcome of any future North Korean interaction with both the United States and Japan within the Six-Party talks framework. If tensions between the United States and North Korea eased, as Pyongyang's bargaining position dramatically improved after the latter's recent nuclear test, China's role would still be more favorably recognized. Should that occur, the countries involved in the process might even consider expanding the six-party mechanism into a permanent Northeast Asian security arrangement, a development that would indicate a shift to U.S. acceptance of multilateralism as an approach to East Asian security problems. Under the 2000s circumstances, however, such a possibility was slim. The more likely outcome was that tensions between Washington and Pyongyang would persist, although without necessarily an actual war breaking out.

The waning American leverage on Taiwan, for instance, was also an additional indication of America's weakening influence and preponderance in East Asia. Washington could not stop Taiwan's "provocative" bid for a referendum on independence in 2004, which was followed by China's prominent February 2005 anti-secession law that closed the door before all attempts to Taiwan's independence. Moreover, President Chen's sudden decision on February 27, 2006, to discard the National Unification Council (NUC), which was established in 1990 by his predecessor to ease tension across the Strait, was also telling of how much the U.S. leverage weakened in East Asia. These were the ominous examples that testified to the fact that the United States could not control the outcome of all of Asia's intriguing political and territorial disputes indefinitely, even those regarding its closest allies, which depended on the U.S. security umbrella. Certainly, there were limits to the U.S. ability to control the outcomes of issues that transcended America's hegemonic attributes in East Asia.

Therefore, a rising China could not only be a security threat to its neighbors, as advanced by the U.S. and Japan, but also represent a strategic dilemma for the United States. Subsequently, the U.S. policy options in the future were not too many; they varied between relying on the existing alliance structure, or seeking other alternatives. Alternative policies ranged from an "off-shore" strategy, as Christopher Layne advocated almost a decade ago (8-28), to accepting a regional multi-polar balance of power among the major actors such as Japan, China, North Korea, South Korea, and Russia, to even an outright withdrawal from East Asia, which was a far-fetched scenario by the then standards.

Nevertheless, Ted Galen and Doug Bandow, from the Cato Institute, did call for a complete disengagement from East Asia, in view of the current security situation in East Asia. North Korea had already gone nuclear; there was an increasingly anti-American sentiment in South Korea, along with a rising powerful and potentially assertive China, and rising calls even from Japan for the United States to leave the archipelago (Galen et al. 163). They argued that "the time had come for Northeast Asians to manage their own affairs-for the United States to withdraw its troops from both South Korea and Japan and to notify both governments that the "mutual" defense treaties would be terminated" (Galen et al. 163).

An outright withdrawal, however, would be a remote probability, given the degree of America's involvement in East Asia and the myriad of economic, political, and strategic interests the U.S. had in a region where the future of the world order would be largely defined. Theoretically, the United States might substantially reduce its military presence in East Asia, relying instead on high-tech, long-range weaponry and missile defense systems (*New York Times*, May 17, 2001). But this would consequently reduce American leverage in the region and seriously undermine U.S. credibility as a reliable ally, namely for Japan and Taiwan, leaving both of them more vulnerable to Chinese coercion. This could also result in regional states accommodating China's potential assertive posture rather than following their preference to balance against Chinese probable pressure.

As China was developing the power inventories to become a future superpower and probably hegemon, as people like **Interviewee 1** argue, even if this would take longer than we tend to think, the United States was highly likely to further deepen its involvement in East Asia in order to maximize its current preponderant position vis-à-vis Beijing. China, in view of its size, potential, and ambitions, would be the most likely nation that would seek to compete with the United States for regional if not for world hegemony, and the United States would have to recognize the new realities of power distributions in East Asia, where at least one rising potential competitor for regional influence was already in the making (Ross 81-117).

This eventuality led the whole discussion about how the United States perceived its security role in East Asia after the Cold War. The way the United States managed the security situation in post-Cold War East Asia was heavily influenced by a background of unilateralism and limited bilateralism, instead of a new mentality of multilateralism that recognized the security concerns of fearful nations which felt they were targeted by the U.S. hegemony in the region. **Interviewee 2**, one of the most recognized world scholars on Korean affairs, told me that the United States missed the opportunity to strike a modus operandi with Pyongyang in the late 1990s, when the two nations were on the verge of diplomatic recognition, following Madeleine Albright's historic visit to North Korea in 1998 (My Interview with **Interviewee 2**, May 15, 2006, University of Chicago, IL).

During my interview with him at the University of Chicago in 2006, **Interviewee 2** argued that the sense of being under threat emanating from the

U.S. new doctrine of pre-emption almost precluded the chances of a resolution to the Korean problem, thus, supporting the argument of this book that the U.S. military presence in East Asia was indeed a negative security factor, and that the United States was seeking to extend its hegemonic power in the region, rather than dealing with a specific security problem. This was a view that was shared not only by 'unfriendly' nations, but also by one of the closest allies in the region-South Korea. Johnson asserted that "the prosperous and well-informed people of the South knew that their fellow Koreans- hungry, desperate, oppressed, but well-armed- are trapped by the ironies of the end of the Cold War......but were also being pushed into an exceedingly dangerous corner by the Americans in their newly proclaimed role as the reigning military colossus" (Ch. Johnson 91). Therefore, the policy of cornering North Korea, approaching the East Asia security equation through the prism of the Cold War mentality of the hub-and-spoke strategy, and refusing to acknowledge the new power realities in the region, constituted the basic pillars of the US East Asia strategy in the 2000s. Washington also refused to acknowledge that China would inevitably need to be accommodated as a future world power, all these overtures were clearly not conducive to a U.S. positive security role, as Washington continuously claimed.

4.4. Summary

In conclusion to this chapter, one can see the fact that the United States was indeed, and by its very nature, the sole superpower in the post-Cold War era, going hegemonic in East Asia, though it could be playing the role of a 'pacifier' temporarily. The arrogance of power combined with the desire to perpetuate world domination were the most visible symptoms of hegemony. It was the sense of 'euphoria' or 'victory' over other hegemonic competitors, or in Bush's discourse, victory over 'evil.' Charles Krauthammer, from the conservative *Washington Post*, summed up America's sense of exceptionalism in the post-Cold War era. He said: "America was no mere international citizen. It was the dominant power in the world, more dominant than any since Rome. Accordingly, America was in a position to re-shape norms, alter expectations and create new realties. How? By unapologetic and implacable demonstration of will" (qtd in Ch. Johnson 68).

But the creation of non-existent threats or the exaggeration of existing ones either testified to an obsession with one's security or to the sense of a declining power that was seeking to cling to its preponderant position vis-à-vis others. The strategy of exaggerating perceived security threats and the tactics of fear the

United States followed in dealing with the East Asian security environment, were strong evidence that the U.S. was creating less security for others, and more for itself. Such an overture resulted in more tension and less trust between the region's key players, such as Japan and China, and thus complicated East Asian security problems which were not solvable without these two countries' mutually recognizing what was a domestic and what was a regional security issue, such as the Taiwan question. The fact that the United States was encouraging Japan to expand its security prerogatives beyond the Japanese mainland and was endorsing Tokyo's shift of policy regarding the status of Taiwan, for instance, was an invitation for both neighbors to collide instead of colluding with regards to the region's precarious security environment.

Had it not been for the September 11 attacks, the Sino-American relationship could have deteriorated to the point of a real military standoff. The war on 'terrorism' and the war on Iraq distracted the U.S. focus on the China threat, but both wars did not eliminate the prospects for confrontation between a world hegemon clinging to its unique preponderant position, and an ambitious rising power aspiring to a regional status that was commensurate with its growing military power and economic potential.

Conclusion

C.1. Findings

This conclusion section seeks first to put forward the findings and to present the account of this book as "the last stage in the qualitative research process", in Russell Schutt's words (18-19). This work has drawn upon a panoply of disciplines such as U.S. history, American Studies, American foreign policy and, related to the latter, political science and international relations. It sums up the argument about the trend of U.S. policy in East Asia in the first two decades after the Cold War, and has explored the security value of the U.S. military presence, which was controversial as to its positive or negative impact on the already precarious security situation in the region. The final objective of this book was achieved by arguing that the two dependent variables of power and security had governed the rules of interaction between the U.S., Japan, and China after the end of the Cold War, especially during the two immediate decades following the disintegration of the Soviet Union.

As for the methodology used to achieve the abovementioned objective, this book has adopted and applied the models of the three realist approaches in political science to the U.S.-Japan-China triangle in the early decades of the post-Cold War era. The theoretical framework of this work has particularly been based on the system of the nation-state in place since the 1648 Westphalia Treaty, which established the maxim of self-interest in international relations between sovereign states that are interacting within an environment of anarchy and competition for power. But there remains the question of how to measure core concepts like power and security on the basis of which these nation-states interact. The analytic model of this book has provided ways of conceptualizing and measuring power and security in order to show how such vague concepts could be broken down into real and tangible units of measurement. The proposed linkage between the dependent and independent variables of this work has aimed at demonstrating that interaction outcomes are indeed governed by power relations between states, like the ones among the United States, Japan, and China in the 1990s and 2000s, which could lead to more instability in an already unstable triangle. This approach has helped this work in trying to identify who was seeking power in post-Cold War East Asia at the expense of the other, which is a prerequisite to answering the central question of this work as to whether the U.S. military presence in the region played a positive security role, as the United States claimed, particularly after the end of the Cold War. In a press conference in Seoul in the wake of North Korea's nuclear test on October 9, 2006, and the U.N. Security Council Resolution 1698, which imposed limited sanctions on Pyongyang in response, Secretary of State Condoleezza Rice and her South Korean counterpart then Bon ke Mun, the new U.N Secretary General, reiterated that the U.S. military presence in East Asia was a factor of stability and deterrence[1].

This work has consulted a variety of sources, primary as well as secondary, and from different sources, American, Japanese, and Chinese- for the sake of triangulation, which is one of the basic criteria of research authenticity as well as credibility. This has been achieved by studying government documents such as the 1996 and 2000 Congressional Hearings on the U.S. policy trends and recommendations in East Asia, the DPG, and the PNAC; also by referring to a series of interviews conducted in 2005 and 2006 with the founder of one of the three major schools in political science, **Interviewee 1**, who founded the school of offensive realism, and whose insights about international relations and U.S. foreign policy in East Asia enlightened this work. Moreover, interviewing an international authority in Korean Affairs, **Interviewee 2**, provided not only a goldmine of primary data about East Asian affairs, but was also a scientific achievement for this book. **Interviewee 2** supported one of the pillars of the argument of this thesis that North Korea's obsession with security was a result of the U.S. 'threatening', from a Pyongyang standpoint, military posture in East Asia and its bellicose discourse toward North Korea, which substantiates the main argument of this work that the U.S. military presence in East Asia is playing a negative security role.

The series of primary sources used in this work also extends to the meetings with and questions to American as well as Chinese diplomats, including His Excellency Wang Guangya, Permanent representative of the People's republic of China to the United Nations; Peter W. Rodman, former U.S. Assistant Secretary of Defense for International Security Affairs; Christopher R. Hill, U.S. Assistant Secretary of State for East Asian and Pacific Affairs; Ambassador Wu Jianmin, Former Chinese Ambassador to France, the United Nations in Geneva, and current President of China Foreign affairs University; **Interviewee 1**, a prominent political science professor, a founder of a new school of thought in political science and currently co-director of a program on international

---

[1] The Press Conference held by U.S. Secretary of State Condoleeza Rice and her South Korean Counterpart Bon Ky Mon on October 16, 2006 in Seoul, South Korea.

security policy at a major university in Chicago. The opportunity of addressing questions to such high-profile people enabled this work to compare and contrast differing perceptions of all sides, leading to the underlying conclusion that, beyond the diplomatic niceties, there was a highly likely chance of another cold war in the making between the United States and its key ally Japan against China, which has been vindicated by the current open rivalry between the US East Asia bloc and China. Beijing's ambiguous intentions about what it would do with too much power in East Asia, motivated both Washington and Tokyo to prepare for a potentially assertive and defiant China. This lack of trust between the United States and Japan, on the one hand, and China, on the other hand, had a negative bearing on East Asia's security for the foreseeable future, as the region's security problems cannot be solved without the three legs of the triangle (the three countries) having balanced and positive working sides (relationships).

This book started first with a review of the literature about the dialectical relationship between the core concepts of power and security as the major dependent variables which have governed international relations since the foundation of the current nation-state system in 1648. Studying these two key variables from the standpoints of the three major schools in political science-realism, neo-realism, and offensive realism- has enabled this work to provide a deeper overview of how power and security have impacted the way states interact with each other, and how they have governed the outcome of such interactions. Moreover, the study of the blurred line between what is offensive and what is defensive has shown that the difference is more a matter of intention than of preparation. The case study of Japan's "Self Defense Force" proves the significance of understanding these two vague concepts, which are usually used subjectively.

The literature review is also expanded to include energy security in order to show that wars have been and will be fought over energy resources, as the control of the latter was highly likely to become one of the most divisive issues in the U.S.-Japan-China competition for power regionally and globally. Nations like the United States, which consumed almost one-quarter of the world's oil, or Japan were bereft of raw material and were more dependent on foreign oil than the U.S. was, and China, whose oil needs increased three times within a decade or so, all three nations showed an increasing greed for energy resources. Differences between the three countries over attempts of one to monopolize energy resources and prices at the expense of another had a deep impact on the post-Cold War U.S.-Japan-China triangle that was deep in history, but fraught with a record of cyclical conflicts and cooperation.

For a better understanding of what was at stake in post-Cold War East Asia, therefore, it is a prerequisite to look at the two major drivers in post-Cold War East Asian security- the U.S.-Japan alliance and the China factor. This book argues that the 1951 security treaty between the United States and Japan, which has been reviewed many times, has paradoxically provided more power to the U.S. and less security to Japan. It even took away much of Japan's economic sovereignty, because the United States took advantage of its upper hand in the security relationship with Japan to pressure Tokyo into acquiescing to Washington's trade conditions regarding a wide range of contested products such as cars and electronics. This work also questions the accuracy of calling the U.S.-Japan security relationship an "alliance", because an alliance is usually meant to equally serve the interests of its signatories.

By this token, what was between the United States and Japan in the immediate years of the post-Cold War era could hardly be called an alliance, because for fifty-five years after the signing of the U.S.-Japan Security Treaty, Japan became less and less secure and America more and more powerful. This was an alliance that enabled the U.S. to further project its power in East Asia, to contain potential Chinese aspirations to regional or world prominence, and, last but not least, to keep Japan in an inferior status, largely dependent on America's security guarantees and subsequently more acquiescent to Washington's economic and trade conditions. In short, Washington used this alliance as an instrument to perpetuate its preponderant power position in Asia and to prevent the rise of potential rivals for regional ascendancy, that is, to "forestall any undermining of Washington's power" (DiFilippo 95-96), thus supporting one of the main claims of this work that states are always after power and that states' appetite for power is insatiable, no matter how powerful they are in relation to others.

Moreover, the U.S.-Japan alliance was subject to a great deal of criticism and suspicion from Japan's neighbors, who had their own respective security calculations of how the complex security equation in East Asia ought to be handled. The degree of disapproval of the U.S.-Japan alliance from Japan's neighbors resulted in less stability and weakened the prospects of establishing a robust security environment in the region, leading to less security for Japan and more resentment of the alliance. Japan, in turn, accepted to alienate its neighbors by allying itself with the United States, largely perceived by most East Asian nations as hegemonic and playing a negative security role in the region.

In return, Japan did not want to face on its own the rising power of China or a nuclear North Korea.

Pyongyang had warned Tokyo on many occasions that, in case of an American attack on North Korea, Pyongyang would target not only American bases in the region, but also Japan as the country that hosts the bulk of U.S. troops in the world. Equally interesting, there was good reason to believe that North Korea's 1993 and 1998 controversial missile tests, which invited a U.S.-Japan uproar about Pyongyang's security threat to Japan and American interests, were primarily motivated by Pyongyang's security concerns. North Korea's fears emanated from the U.S.-Japan alliance and the strong U.S. military presence in East Asia, supporting the main claim of this book that the U.S. military presence in East Asia played a negative security role because it pushed insecure states to destabilize the status quo out of survival concerns (Suskind 114-15). Pyongyang's nuclear test on October 9, 2006, was said to be provoked by "American belligerency", as the state TV station put it, which could further substantiate the argument of this work that the U.S. military presence in East Asia, regardless of the reality of Washington's intentions, was a destabilizing factor, as most of the region's actors, rightly or wrongly, view it negatively.

China, which perceived the U.S.-Japan alliance with as much suspicion, had mixed views of the U.S.-Japan security connection. On the one hand, Beijing implicitly had some blessing of this alliance because it practically and legally kept Japan's trends of rearming and even Japanese militarism under control. America's security umbrella took away from Tokyo the need to seek to build an offensive military, and the American-dictated Japanese constitution precluded the chances of such an eventuality, notwithstanding the repeated calls from within Japan to review the so-called peace constitution, which had even come from the late Prime Minister Shinzo Abe. The alliance allowed Japan to avoid its neighbors' reaction to a prospective Japanese rearmament, especially in view of Japan's militarism and actions in Asia during WWII.

On the other hand, China was the most critical of the U.S.-Japan security alliance, and claimed that its envied military modernization program was then, after the disintegration of the Soviet Union, the new primary target of this alliance. China barely concealed its desire to weaken the U.S.-Japan bilateral relationship, and repeatedly called for the need for a new multipolar world order and the end of Cold War security arrangements. As Beijing saw it, Washington and Tokyo together presented a far more formidable challenge to Chinese regional security interests than China did to those of the United States and Japan. China was highly sensitive to anything pertaining to Japan and its changing international role, because the broadening of Japan's regional role, as the 1997 U.S.-Japan Defense Cooperation Guidelines stipulate, would open the door to probable Japanese involvement in choking points like Taiwan, the South China Sea, the Spratly Islands, and the Strait of Malacca.

As for Japan, China's rising power presented multiple challenges to Japanese foreign policy. The paradox between Japan's economic largesse and its weak political influence has exacerbated Tokyo's security concerns and gave the Japanese little choice but to cling to their alliance with the United States for better or for worse. The balance of power between Tokyo and Beijing was already imbalanced. Militarily, China had nuclear weapons, and the potential for power projection; Japan, a comparatively weak and a dependent country for its own security on an alliance that was so controversial in Japan and East Asia alike, had thereby paradoxically brought less security and less stability to the region at large.

Though Tokyo had a sophisticated SDF and theoretically the capability of producing nuclear weapons within months (Bergner 170- 194), Japan had its hands tied behind its back by Article 9 of the Japanese peace Constitution which precluded the country even from raising an army. Politically, China had its permanent seat in the U.N. Security Council while Japan had failed to secure such a place over the last two decades, though it was ironically a major benefactor of the United Nations itself and other international institutions. Economically, Japan was the second largest economy in the world up to 2010, but China was catching up, and expected to outsize even America's economy by the year 2030 (Dibb 27).

The post-Cold War Sino-Japanese relationship was bound to remain unstable and fragile, as Tokyo and Beijing diverged on the political, security, and trade levels. The alleged accidental intrusion of a Chinese submarine into Japanese territorial waters in November 2004, for instance, the former Taiwanese president and independence activist Lee Teng-hui's visit to Japan in December 2004; Japan's publication of textbooks that whitewashed its World War II misdoings, all showed how quickly the Sino-Japan relationship could spiral down to a real crisis. "As such cases show, the historical conflicts between China and Japan and the mutual antagonism of their peoples could easily become political problems. Unless the issues were handled with care, they could evolve into serious crises" (*Jisi*, "China's Search for Stability with America" 44).

Japan and China had particularly and strategically differed over their respective relations with the United States and about the latter's military presence in East Asia. Their different approaches to the security of the region, together with their opposite views of the U.S.-Japan alliance had a negative effect on the China-Japan relationship. Beijing charged that Tokyo had failed to honor the 1976 Sino-Japan Treaty of Peace and Friendship, which emphasized Japan's commitment not to support hegemony in Asia, whereas Japan argued that it was China's post-Cold War ambiguous intentions that justified Japan's need for the security alliance with the United States. It was clear that there was a problem of definition between Japan and China about what was 'hegemony' and what was 'security'. "While Beijing viewed the Japan-U.S. security arrangement as a destabilizing force in the Asia-Pacific area, Tokyo, like Washington, argued that the alliance was necessary for stability in the region" (DiFilippo 72).

Furthermore, attempts by the two major corners in East Asia's post-Cold War triangle of a genuine rapprochement were compromised by the mutual perception that China and Japan are natural rivals, paving the way for an unstable and unequal triangle in East Asia between Japan, China, and the United States. As China's role on the world stage was getting greater attention, Japan's star was on the wane, and America's determination to preserve its preponderant position in the region, using its alliance with the latter for that purpose, added fuel to the fire in the Sino-Japanese equation. Therefore, the potential for conflict and competition over East Asian domination, together with the pending unresolved issues between Japan and China challenge the U.S. claim that it was playing a positive security role in East Asia. On the opposite, this book advances that the U.S. policy in the region, be it military, political or economic, was perceived by most of the regional actors as threatening and even hegemonic.

The opposition to the U.S. military presence came not only from America's foes in East Asia, but also from its friends, such as South Korea, where "a survey showed that six times as many South Koreans feared the United States as feared North Korea" (*The Economist*, London, June 1994). However, one needs to explore the different uses of the term, as the charge of being hegemonic was traded between China, on the one hand, and the United States and Japan, on the other hand. Therefore, the chances of a positive Sino-Japanese relationship were quite slim because when two nation-states want the same thing–that is East Asian domination, it became highly unlikely that they would trust each other. The lack of trust, as advanced before, was further deepened by the way the United States dealt with Japan as a key ally, and with China as a potential adversary.

The last Chapter of this book is about the mutually perceived hegemony between China, on the one hand, and Japan and the United States, on the other hand. It is built into the form of closing off this work by trying to answer its main question of whether the U.S. military presence in East Asia in the immediate decades after the Cold War contributed to the security of the region, or was a destabilizing variable in the region's complex security equation, as it was viewed hegemonic rather than balanced. This chapter has also looked at the concept of hegemony from a theoretical point of view and how the two kinds of hegemony–structural and surface–apply to Japan and China in their respective relations with the United States.

Interviewee 1 told me in 2006, during my interview with him at the University of Chicago, that the ideal situation for any state was to be the hegemon. States' interactions are basically about the competition for power that is animus dominandi. Paradoxically, however, the more powerful a state is, the more likely it is that another state will threaten it, and since states first seek to survive, they, therefore, have the incentive to be as powerful as possible, that is, the hegemon. But whether **Interviewee 1**'s argument justified the U.S. perceived hegemony in East Asia and in the world at large is not the issue here, as the main focus of this work is not hegemony per se, but the security role of the post-Cold War U.S. military presence in a region which was drawing more and more attention, since its economic importance, its political diversity, and its security challenges kept growing. Nevertheless, according to some government documents, such as the DPG and the PNAC, the United States should go and consequently went hegemonic since the end of the Cold War.

The twenty-first century was believed by the neo-conservatives in the United States to be the American New Century, wherein the United States would go on a crusade ostensibly to eradicate "evil", but strategically to perpetuate its hegemonic position in the existing balance of power. Over the first decade or so of this century, however, there was a growing imbalance between U.S. military might and its economic prowess. This paradox shed substantial doubts about the United States' ability to continue to enjoy a strategically preponderant position with regard to other nations like China and Japan. This pushed the United States to go economically hegemonic, using its politically and militarily privileged position to gain economic concessions even from its closest allies, such as Japan. This book has argued that this was not the posture that was conducive to more security and stability in East Asia, which drew more questions than answers regarding the post-Cold War U.S. military presence there, since one of its basic premises, the monolithic Communist threat, disappeared.

After examining some primary sources such as government documents, which include the 1992 Defense Policy Guidance (DPG) and the 1997 Project for a New American century (PNAC), one can argue that the post-Cold War

American views of the role of the United States not only in East Asia but also in the world were rather hegemonic and assertive, instead of being conducive to more security. Both documents, devised by people who were then called neoconservatives, clearly showed that the U.S. would seek to perpetuate Pax Americana well into the twenty-first century, which they called the American century. The PNAC advanced that American power was a righteous one and, therefore, ought to be used for righteous purposes, such as spreading democracy in the world as an American virtue. As far as the focus of this work is concerned, the PNAC and the DPG are looked at from the angle of their significance to understanding the post-Cold War U.S. policy and the value of its military presence in Northeast Asia.

The United States policy of working to prevent the rise of a rival power, as the DPG and the PNAC ostensibly called for, meant so far the consolidation of the U.S.-Japan alliance in East Asia to discourage potential Chinese assertive conduct in the region, which resulted in a negative feedback from both the Chinese and the North Koreans, who themselves saw this alliance as more threatening than stabilizing. Moreover, the U.S. National Security Strategy of September 17, 2002, reads, "the United States would require bases and stations within and beyond Western Europe and Northeast Asia, as well as temporary access arrangements for the long-distance deployment of U.S. forces." These widespread military deployments aimed at preparing for perceived "security challenges" which primarily included the rising power of China and its security and strategic implications for the United States as the sole world superpower in East Asia.

The U.S. continued reliance on a network of alliances and military bases meant that East Asia then hosted the bulk of the U.S. 254,000 troops deployed in 38 countries, together with the majority of the 725 American military bases (Ch. Johnson 154). Therefore, the high level of troop presence in East Asia, from experts' perspectives such as Chalmers Johnson, combined with the controversial U.S. alliance with Japan, challenged the U.S. claim that the American military presence in the region was a positive security factor. As this work has shown, from a Sino-North Korean view point, the 'excessive' U.S. military deployments and their attendant ramifications, such as the yearly South Korean-American military exercises and the expansion of the Japanese role to "areas surrounding Japan" to include Taiwan, could only lead to the conclusion that the security situation in East Asia was getting more and more unstable.

The post-Cold War U.S. military "over-presence" in the region meant that it was 'protecting' some but, paradoxically, threatening others. For those who felt they were being protected, however, it was not sure whether they really believed in Chinese and North Korean threats or they were made to believe in such threats, as "the pentagon [had to] constantly invent new reasons for keeping in [U.S.] hands as many bases as possible long after the wars and crises that had led to their creation have evaporated" (Ch. Johnson 152). It was the crescent-shaped network of alliances in East Asia that allowed the United States to keep in its hands too "many bases", but drew much criticism and suspicion from countries like China, South Korea, and Russia.

Due to the lack of regional institutional traditions combined with lingering historical and security issues between Asia's two major actors–Japan and China (Vogel et al. 2002), East Asia was a volatile region where Washington had a hard time drawing most of the region's countries into one single military and/or political grouping. A NATO-like security apparatus in Asia was still not feasible. As NATO has rather muted some open inter-European conflicts on the scale of those that opposed France or Britain and Germany during the first half of the twentieth century over the domination of the continent, the U.S.-Japan alliance exposed East Asia's inter-regional conflicts.

However, the U.S. reliance on a group of alliances in East Asia did not necessarily mean support of multilateralism, since the United States came to view some international organizations and a few multilateral treaties with a great deal of suspicion and skepticism. The U.S. policy of U.N. bashing, the sabotage of international agreements, such as the Kyoto Protocol, the International Criminal Court, and the 2002 unilateral withdrawal from the 1972 Anti-Ballistic Missile treaty (ABM), showed a recent American negative perception of the legitimacy of international law and institutions (Suskind 81-86).

But the policy of unilateralism was not without price. It cost the United States the defection of some historical allies, such as Germany and France during the buildup of the Iraq War in 2003, for instance. It also damaged Washington's credibility and image all over the world, leading some to ask a common rhetorical question "why did they hate us?," and inviting a rhetorical answer in the form of another question "why *didn't* they hate us?."[2] Hoffman said: "the most flagrant and widely deplored contradiction was between America's self-image as a force

---

[2] In an interview published on Wednesday, January 28, 2004 by CTV.ca – Canada, and under the title "Michael Moore Prepares Provocative 9-11 Project", Moore said: "You know the question which a lot of people were asking after Sept. 11 -- 'Why do they hate us?' The question I want to ask is, 'Why DON'T they hate us?' -- and then take my camera around the world a bit and show what's done in our name".

for democracy and human rights… with the torture of enemy combatants, while the U.S. repudiated the international laws of war" (Hoffman 60).

In short, the time of Theodore Roosevelt's "Big Stick" strategy was not applicable any more in a post-Cold War era when the United States was then dealing with at least three declared nuclear powers in East Asia. Cumings argued that "hegemony was most effective when it was indirect, inconclusive, plural, heterogeneous and consensual- less a form of domination than a form of legitimate global leadership" (*Parallax Visions* 484). Legitimacy could only be earned by setting the example, and not by acting as Big Brother. But instead of being an example, the United States "pursued a hegemonic strategy-one that reserved a special role for the United States as the principal guarantor of regional order" (Ikenberry, ed. *America Unrivaled* 193).

As for Taiwan, in pursuing unification, Beijing invoked national security interests, but in addition to the regional strategic stakes involved, the reality of Taiwan's democracy and China's autocracy would ensure that the issue remained a delicate matter in China's relationship with Japan and the United States, since both countries stated time and again that Taiwan was a "common security challenge" for them. But for the time being, the United States was very much consumed by the global war against "terrorism", and thus sought to prevent either side from precipitating a crisis across the Strait of Taiwan that would distract from its focus on the Middle East. The situation as such left East Asia's security, which the United States claimed it was protecting, especially since the end of the Cold War, with an uncertain and precarious destiny, one that is similar to that of Taiwan.

The problem of Taiwan, as advanced in the introduction of this book, would not be solved by just Beijing and Taipei, because the Taiwan issue was by then to be tackled, not as a Chinese domestic secessionist problem, but as a regional security question. In my interview with **Interviewee 1**, he told me that the United States and Japan would never let China take Taiwan back because of the strategic importance of the Island to the American-Japanese common long-term strategy to contain the rise of China to a world power status. Taiwan would always be used against China first as a strong political card, and second as a threat to the sustainability of China's economy in terms of oil shipments and China's future secret plans in the South China Sea.

Regarding its approach to the China factor, instead of trying to integrate the biggest nation on earth into the U.S. web of bilateral alliance structures in East Asia, the United States dealt with Communist China as an outsider to East Asia's post-Cold War triangle instead of one of its cornerstones (Lin 17). In describing its erratic policies vis-à-vis China, Washington used "doublespeak" (Orwell) such as "comprehensive engagement", "constructive engagement", and "strategic partnership" with the PRC. The continued absence of a real political vision and initiative, particularly vis-à-vis China's future role in East Asia, remained at the heart of the U.S. vision impasse. In my meeting with **Interviewee 1**, he told me that the United States had in a very important way become obsessed with the Middle East and consequently took its resources away from Asia and away from Europe and transferred them to the Middle East. Most of America's allies in East Asia think that the U.S. did not "foolishly" devote enough attention to Asia. "The U.S. was not worried enough about the Chinese threat and spent too much time worrying about the threat in the Middle East".

The U.S. management of the post-Cold War triangle in East Asia, however, showed a biased tilt toward Japan as the historically preferred strategic ally in the region, which was key for the United States to play the role of the hegemon, since the U.S. became the unrivaled power in the region. And this was not the overture of a positive security actor, as it was considered by key regional actors as threatening and biased. It was widely believed in the United States that showing the Chinese the strategic significance of the U.S.-Japanese security partnership would discourage Beijing from challenging the U.S.-led status quo in the region. This was exactly a policy prescription for more instability and less security in East Asia. The mismanagement of the triangle on the part of Washington, together with the policy to prevent a Sino-Japanese genuine rapprochement, or sabotage a North and South Korean reconciliation, could only lead to more instability and tension between the region's two major drivers. It was the old-new policy of divide and rule (Suskind 114-15).

Though the U.S. post-Cold War security culture in East Asia was that the United States was wary of Beijing's growing role in the region, this did not lead automatically to the conclusion that the Sino-U.S. relationship was one of confrontation and rivalry for primacy in the sense the U.S.-Soviet relationship was during the Cold War. But, the whole U.S.-Japan-China triangle did contain some of the characteristics of the U.S.-China alliance against the Soviet Union in the early 1970s. Then, the United States did not have such a strong security alliance with Beijing after Richard Nixon's February 1972 surprise visit to China. It was a calculated American move to contain and weaken the Soviet Union politically and militarily. It was called playing the China card to contain the Soviet intransigence in arms negotiations. Moreover, the U.S. did not enjoy the privilege of being the unrivalled military power in East Asia in the 1970s, nor was it the only superpower in the world as it was in the post-Cold War first decades. then, the United States not only was the hegemon in the region, but also it was highly unlikely that it would have a rival for hegemony at least for the foreseeable future. China was a long way off from challenging the U.S. hegemonic position in East Asia, a position that was manifested through a widespread American military presence, while Japan's road to becoming a normal and independent country was still long and hard.

But, the U.S.-China relationship could not be described as one that is similar to the U.S.-Soviet relationship during the Cold War in terms of economic assets and military parity. The tremendous gap between the two countries in national power and international status did not make China a peer of the United States (Vogel et al., 2002). China's political, economic, social, and diplomatic leverage and influence on the United States were far smaller than the latter on the former, making the balance of power among the two nations rather unequal. The United States had most of the time taken the initiative regarding their bilateral or world issues. But China simply reacted either by abstaining or by acquiescing to American pressures with respect to issues as serious as China's future sovereignty over Taiwan and European and Middle East security problems, such as respectively the 2000 bombing of the Chinese embassy in Belgrade or the 2003 controversial U.S. invasion of Iraq.

What China actually wanted was to curb U.S. influence regionally as well as globally by promoting a multipolar international order, with China as one of the great powers, but this work has argued that this was not necessarily a threat to regional or international security (Schwartz). In fact, a three-power multipolar system had already been advocated by President Nixon and his secretary of State Henry Kissinger in the early 1970s in what was called the Strategic Triangle, with China serving as one of the tripartite powers in this system along with the United States and the Soviet Union. In the post-Cold War, with the United States as the sole post-Cold War predominant power, China's support for the emergence of multipolarity was perceived in Washington as a threat because it was understood as a potential tendency to challenge the status quo. Still, one could question the validity of the argument of the China threat.

However, **Interviewee 1** argued that if there was any country that was going to dominate Asia in the future, it would not be the United States; it would be China, because it is an Asian power. It is physically located in the region and has a great deal of potential. Interviewee 1 believed that China would try to dominate Asia the way the U.S. was dominating the western hemisphere during and after the Cold War. As China's economic power was growing in double digit figures, so was its military power. The International Monetary

Fund (IMF) in the late 1990s "calculated that China's economy was slightly smaller than Japan's and larger than those of France and the United Kingdom combined. The size of China's economy would surpass that of the U.S. by 2030" (Dibb 27). Economic success would allow Beijing to fully develop power projection capabilities with which to threaten more than its immediate neighbors if it chose to do so. An economically successful China would likely develop significant military capabilities by 2020-25 by which it could seriously threaten the security of most of its regional neighbors as well as challenge U.S. ascendancy in East Asia. If this happened, Chinese interests would likely change, and China might well become more of a threat to its neighbors and to U.S. interests in the region. The interests that China would develop, through its enhanced dependence on international trade and energy imports, could lead it into conflict with its neighbors and with the United States over energy resources and important sea lanes.

What would the rise of China mean for the U.S.-constructed preponderant position in East Asia? We could see some vulnerable countries in the region ingratiating themselves with a potentially rising hegemon to the detriment of the United States interests, as China was likely to assert itself as East Asia's great power. Doubts about U.S. credibility and reliability, combined with continuous Chinese pressure, could break up the U.S. network of alliances with Japan, South Korea, and Taiwan and may well lead smaller and vulnerable states to readjust their policies to Chinese coercion. This was more likely to be the case for countries which were immediately on China's borders, namely Japan and Taiwan, the two immediate targets of the perceived Chinese security threat in the region. But in this case, we could also expect important implications for the U.S. defense strategy in the region and its alliance structure. So, the extent that Japan and the U.S., the other two corners in the triangle, were concerned about the future of the security architecture in Asia was largely seen as a response to the rise of China. What we saw happening in East Asia then was that China was growing more and more powerful, and, in response, countries like the United States and Japan were coming together and thinking about how to deal with a very powerful China down the road.

Therefore, China deemed unlikely to become America's strategic partner again in the manner that it had been during the Nixon years. As a major regional actor and a rising power with vital interests in Asia, China would occasionally collide with the United States, but it was also likely to find that its long-term interests were better served by pursuing a cooperative relationship with America and Japan. China might thus become neither a formal ally, because it was always hostile to the perceived U.S. "hegemony", nor a declared enemy of America, since it would be in nobody's interest in Asia, for a cooperative China would have an important geo-strategic effect on regional and international security. After all, a stable China would reinforce Japan's stake in a defensive alliance with America without frightening Tokyo either into rapid re-armament or into divisive tensions with the United States.

In short, the engagement of China, together with the maintenance of Japan's "civilian power" role by turning the U.S.-Japan alliance into an inclusive one, while avoiding making such an alliance appear to be directed against the Chinese, was likely to become the cornerstone of America's Asian strategy for the foreseeable future. If the U.S. military presence in East Asia had any positive security role, Washington would have a profound stake in ensuring that China saw this military presence as contributory to the overall stability of the Asia Pacific region, rather than directed against its rising power.

It was the post-Cold War rise of China that engaged American attention because it had tremendous implications for the United States. The continuing rise of China affected the United States in a strategic and political way, and long before it affected America, it had affected America's friends in Japan in a much more direct and significant fashion. When the Cold War ended in 1989, many people thought that the U.S. would significantly reduce, if not eliminate, its military presence in Asia.

Throughout the 1990s, however, America kept its forces in Asia, not to deal with any particular threat, but to prevent potential conflicts in the region. But by the end of the 1990s and in the early 2000s, the focus began to shift to the rising power of China which mandated, from a U.S. perspective, that the U.S. keep its troops in Asia (Kaplan, "How We Would Fight China" 49-65). **Interviewee 1** told me: "So, as far as the future was concerned, I think the main reason that the U.S. would stay in Asia was not to keep the peace or to play the role of a pacifier but instead to *counter* China". Therefore, stability was likely to remain a wild goose chase unless the three great powers of Asia- the U.S., Japan, and China could somehow find a way to work together instead of working at cross purposes.

The United States claimed that its military presence in East Asia was subject to a robust consensus among the majority of the region's nations, both in Northeast and Southeast Asia that were suspicious of China's strategic intentions to project its coercive power against them. This work, however, contends that one of the root reasons why the U.S.-Japan-China triangle was quite unstable was the controversy over the U.S. military presence in East Asia.

It was a presence that was viewed differently by the regional actors, according to their respective power and security considerations, on the basis of which the three parties interacted in the post-Cold War era. Although there was some evidence that nations such as Japan, the Philippines, Thailand, and Indonesia were indeed more comfortable with an American hegemony than with a would-be Chinese one, one can argue that in no way could this relative regional consensus about the need for a preponderant power in the region which played the role of a stabilizer, be a majority consensus.

The bulk of the Asia Pacific peoples' aspirations of seeing their region develop into a European Union-like forum were disappointed by an excessive and rather threatening military presence. To put it bluntly, "tensions and instabilities particularly in the Korean Peninsula, between China and Taiwan, and other hot spots in the region were heightened because of U.S. interventionism" (Tuazon, "Current U.S. Hegemony in Asia Pacific", Lecture March 1, 2003).

Finally, while maintaining the largest American military presence in an East Asia that was overshadowed by the rapid rise of China and the potential power rivalry between Beijing and Tokyo, the United States had, rightly or wrongly, confused between the considerations of power and the considerations of security, resulting in less security in a region overladen with historical enmities, economic competition, territorial disputes, and power greed. The paradox between what the U.S. was claiming and what East Asia was experiencing, revealed a serious problem either of policy design or of a conceptual deficit regarding concepts like power and security. While many governments in East Asia approved of the U.S. military presence and sought to use it to advance their own interests against an unpredictable China, an already nuclear North Korea, and an increasingly assertive Japan, other regional actors tried to undercut the U.S. forward military presence in the region.

With so much controversy around the U.S. military presence in East Asia after the end of the Cold War, it was a wonder how the United States could have played a positive security role, which would be appreciated by the nations involved in the power and security game in the region. The United States continued to magnify the China threat. David M. Lampton, Dean of the School of International Studies at Beijing University and Director of the Institute of International Strategic Studies at the Central Party School of the Communist Party of China, supported one of the basic arguments of this thesis. Lampton argued that

U.S. policymakers often overestimate China's military might. And if they continue to view China's power in substantially coercive terms when it is actually growing most rapidly in the economic and intellectual domains, they will be playing the wrong game, on the wrong field, with the wrong team (23).

There was a prevailing regional view, "in the long term, the decline of U.S. primacy and the subsequent transition to a multipolar world was inevitable; but in the short term, Washington's power was unlikely to decline, and its position in world affairs was unlikely to change" (Jisi, "China's Search for Stability with America" 40). So, nations in East Asia, friendly and unfriendly to the U.S. military presence in the region, were aware that they would have to cooperate or, in the best scenario, seek a modus vivendi with the Unites States for a long time to come, but were, at the same time, consoled by the historical lesson of the inevitable decline of hegemonic powers.

C.2. Implications

This book has tried to shed light on the post-Cold War security role of the United States in East Asia, and how key variables in international relations, like those of power and security, governed the relationship between the United States, Japan, and China in the early decades of the post-Cold War era. Though this work does not claim to be exhaustive, it has not limited its focus only to the three countries mentioned in the title, but it has included North Korea, South Korea, and Taiwan, in particular, and Russia occasionally, depending on the relevance and the significance of each country to the triangle under study.

On many occasions, this work has demonstrated that neither the North Korean nuclear and security problem, nor the Taiwan question could have been solved bilaterally. Rather, in view of the Chinese historical, ideological, and economic leverage on Pyongyang, the United States and Japan heavily relied on China's key role in bringing the North Koreans to the table of negotiations before and even after the latter tested its first nuclear device on October 9, 2006. This was true in view of China's special and historic relationship with the North Koreans, and the political and economic dependence of the latter on the former.

As for Taiwan, Taipei was in no position to take any unilateral political decisions regarding the Island's future status without receiving the sanction of Washington and Tokyo, given the American military security guarantees as stipulated in the 1979 Taiwan relations Act, and the U.S.-Japanese joint but implicit political and psychological support of the Taiwanese defiant demeanor. As section 2 of Chapter Four showed, even in times of an American-Japanese drift with Taiwan over some separatist Taiwanese declarations or decisions, the drift was about the modalities or the timing, and not about the 'righteousness' of Taiwan's question. Therefore, post-Cold War politics in East Asia did not take a pentagon shape; rather, it would always be a triangle driven by the power and security calculations of the two major regional powers-Japan and China- in relation to their respective interaction with the United States as the only superpower that kept an empire of military bases not only in Asia, but also all over the world.

As the value of this book can only be assessed by the reader, it is safe to claim that it has drawn some attention to the importance of the post-Cold War U.S.-Japan-China triangle regarding the future of the international system on the basis of which small and big, rich and poor, and strong and weak states have interacted thereafter. As the United States was recognized as the sole superpower then, Japan was also key to the security and stability of East Asia in view of its economic prowess and its special security relationship with the U.S. As for China, Tokyo and Washington feared that it could be tempted by its rising power into trying to challenge the political, military, and economic status quo in the region. The growing power of China and the U.S.-Japanese concerns about what China would do with its increasing power shaped post-Cold War politics in East Asia and continued to govern the power relations and the respective security calculations of three major actors in the region well into the second decade of the twenty-first century.

The value of this work also emanates from the challenge to assess the validity of the U.S. claim that the American military presence in East Asia was playing a positive security role and was a force of stability rather than insecurity. The challenge stemmed from the inextricable link between the U.S. policies in the region, and those of China and Japan, which required further efforts to study Chinese and Japanese histories and policies vis-à-vis each other and respectively towards the United States, largely perceived as an intruder into East Asian affairs by the former, and as a strategic ally by the latter.

Furthermore, in the attempt to explore the U.S. security role within the triangle, and in relation to Japan and China during the early decades of the new world order of US unipolarity, this book consulted some political science theories about states' interaction within a system that was always governed by the balance of power which deeply impacted the outcome of such interactions. To achieve this purpose, some cases of interaction outcomes among the sole superpower then, the second largest economy in the world, and the rising power of the twenty-first century, respectively, the U.S., Japan, and China were studied to demonstrate that virtually in all cases the strongest prevailed and the weakest blinked. These cases included the 1996 and the 2000 presidential elections in Taiwan, or the April 2001 E-P 3 U.S. plane incident, where in all three cases, China conceded, as the cost-gain calculus was not in its favor, since the Chinese were not in a position to withstand U.S.-Japanese concerted pressure and their joint show of force.

Moreover, as Ezra Vogel suggested a quarter of a century ago, the building of a three-way equal partnership between the United States, Japan, and China ("It Takes Three for This Tango" 60-61), part of this work has taken a different view by crafting its own argument based upon the thesis that such a three-way equal partnership was not feasible since it would give China and Japan an equal status and importance in America's Asia calculus. And this fueled Japanese suspicions about the geo-political and geo-strategic intentions of the United States in East Asia, and subsequently heated up Japan's security apprehensions. The Japanese feeling that the U.S. was playing fast and loose with its special relationship with Japan did play well into the hands of the anti-American Japanese political party (JSP), which was working on heating the domestic sentiments to question the need for Tokyo's close ties with the United States.

Eventually, this book has also brought to the fore the value of studying the Pacific Rim region, a part of the world that, over the following decades, acquired increasing importance for and attention from the world as a whole. This work aspires to be a potentially useful contribution to the scholarship which seeks to further understand the pushing and pulling variables of East Asia's politics in the 1990s and 2000s, as one can only see little research about the post-Cold War U.S.-Japan-China triangle from the prism of power and security during this specific period. In the study of the U.S. vision of its future role in East Asia, this work has also shed light on important historical, economic, and political facts which governed and would continue to govern the interaction not only among America, Japan, and China, but also among most regional actors.

C.3. Limitations of the Study

This book is not an attempt to present a comprehensive and theoretical analysis of the impact of the variables of power and security on the interaction outcomes in international relations. As this work is not exclusively about theory, it can be a starting point for a more specialized and specific approach to these two defining variables in political science. In this respect, it is an effort to determine how important the variables of power and security were in dictating states' actions with and reactions to each other within a certain environment of competition and distrust due to the lack of a central world government. Though only one case -the post-Cold War U.S.-Japan-China Triangle- of power-security interconnectedness in states' interactions is studied, it is hoped that the results may be used for analysis of other case studies in Europe, Asia and Africa as well.

Moreover, the case, which is the main focus of this book, involves the actions of nation-states rather than the impact of regional or international forums, such as respectively ASEAN, WTO, or the United Nations, on considerations of power and security of the parties concerned. This work deals with the key East Asian countries-China and Japan- as the two major regional actors in their respective relationships with the United States, and the impact of their triangular interaction on regional security in the immediate decades of the post-Cold War era.

Russia was not referred to as a major security driver in East Asia as far as the China-Japan-U.S. triangle was concerned. Though Russia still occupied the Japanese Kuril islands, and still had some border problems with China, Moscow did not play a key security role in the region during the early years after the Soviet Union was gone, its historical relationship with North Korea, notwithstanding. After the disintegration of the Soviet Union, Pyongyang shifted its security calculations from complete reliance on Russia to a strategic partnership with China to constitute the last handful of communist political systems. But Russia was mentioned in this work whenever it was relevant, as in the case, for instance, of Moscow's dissatisfaction with Japan's participation in an American-sponsored missile program in Asia called the 1993 Theater Missile Defense (THAD) system, or when dealing with Pyongyang's nuclear standoff with the United States, given Russia's remaining leverage on North Korea.

On another note, the methodology Chapter centers upon theoretical frameworks such as realism, neo-realism, and offensive realism, and on abstract concepts like power and security, or offensive and defensive postures. This work argues that this chapter is significant because it provided this work with a clear vision thanks to the theoretical framework within which the central question of this thesis was dealt with, as the triangle under study is a case of international relations within a certain international order which needs such a framework so that it would not be operating vaguely with a potential loss of focus.

As part of this book examined the impact of the two core concepts of power and security on the interactions between the U.S., Japan, and China in the post-

Cold War era, this work adopted the French and Raven approach to conceptualizing power and that of Jeffrey Hart to measure it. But it did not deny the existence of other definitions of power, like those of Prince Machiavelli and Thomas Hobbes. Furthermore, as this work is a case study of international relations among sovereign states, it has also dealt with the post-Cold War U.S.-Japan-China triangle from three different political science approaches to interstate relations as well as the significance of power politics -the animus dominandi- as the motive behind states' interactions. The choice of the triangle under study was motivated by the fact that this triangle represented a sample of how states interacted within an international system of self-help and anarchy. For this purpose, Reynolds's definition of the notion of 'interaction' as the relative power of the unit, the costs-gains calculus, and the freedom of alignment was adopted (Reynolds 219).

Lastly, the use of variables such as power and security to analyze different levels of analysis, or the use of the independent variables of the balance of power and interaction outcome to explain the dependent ones, was used as a means, rather than an end, to contribute to answering the overall objective of this book about the reality of the U.S. military presence in East Asia in the post-Cold War early decades, and eventually to dispute the claim that this presence was a stabilizing factor in an unstable East Asian security environment. Therefore, as no major security challenge in East Asia could be managed without cooperation among Beijing, Tokyo, and Washington, the most critical challenge that remains today is how to foster a tradition of security cooperation between China, Japan, and the United States; a cooperation that is not premised on a "two-against-one" triangular logic, leading one party to feel it is the odd man out.

Bibliography

Primary Sources

Conference on "China and the Future of the World", April 28-29, 2006, organized by the Chicago Society, University of Chicago. Among the guest speakers were His Excellency Wang Guangya, Permanent representative of the People's republic of China to the United Nations; Peter W. Rodman, U.S. Assistant secretary of Defense for International Security Affairs; Christopher R. Hill, U.S. Assistant Secretary of State for East Asian and Pacific Affairs; Ambassador Wu Jianmin, Former Chinese Ambassador to France, the United Nations in Geneva, and current President of China Foreign affairs University; **Interviewee 1**, a prominent political science professor, a founder of a new school of thought in political science and currently co-director of a program on international security policy at a major university in Chicago.

Congressional Research Service Report 94-422S, Washington, D.C.: The Library of Congress. Sutter, Robert G. "Chinese Nuclear Weapons and Arms Control Policies: Implications and Options for the United States". 25 March 1994.

Department of State Bulletin. "Crisis in Asia-an Examination of U.S. Policy". No.55, January 12, 1950, 111-118.

Excerpts From President Nixon's 1972 Report to Congress. "United States Foreign Policy For the 1970s: The Emerging Structure of Peace". February 9, 1972.

Hearings Before the Committee on Armed Services House of Representatives of the One Hundred Sixth Congress. 2nd Session. July 19, 2000, U.S. Government Printing Office. "Military Capabilities of the Peoples Republic of China". Washington. 2001.

Hearings Before the Committee on National Security of the House of Representatives of the One Hundred Fourth Congress. 2nd Session. U.S. Government Printing Office, 1996. "Security Challenges Posed by China". Washington. March 20, 1996.

Hearings of the Committee on Armed Services of the House of Representatives, the One Hundred Sixth Congress. "Security Challenges Posed by China." July 19, 2000.

Information Office of the State Council of the People's Republic of China. "China's National Defense in 2004". Beijing, December 2004.

Japan's Defense Agency. "Basic Policy for National Defense". Tokyo, May 20th, 1957.

Japan's Ministry of Foreign Affairs. "Announcement by the Chief Cabinet Secretary on Japan's Immediate Response to North Korea's Missile Launch". Tokyo, September 1st, 1998.

Kaneda, Hideaki. "The U.S. is threatened by 'Aggressive Chinese Sea' Power". Report commissioned in 2005 by the U.S. Department of Defense's Office of Net Assessment. 2005.

Ministry of Foreign Affairs of Japan. "Joint Statement: U.S.-Japan Security Consultative Committee." 21 February 2005.

Office of the Assistant Secretary of Defense for International Security Affairs-East Asia and Pacific Region. Washington D.C., Department of Defense. "United States Security Strategy for East Asia-Pacific Region". February 1995, p.18.

Office of the Assistant Secretary of Defense for International Security Affairs, East Asia Pacific Region. Washington D.C: Department of Defense. "Strategic Framework for the Asian Pacific Rim". 1992.

Office of the Assistant Secretary of Defense for International Security Affairs-East Asia and Pacific Region- United States Security Strategy for East Asia-Pacific Region. Washington D.C., Department of Defense. Nye, Joseph. "The 1995 Nye Report". February 18, 1995.

Polls by Nihon Keizai Shimbun (WSJ/NKS), by the CBS News/ Tokyo Broadcasting System collaboration (CBS-TBS), by CBS/New York Times/TBS, and by the Japanese Jiji Press.

President Nixon's 1972 Report to Congress. "United States Foreign Policy For the 1970s: The Emerging Structure of Peace". February 9, 1972.

Quadrennial Defense Review Report, Department of Defense, Washington, DC., September 30, 2001, p.1.

The Pentagon Quadrennial Defense Review. *The Brookings Policy Brief* no.15, 1997.

U.S.-Japan Security Consultative Committee Joint Statement. "Completion of the Review of the Guidelines for U.S.-Japan Defense Cooperation". New York, September 23, 1997.

U.S. Department of Defense, Annual Report on the Military power of the People's Republic of China: Report to Congress, National Authorization Act 2002.

U.S. Department of Defense, Report of Office of International Security Affairs, Washington, D.C.: Government Printing Office. "United States Security Strategy for the East-Asia Pacific Region". 2000.

Books

Abramowitz, Morton. *China-Japan-U.S.: Managing the Trilateral Relationship.* Tokyo; New York: Japan Center for International Exchange, c 1998.

Allen, Mary J. *Introduction to Measurement Theory.* Calif., Pacific Grove: Brooks/Cole, 1979.

Arbatov, Alexei G. Multilateral Nuclear Weapons Reductions and Limitations in Strategic Views from the Second Tier: The Nuclear Weapons Policies of France, Britain, and China. New Brunswick, NJ: Transaction Publishers, 1995.

Barber, Benjamin R. *Fear's Empire: War, Terrorism, and Democracy.* New York: Norton Books, 2003.

Barr, Pat. The Coming of the Barbarians: the opening of Japan to the West, 1853-1870. 1ˢᵗ ed. New York: Dutton, 1967.

Bergner, Jefferey T. *The New Superpowers: Germany, Japan, the U.S., and the New World Order.* 1ˢᵗ ed. New York: St. Martin's Press, 1991.

Bernstein, Richard and Ross H. Munro. *The Coming Conflict with China.* 1ˢᵗ ed. New York: A. Knopf, Distributed by Random House, 1997.

Bertaux, Daniel and Paul Thompson. *International Handbook of Oral History and Life Stories.* Vol. 2. New York: Oxford University Press, 1993.

Boulding, Kenneth E. *Conflict and Defense.* New York: Harper Torch Books, 1962.

Breisach, E. *Historiography: Ancient, Medieval, and Modern.* Chicago: University Press, 1983.

Bridge, F.R. and Bullen, Roger. *The great Powers and the European State System.* Harlow, Longmans, 1980.

Brown, Michael. E. *Grave New World: Security Challenges in the 21ˢᵗ Century.* Ed. Washington, D.C.: Georgetown University Press, 2003.

Buzan, Barry. *People, States and Fear.* Boulder, Co.: Lynne Rienner, 1983.

Buzan, Barry, et al. *Security: A New Framework For Analysis.* Boulder, Colo.: Lynne Rienner Pub., 1998.

Baker, James A. *The Politics of Diplomacy.* New York: G.P. Putnam's Sons, 1995.

Blainey, Geoffrey. *The Causes of War.* New York: Free Press, 1973.

Blum, William. *Rogue State: A Guide to the World's Only Superpower.* Monroe, ME: Common Courage Press, 2000.

Bridge, F.R. and Bullen, Roger. *The Great Powers and the European State System.* Harlow, Longmans, 1980.

Bush, Richard C. *At Cross Purposes: U.S.-Taiwan Relations Since 1942.* Armonk, M. E: Sharpe, 2004.

Carter, Jimmy. *Our Endangered Values: America's Moral Crisis.* New York: Simon & Schuster, 2005.

Chen, Chin-Yuen. *American Economic Policy Toward Communist China, 1950-1970.* Ann Arbor, Mich.: University Microfilm, 1974.

Chomsky, Noam. New York: Henry Holt &Company Inc., 2003.

Claude, Inis. *Swords into Plowshares.* New York: Random House, Inc, 1964.

Clements, Kevin P. *Peace and Security in the East Asia Region: Post-Cold War Problems and Prospects.* Tokyo, Japan: United Nations University Press; Palmertson North, New Zealand: Dunmore Press, 1993.

Cobden, Richard. *Speeches on Questions of Public Policy.* Eds. John Bright and James E. Thorold Rogers. Vol 2.: London: Macmillan& Co., 1870.

Cohen, Warren I. *Pacific Passage: The Study of American-East Asian Relations on the Eve of the Twenty-First Century.* New York: Columbia University Press, 1996.

Cumings, Bruce. *Parallax Visions: Making Sense of American-East Asian Relations at the End of the Century. Asia-Pacific, Culture, Politics and Society.* London: Duke University Press, 1999.

Davis, John F. *China During the War and Since the Peace.* Delmington, Delaware: Scholarly Resources, 1972.

Deller, Nicole. Ed. "Rule of Power or Rule of Law? An Assessment of U.S. Policies and Actions Regarding Security-Related Treaties." New York: Apex Press, 2003.

Denning, Margaret B. *The Sino-American Alliance in World War II: Cooperation and Dispute among Nationalists, Communists, and Americans.* Bern, New York: P. Lang, 1986.

DiFilippo, Anthony. *The Challenges of the U.S.-Japan Military Arrangement: Competing Security Transitions in a Changing International Environment.* Armonk, N.Y.: M.E. Sharpe, c2002. DiFilippo, Anthony. *The Golden Age of the U.S.-China-Japan Triangle, 1972-1989.* Cambridge, Mass.; London: Harvard University Asia Center: Distributed by Harvard University Press, 2002.

Dorwart, Jeffrey M. *The Pigtail War: American Involvement in the Sino-Japanese War of 1894/95.* Amherst, Lamas: University of Massachusetts Press, 1975.

Dunn, Fredirick S. *Peaceful Change.* New York: Council on Foreign Relations, 1937.

Eldridge, Robert D. *Beyond Bilateralism: U.S.-Japan Relations in the New Asia Pacific.* Stanford, Calif.: Stanford University Press, 2004.

Fairbank, John King. *The United States and China.* Cambridge, Mass: Harvard University Press, 1983.

Ferguson, Niall. *Colossus: The Price of America's Empire.* New York: Penguin Press, 2004.

Ferguson, Niall. *The Rise and Demise of the British World order and the Lessons for Global power.* n.p: Basic Books, 2004.

Fulbright, J. William. *The Arrogance of Power.* New York: Random House, 1966.

Finel, Bernard I. and Kristin M. Lord. *Power and Conflict in the Age of Transparency.* 2nd ed. New York, N.Y.: Palgrave, 2000.

Fingleton, Eamonn. *Blindside: Why Japan is Still on Track to Overtake the U.S. by the Year 2000.* Boston: Houghton Mifflin Co.,1995.

Fishman, Ted C. *China, Inc.: How the Rise of the Next Superpower Challenges America and the World.* Scribner, 2005.

Foot, Rosemary. *The Practice of Power: U.S. Relations With China Since 1949.* Oxford, New York: Oxford University Press, 1995.

Frash, Bill. The Relationship Between North And South Korea and Four Powers: China, *Japan, America, and Russia In the post-Cold War.* Nanking, Taipei, R.O.C.: Program for Northeast Asian Studies, Academia Sinica, 1999.

Friedman, George and Meredith Lebard. *The Coming War with Japan.* New York: St. Martin's Press, 1991.

Fukuyama, F. *America at the Crossroads: democracy, Power, and the Neo Conservative Legacy.* n.p. Yale University Press, 2006.

Fukuyama, F and Kongdan Oh. *The U.S.-Japan Security Relationship After the End of the Cold War.* Santa Monica, CA: RAND, 1993.

Funabashi, Yoichi. *Alliance Adrift.* New York: Council On Foreign Relations Press, c1999.

Galen, Ted and Doug Bandow. *The Korean Conundrum: America's Troubled Relations with North and South Korea.* New York: Palgrave Macmillan, 2004.

Gardiner, P, ed. *Theories of History.* New York: n.p., 1959.

Garten, Geffrey E. *A Cold Peace: America, Japan, Germany, and the struggle for supremacy.* 1st paperback ed. New York: Times Books, c 1993.

Geoff, Simons. *Iraq: From Sumer to Saddam.* London: St. Martin's Press, 1994.

Gertz, Bill. *The China Threat: How the People's Republic Targets America.* Washington, D.C.: Regnery Publishing, Inc., 2005.

Gilbert, F. *History: Politics or Culture?* Princeton: Princeton University Press, 1990.

Gilpin, Robert. *The Challenge of Global Capitalism: The World Economy in the 21st Century.* Princeton: Princeton University Press, 2000.

Girard, P. Jolyon. *America and the World.* CT: Greenwood Publishing group Inc., 2001.

Glaser, Bonnie S. and Garrett Banning. *China and the U.S. Japan Alliance at a Time of Strategic Change and Shifts in The Balance of Power.* Stanford, California: Asia-Pacific Research Center, 1997.

Goldstein, Avery. *Rising to the Challenge: China's Grand Strategy and International Security.* CA: Stanford University Press, 2005.

Goldestein, Donald M. *The Rain of Ruin: A Photographic of History of Hiroshima and Nagazaki.* UK: Brassey's Inc., 1995.

Goldstein, Joshua S. *Three-Way-Street: Strategic Reciprocity in World Politics.* Chicago: University of Chicago Press, 1990.

Gooch, Brison D. *The World of Europe: The Nineteenth Century 1815-1914.* Saint Louis, Missouri: Forum Press, 1973.

Gudy Kunst, William B. and Tsukasa Nishida. *Bridging Japanese/North American differences.* Thousand Oaks, Calif.: Sage Publications, c1994.

Gulliver, P.H. *Disputes and Negotiations A Cross-Cultural Perspective.* New York: Academic Press, 1997.

Harding, Harry. *A Fragile Relationship: The United States and China Since 1972.* Washington, D.C.: the Brookings Institution, 1992.

Harris, Cooper M. *Research Design: Strategies and Choices in the Design of Social Research.* New York: Toutledge, Chapman & Hall, 1987.

Hay, D. *Analysts and Historians: Western Historiography from the Eighth to the Eighteenth Centuries.* London: n.p., 1977.

Hayashida, Hiroaki. *The Triangle of East Asian Security: The United States, China, and Japan.* Cambridge, MA: Harvard University, the Program on U.S.-Japan Relations: the Center for International Affairs and the Reischauer Institute of Japanese Studies, 1997.

Herbert, Jacob. *Using Published Data: Errors and Remedies.* Calif., Sage: Thousand Oaks, 1984.

Herz, Jervis. *International Politics in the Atomic Age.* New York, NY: Columbia University Press, 1959.

Hinton, Harold C. *The China Sea: The American Stake in its Future.* New York, N.Y: National Strategy Information Center, New Brunswick, Distributed by Transaction Books, 1980.

Hoff, Joan. *Nixon Reconsidered.* New York, NY: Basic Books, 1994.

Holsti, Ole R. *Image and Reality in World Politics.* Ed. John C. Farrell and Asa P. Smith. New York: Columbia University Press, 1968.

Hsiao, Gene. *Sino-American Normalization and its Policy Implications.* New York, NY: Praeger Publishers, 1983.

Hunsberger, Warren S. *Japan's Quest: The Search for International Role, Recognition, and Respect.* Armonk, N.Y.: M.E. Sharpe, 1997.

Hunt, Michael H. *The Making of a Special Relationship: The United States and China to 1914.* New York: Columbia University Press, 1983.

Ikenberry, G. John, ed. *America Unrivaled.* Ithaca, New York: Cornell University Press, 2002.

Isaak, Alan C. *Scope and Methods of Political Science.* 4th ed. Belmont, Calif.: Wadsworth, 1988.

Isaac, Stephen and William Burton Michael. *Handbook in Research and Evaluation: A Collection of Principles, Methods, and Strategies useful in the Planning, Design, and Evaluation of Studies in Education and the Behavioral Sciences.* San Diego, Calif: EDITS Publishers, 1981.

Ishihara, Shintaro. *The Japan That Can Say 'No': The New U.S.-Japan Relations Card.* New York: Simon & Schuster, 1991.

Ito, Go. *Alliance in Anxiety: Détente and the Sino-American-Japanese Triangle.* Lanham, Md.: Lexington Books, c2004.

Johnson, Chalmers. *The Sorrows of Empire: Militarism, Secrecy, and the End of the Republic.* New York: Metropolitan Books, 2004

Johnson, Janet B. *Political Science Research Methods.* 2nd ed. Washington, D.C.: CQ Press, 1991.

Johnston, Douglas W. *Who's Next?: Ends, Ways, Means: Analysis of the Rise of Potential Hostile Competitions.* Carlisle Barracks, Pa.: U.S. Army War College, 1999.

Jordan, Amos A., et al. *American National Security: Policy and Process.* 4th ed. London: The Johns Hopkins Press, 1993.

Joseph, Jonathan. *Hegemony; a realist Analysis.* New York: Routledge Studies in Critical Realism, 2002.

Kanet, Roger E. *Resolving Regional Conflicts.* n.p.: University of Illinois Press, c1998.

Kaplan, M.A. *System and Process in International Politics.* Washington, D.C.: Wiley, 1957.

Kawakami, Kiyoshi Karl. *Japan Speaks on the Sino-Japanese Crisis.* New York: the Macmillan Company, 1932.

Ken, Booth. *The Cold War and Beyond.* Cambridge (UK, New York): Cambridge University Press, 1998.

Kihl, Young W. *Korea and the World: Beyond the Cold War.* Boulder: Westview Press, 1994.

Kim, Samuel S. *North Korean Foreign Relations in the post -Cold War Era.* Hong Kong, New York: Oxford University Press, 1998.

Kissinger, Henry. *A World Restored: Metternich, Castelreagh, and the problems of Peace1812-1922.* NY: Grosset and Dunlap, 1964.

Klare, Michael T. *Resource Wars: The New Landscape of Global Conflict.* New York: Henry Holt, 2002.

Kolodziej, Edward A. *Coping with Conflict After the Cold War.* Baltimore: Johns Hopkins University Press, 1996.

Kosaka, Masataka. *Options for Japan's Foreign Policy.* London: International Institute for Strategic Studies, 1973.

Koshiro, Yukiko. *The U.S.-Japan Alliance: Past, Present, and Future.* New York: Council on Foreign Relations Press, c1999.

Kueh, Y.Y. *The Political Economy of Sino-American Relations: A Greater China Perspective.* Hong Kong: Hong Kong University Press, 1997.

Kunz, Diane B. *The Diplomacy of the Crucial Decade: American Foreign Relations During the 1960s.* New York: Columbia University Press, 1994.

LaFeber, Walter. *The Clash: U.S.-Japanese Relations Throughout History.* New York: W. W. Norton, 1998.

LaFeber, Walter. *The Clash: A History of U.S.-Japan Relations.* New York: W.W. Norton & Company, c1997.

Lakatos, Irme. *The Methodology of Scientific Research Programs.* Cambridge: Cambridge University Press, 1978.

Latané, John Holladay. *A History of American Foreign Policy.* New York: Doran and Company, Inc., 1927.

Lebow, R.N. *The Art of Bargaining.* Baltimore: Johns Hopkins University Press, 1996.

Le Prestre, Philippe G. *Role Quests in the Post-Cold War Era: Foreign Policies in Transition.* Montreal, Buffalo: McGill, Queen's University Press, 1997.

Lewis, John P. *The Goliath Problem: The Wages of Hegemony.* NJ, US: Pinninti Publishers, 2004.

Lieber R.J. *No Common Power: Understanding International Relations.* New York: Harper Collins College Publishers, 1995.

Liu, Xiaoyuan. *A Partnership for Disorder: China, the United States, and Their Policies for the Post war Disposition of the Japanese Empire, 1941-1945.* Cambridge, New York: Cambridge University Press, 1996.

Long, Robert Emmet, ed. *Japan and the U.S.* New York: H.W. Wilson Co., 1990.

Luther, Catherine A. *Press Images, National Identity, and Foreign Policy: A Case Study of U.S.-Japan Relations from 1955-1995.* New York: Routeledge, 2001.

Macchiarola, Frank J. and Robert, B Oxnam. *The China Challenge: American Policies in East Asia.* New York: the Academy of Political Science in Conjunction with the Asia Society, 1991.

Malik, Hafeez. *The Roles of the United States, Russia, and China in the New World Order.* New York: St. Martin's, 1997.

Mandelbaum, Michael. *The Case for Goliath: How America Acts as the World's Government in the Twenty-First Century.* NY: Public affairs, 2006.

Mann, Michael. *Incoherent Empire.* New York: Verso, 2003.

Mathisen, T. *Methodology in the Study of International Relations.* New York: Macmillan, 1959.

Mathoma, Pandelami T. *Ripeness and Conflict Resolution Through Direct Negotiations.* Pittsburgh, Pa: University of Pittsburgh, GSPIA, 1998.

Matray, James I. *Japan's Emergence as a Global Power.* Westport, Conn.: Greenwood Press, 2001.

Mcintosh, Malcom. *Japan Re-armed.* New York: St Martin's, 1986.

Mearsheimer, John J. *The Tragedy of Great Power Politics.* New York: Norton, 2001.

Montesquieu, Charles Louis de Secondat. *The Spirit of Laws.* Trans. Nugent, Book I. New York: Hafner Publishing Co., 1949.

Morgenthau, Hans. J. *Politics Among Nations.* 5th ed. New York: Alfred A. Knopf, 1973.

Morse, Hosea B. *The International Relations of the Chinese Empire.* Vol 2. New York: Longmans, Green & Company, 1910-1918.

Munakata, Takayuki. *The True Nature and Solution of the Taiwan Problem.* Taipei, Taiwan: International Interchange Foundation, 1998.

Muraoka, Kunio. *Japanese Security and the United States.* London: International Institute for strategic Studies, 1973.

Murphy, John. *The United States and the Rule of Law in International Affairs.* New York: Cambridge University Press, 2004.

Murphy, Ann Marie. *U.S-Japan Policy Dialogue on China: Economic Issues.* New York, NY: Asia Society, 1992.

Murray, Douglas J, and Paul, R Viotti. *The Defense Policies of Nations: A Comparative Study.* 3rd ed. Baltimore: Johns Hopkins University Press, 1994.

Nachmias, David. *Research Methods in the Social Sciences.* 5th ed. New York: St. Martin's Press, 1996.

Nelson, Harvey W. *Power and Insecurity: Beijing, Moscow, and Washington, 1949-1988.* Boudoir: Lyne Rienner Publishers, 1989.

Nye, Joseph Jr. *Bound to Lead: The Changing Nature of American Power*. New York: Basic Books 25 Inc, 1990.

O'Brien, Patrick K., and Armand Clesse, eds. *Two Hegemonies: Britain 1846-1914 and the United States 1941-2001*. Aldershot, U.K.: Asghate, 2002.

Odom, W. *The Emerging Ballistic Missile Threat to The United States*. Washington, D.C: U.S. Proliferation Study Team, 1993.

Olson W.C., and F.A. Sonderman. *The Theory and Practice of International Relations*. 2nd ed. Prentice Hall, 1966.

Organski, A.F.K. *World Politics*. 2nd ed. New York, N.Y.: Alfred Knopf, 1968.

Osius, Ted. *The U.S.-Japan Security Alliance: Why it Matters and How to Strengthen it*. Washington, D.C.: Westport, Conn.: Praeger: Published with the Center For Strategic and International Studies, 2002.

Overholt, William H. *China: The Next Economic Superpower*. London: Weidenfled and Nicolson, 1993.

Oye, Kenneth A. *Eagle in a New World: American Grand Strategy in the Post - Cold War Era*. New York: Harper Collins Publishers, 1992.

Page, Edward A, and Michael Redclift, ed. *Human security and the Environment: International Comparisons*. Cheltenham, UK; Northampton, MA: Edward Elgar, c 2002.

Paul, T.V. *Power Versus Prudence: Why Nations Forgo Nuclear Weapons*. Montreal: McGill-Queen's University Press, 2000.

Perry, Charles M. *The U.S.-Japan Alliance: Preparing for the Korean Reconciliation and Beyond*. Dulles, Va.: Brassey's, 2003.

Perstowitz Jr, Clyde V. *Trading Places: How We allowed Japan to Take the Lead*. New York: Basic Books, 1988.

Perstowitz Jr, Clyde V. *Rogue Nation: American Unilateralism and the Failure of Good Intentions*. New York: Basic Books, 2003.

Prescott, J.R.V. *Maritime Jurisdiction in Southeast Asia: A Commentary and Map*. Honolulu: East-West Center, 1981.

Prueher, Joseph. *Shaping Our Future in the Asia-Pacific*. Washington, D.C.: United States Joint Chiefs of Staff, 1998.

Purcell, Victor. *The Boxer Uprising Study: a Background Study*. Cambridge: Cambridge University Press, 1963.

Rai, Kul B. *America in the 21st Century: Challenges and Opportunities in Foreign Policy*. Upper Saddle River, N.J: Prentice Hall, 1997.

Reason, Peter, and John Rowan. *Human Inquiry: Developments in New Paradigm Research*. Sage, Calif.: Thousand Oaks, 1989.

Reynolds P.A. *An Introduction to International Relations*. 3rd ed. London & New York: Longman, 1994. Reischauer, Edwin O. Japan. Ed. New York: Arno Press, 1974.

Rhaiem, Jalel. *The United States and China: Cooperation or Confrontation?* D.E.A Thesis. Tunisia: Manouba University, 1999 (unpublished).

Roleff, Tamara L, ed. *War: Opposing Viewpoints*. San Diego, Calif.: Greehaven Press, 1999.

Ross, Robert S. *East Asia in Transition: Toward a New Regional Order*. Armonk, N.Y.: M.E. Sharpe, 1995.

Rourke, John T. *Taking Sides Clashing Views on Controversial Issues in World Politics*. 4th ed. Guilford, CT: Dushkin Pub. Group, 1992.

Rousseau, J.J. *A Lasting Peace Through the Federation of Europe and the State of War*. London: Constable & Co., 1977.

Sands, Philippe. *Lawless World: America and the Making and Breaking of Global Rules from FDR's Atlantic Charter to George W. Bush's Illegal War*. USA: Viking Adult, 2005.

Schaller, Michael. *The U.S. and China in the Twentieth Century*. 2nd ed. NY: Oxford University Press, 1990.

Schelling, T. C. *The Struggle of Conflict*. Harvard: Harvard University Press, 1960.

Schonberger, Howard B. *Aftermath of war: Americans and the Remaking of Japan, 1945-1952*. Kent, Ohio: Kent State University Press, c1989.

Schutt, Russell K. *Investigating the Social World, the Process and Practice of Research*. 3rd ed. Boston: University of Massachusetts, 2001.

Shaw, Chonghal Petey. *The Role of The United States in Chinese Civil Conflicts, 1944-1949*. Salt Lake City, Utah: C. Schlacks, Jr., 1991.

Shuman, Frederick L. *International Politics*. 5th ed. New York: McGraw-Hill Book Co., 1953.

Snyder, Scott. *"Trialogue": U.S.-Japan-China Relations and Asian Pacific Stability*. Washington, DC: United States Institute of Peace, 1998.

Soderberg, Nancy. *The Superpower Myth: The Use and Misuse of American Might*. Hoboken, NJ: John Wiley& Sons, 2005.

Spanier, John. *American Foreign Policy Since World War II*. 11th ed. New Delhi: Tata McGraw-Hill Publishing Company Limited, 1988.

Spence, Jonathan D. *The Search for Modern China*. New York: W. W. Norton & Company, 1990.

Steinbruner, John D. *Principles of Global Security*. Washington, D.C.: Brookings Institution Press, c2000.

Sugihara, Seishiro. *Reconstructing The U.S.-Japan Alliance: Toward A More Equal Partnership*. Washington, D.C.: Center for Strategic and International Studies, c1997.

Suskind, Ron. *The Price of Loyalty*. New York: Simon & Schuster, 2004.

Taft, Robert A. *A Foreign Policy for Americans*. New York: Doubleday & Co., 1951.

Talentino, Andrea Kathryn. *Military Intervention After the Cold War: The Evolution of Theory and Practice*. Ohio: Ohio University Press & Swallow Press, 2005.

Thompson, Kenneth W. *China, Taiwan, Japan, the United States, and the World*. University Press of America, 1997.

Thucydides. *History of the Peloponnesian War*. Trans B. Jowett. 2nd ed. London: Oxford University Press, 1900.

Todd, Emmanuel. *After the Empire: The Breakdown of the American Order.* Columbia: University Press, 2003.

Tucker, Nancy B. *Taiwan, Hong Kong, and the United States, 1945-1992.* New York: Twayne Publishers, 1994.

Tucker, Nancy B. *Dangerous Strait: The U.S.-Taiwan-China Crisis.* Washington, D.C., Columbia University Press, 2005.

Tse-Tung, Mao. *Selected Works of Vol. I.* Beijing: Foreign Languages Press, 1965.

Vagts, Alfred. *Defense and Diplomacy.* New York: King's Crown Press, 1956.

Viotti, P.R. and M.V. Kauppi. *International Relations Theory: Realism, Pluralism, Globalism.* 2nd ed. New York: Macmillan, 1993.

Vogel, Ezra, et al., eds. *The Golden Age of the U.S.-China-Japan Triangle 1972-1989.* Harvard, MA.: President and Fellows of Harvard College, 2002.

Walt, Stephen M. *Taming American Power: The Global Response to U.S. Primacy.* New York: W.W. Norton & Company Inc., 2005.

Waltz, Kenneth. N. *Man, the State, and War.* New York: Columbia University Press, 1959.

Wan, Ming. *A Comparison of Sino-Japanese and Sino-American High-Level Official Contacts Since 1972.* Cambridge, MA: Program on U.S.-Japan Relations, Harvard University, 1994.

Wang, Jianwei. *The Chinese Perspective of America's Alliances with Japan and Korea.* Stanford, CA: The Asia-Pacific Research Center, 1998.

Wang, Qingxin Ken. *Hegemonic Cooperation and Conflict: Postwar Japan's China Policy and the United States.* Westport, Conn.: Praeger, 2000.

Weber, M. *The Protestant Ethic and the Spirit of Capitalism.* New York: n.p., 1958.

Webster, C.K. *The Foreign Policy of Castlereagh 1815-1822.* New York: Bell, 1925.

Wedeman, Andrew Hall. *U.S.-Japan Policy Dialogue on China: Security Issues.* New York, NY: Asia Society, 1993.

Weltman, John J. *World Politics and the Evolution of War.* Baltimore: The John Hopkins University Press, 1995.

Whitrow, C. J. *Time in History: Views of Time from Prehistory to the Present Day.* Oxford: n.p., 1988.

Williams, Phil, Jay M. Shafritz, and Roland S. Calinger. *The Dictionary of 20th-Century Politics.* New York: Henry Holt & Company, 1993.

Williams, Phil, Donald Goldstein, and Jay M. Shafritz. *Classic Readings of International Relations.* Belmont, California: Wadsworth Publishing Company, 1994.

Wiltse, Jeffrey S. *"China Factor" in Japanese Military Modernization for the 21st Century.* n.p.: Armstrong Press, 1997.

Winkler, Allan M. *The Recent Past: Readings on America Since World War II.* New York: Harper & Row Publishers, 1989.

Wittkopf, Eugene R. *The Future of American Foreign Policy.* 3rd ed. New York: St Martin's Press, 1999.

Yabunaka, Mitozi. *Economic Negotiations with the U.S.: Real picture of Frictions.* Tokyo: The Simul Press, 1991.

Yin, R.K. *Case Study Research: Design and Methods.* 2nd ed. Ca.: Sage: Thousand Oaks, 1994.

Young, Kenneth Todd. *Diplomacy and Power in Washington-Peking Dealings, 1953-1967.* Chicago: University of Chicago, Center for Policy Study, 1967.

Zeng, *Ka, et al.* "*Trade Threats, Trade Wars: Bargaining, Retaliation, and American Coercive Diplomacy.*" Michigan: University of Michigan Press, 2004.

Zhang, Ming, and Ronald N. Montaperto. *A Triad of Another Kind: the United States, China and Japan.* Basingstoke: Macmillan, 1999.

Zhao, Suisheng. *Power Competition in East Asia: From the Old Chinese World Order to Post-Cold War Regional Multipolarity.* New York: St. Martin's Press, 1997.

Articles

Acharya, Amitav. "A concert of Asia?" *Survival* 1999: 84-101, vol. 41, no. 3.

Acharya, Amitav. "A New Regional Order in South-East Asia: ASEAN in the post-Cold War Era". *ADELPHI PAPER* 269: 1993.

Arundhati, Roy. "The Loneliness of Chomsky." *The Hindu* 24 August 2003.

Bullock, Todd. "Asia Most likely to shape U.S. Defense Policy." *The Washington File.* The Bureau of International Information Programs, September 2005.

Baker, James A. "America in Asia: Emerging Architecture for a Pacific Community." *Foreign Affairs* 70, No.5. 1991/1992: 5.

Bosworth, Stephen. "The United States and Asia." *Foreign Affairs* September /October 2005, Vol 71, N° 1.

Burton, J.W. "The Means to Agreement: Power or Values?" *Perspectives on negotiation.* Report of visit of J.W. Burton and M. Light to Moscow, 4-10 Feb. 1980, National Library of Australia.

Burton, Sandra, et al. "The Next China." *Time,* March 1997: 52.

Calder, Kent E. "China and Japan's Simmering Rivalry." *Foreign Affairs March/ April,* 2006: 129-139. Vol. 85, no.2.

Campbell, Kurt M. and Derek J. Mitchell, "Crisis in the Taiwan Strait." *Foreign Affairs* July/August 2001, Vol. 80, N°4.

Catley, Bob. "The Bush Administration and Changing Geopolitics in the Asia-Pacific Region." *Contemporary Southeast Asia.* April 2001, Vol. 23, Issue. No.1.

Cooper, Richard N. "The United States and the World Economy: Foreign Economic Policy for the Next Decade." *Foreign Affairs* September/October 2005, Vol.84, Number 5.

Crampton, Thomas. "Neither China nor U.S. is Telling Everything About Spy Plane." *International Herald Tribune* 19 Apr. 2001:8.

Crock, Stan, et al. "Yankee, Don't Go Home: Asia Looks to the U.S. for Security Again." *Business Week* 1 April 1996: 46, n° 3469.

Christensen, Thomas J. "China, the U.S.-Japan Alliance, and the Security Dilemma in East Asia." *International Security* 23 Spring 1999 no.4: 52.

Chong, Pin Lin. "Chinese Military Modernization: Perceptions, Progress, and Prospects." *Security Studies* 13. 1994: 718-53.

Cumings, Bruce. "Is America an Imperial Power?" *Current History* November 2003: 355-360.

Dibb, Paul. "Towards a New Balance of Power in Asia." *ADELPHI PAPER* 295: 26-29.

Dillon, Dana R., Balbina Y. Hwang, and John J. Tkacik, Jr. "ASEAN Regional Forum: Promoting U.S. Interests." *The Heritage Foundation Backgrounder* 10 June 2003 No.1659.

Durkee, F. "Oily Claims." *Far Eastern Economic Review* 30 Mar. 1955: 4.

Eland, Ivan. "The China-Taiwan military Balance: Implications for the United States." Cato's *Foreign Policy Briefing* 5 February 2003: 3, no.74.

Eckholm, Erik, "China Complains About U.S. Surveillance Ship." *The New York Times* 27 September 2002: 13.

Faoila, Anthony. "Japan-Taiwan Ties Blossom as Regional Rivalry Grows." *Washington Post,* 24 March 2006: A12.

Ferguson, Niall. "Hegemony or Empire?" *Foreign Affairs* September/October 2003: 155 Vol 82, n 5.

Freidberg, Aaron. "The Struggle for Mastery in Asia." *Commentary,* 2000: 17-26.

Fukuyama, Francis. "Re-Envisioning Asia." *Foreign Affairs* January/February 2005: 76 Vol.84, no. 1.

Funabashi, Yoichi. "Tokyo's Depression Diplomacy." *Foreign Affairs* November /December 1998: 26-36, Vol.77, no.6.

Garrette and Glaser. "Chinese Apprehensions about Revitalization of the U.S.-Japan Alliance." *Asian Survey* 1997 vol.37, no.4.

George, A.L. "Case Studies and Theory Development: The Method of Structured, Focused Comparison." *Diplomacy: New Approaches in History, Theory, and Policy.* Ed. Paul G. Lauren. New York: Free Press, 1979.

Gertz, Bill. "China Enacts Law Extending its Control." *The Washington Times* 17 January 2003: 1.

Gerson Joseph. "Architecture of U.S. Asia-Pacific Hegemony." *Peace Review* September 1999: 399, Vol.11.

Geyer, George Anne. *International Relations of the Asia Pacific* Vol. 6, no.1, 2006.

Glancey, Jonathan. "Gas, chemicals, bombs: Britain has used them all before in Iraq." *The Guardian* Saturday 19 April 2003.

Gordon, Michael R. "Pentagon Review Puts Emphasis on Long-Range Arms in Pacific." New York Times 17 May 2001.

Green, Michael. "State of the Field Report: Research on Japanese Security Policy." *Access Asia Review,* September 1998: 13-14.

Guoxing, Ji. "SLOC Security in the Asia Pacific." *Occasional Paper Series,* February 2000.

Hart, J. "Three Approaches to the Measurement of Power in International Relations." *International Organization* 1976: 289-305.

Haydock, Michael D. "America's Other Korean War." *Military History* April 1996: 38-44.

Hiroshi, Nakanishi. "Redefining Comprehensive Security in Japan in Challenges for China-Japan-U.S. Cooperation", Tokyo and New York: Japan Center for International Exchange. 1998: 44-69.

Hoffmann, Stanley. "The Foreign policy the U.S. Needs." *The New York Review of Books* 10 August 2006:60.

Holt, James, W., "Twenty Theses on the Chinese Military." *World Policy Institute* 18 April 2001: 1.

Itoh, Makoto. "Japan in a New World Order." London, Merlin Press: 1992.

Ikenberry, John G. "Illusions of Empire: Defining the New American Order." *Foreign Affairs* March/April 2004 Vol 83, N° 2.

Ikenberry, John G. Book Review. *Foreign Affairs*, November/December 2005, Vol 84, *N°* 6.

Jay, John. *The Federalist Paper* no.7. 33-40.

Jervis, Robert. "Cooperation Under the Security Dilemma." *World Politics* 1978 vol.30, no.2.

Jimmy W. Wheeler and Perry L. Wood. "ASEAN and Southeast Asian Security in the 1990's: Implications for U.S Interests." Indianapolis, Indiana: Hudson Institute, 1989.

Jisi, Wang. "Pragmatic Nationalism: China Seeks a New Role in World Affairs." *The Oxford International Review* Winter 1994: 29.

Jisi, Wang. "China's Search for Stability with America." *Foreign Affairs* September/October 2005: 29, Volume 84, No. 5.

Johnston, Alastair I. "China's New 'Old Thinking': The Concept of Limited Deterrence." *International Security* 20, no. 3, Winter 1995-1996: 5.

Kajimoto, Tessuhi. "Constitution Faces long Road to Amendment." *Japan Times* 3 May 2005: 5.

Kaplan, Robert D. "How We Would Fight China: The Next Cold War." *The Atlantic Monthly* June 2005: 29.

Kaplan, Robert D. "The Next Cold War." *The Atlantic* June 2005: 50.

Kaplan, Robert D. "Supremacy by Stealth." *Atlantic Monthly*, July/August 2003: 67-83.

Kelman, H.C. "The Role of The Individual in International Relations: Some Conceptual and Methodological Considerations." *Journal of International Affairs.* 24. 1970.

Kelman, H.C. "The Interactive Problem-Solving Approach." *Managing Global Chaos.* Eds.CA Crocker and FO Hampson, California:1996.

Khoo, Nicholas and Michael L.R, Smith. "A 'Concert of Asia'?" *Policy Review* no.108, August/September 2001: 4.

Knight, J. and J. Ensminger. "Conflict over Changing Social Norms: Bargaining, Ideology, and Enforcement." *The New Institutionalism in Sociology.* Ed. M.C. Brinton and V. Nee. New York: Russel Sage Foundation, 1998.

Kristof, Nicholas D. "The Problem of Memory." *Foreign Affairs* 66, Vol 77, Nov/ Dec 1998: 37-49.

Kokubun, Ryosei. "Challenges for China-Japan -U.S. Cooperation." Tokyo, New York, Japan Center for International Exchange, Washington, D.C.: The Brookings Institution Press, 1998.

Kurlantzick, Joshua. "Beijing's Safari: China's move into Africa and Its Implications for Aid, Development, and Governance." *Policy Outlook* Carnegie Endowment for International Peace, China Program, November 2006, Washington, DC.

Lampton, David. M., "The Faces of Chinese Power." *Foreign Affairs January /February 2007,* Vol. 86, Number 1.

Layne, Christopher. "Rethinking American Grand Strategy: Hegemony or Balance of Power in the Twenty-First Century." *World Policy Journal* Vol. 15, no. 2, Summer 1998.

Layne, Christopher. "Less Is More: Minimal Realism in East Asia." *National Interest* Spring 1996.

Leifer, Michael. "The Issue is ASEAN." *Far Eastern Economic Review* 30 November 1995.

Lemco, Jonathan and Scott B. MacDonald. "Sino-Japanese Relations: Competition and Cooperation." *Current History* September 2002: 290-293.

Levey, David H., and Stuart S. Brown. "The Overstretch Myth." *Foreign Affairs December* 2005: 7.

Levey, Jack, "Contending Theories of International Conflict: A levels-of-Analysis Approach." *Managing Global Chaos.* Washington, D.C.: United States Institute of Peace Press, 1996.

Lim, Robyn. "Persuading China to Rein in Pyongyang." *The Wall Street Journal Online* 18 February 2004: 315.

Lin, Gang. "Who is the Odd Man Out?" *Asia Program Special Report,* June 2003: 17, no. 113.

Luttwark, Edward N. "From Geo-Politics to Geo-Economics." *The National Interest* 20, Sum. 1990.

Makin, John H. and Donald C., Hellman. "Sharing World Leadership? New Era for America and Japan." eds. Washington, D.C.: American Enterprise Institute, 1989.

Mandelbaum, Michael. "David's Friend Goliath." *Foreign Policy* January/ February 2006: 51-56.

Mclennan, A.D. *The National Interest* Fall 1997, no.49: 52.

Mufson, Steve. "U.S.-Japan Accord Fans China's Fears." *Washington Post* 19 April 1996: 96.

Nye, Joseph. "'The Nye Report' Six Years later. *International Relations of the Asia-Pacific* no.1, 2001: 95-104.

Nye, Joseph. "China's Re-mergence and the Future of the Asia Pacific." *Survival* 39, no.4, Winter 1997.

Phillips, John. "Japan's Military Plan Stresses Cooperation with the U.S." *Armed Forces Journal International* June 1989: 104.

Pomfret, John. "U.S. Now a 'Threat' in China's Eyes." *Washington Post* 15 October 2000: A 01.

Preble, Christopher. "Two normal Countries: Rethinking the U.S.-Japan Strategic Relationship." *Policy Analysis* 18 April 2006: 8-28, no.566.

Przystup, James J. and Saunders, Phillip C. "Visions of Order: Japan and China in U.S. Strategy." No. 220, June 2006, *Strategic Forum*, Institute for National Strategic Studies National Defense University.

Pye Lucian W., Book Review: *Dangerous Strait: The U.S.-Taiwan-China Crisis.* Edited by Nancy Bernkopf Tucker: Columbia University Press, 2005, *Foreign Affairs, September/October 2005*, Volume 84, No.5.

Rosenthal A. M. "The Chinese Missiles." *New York Times* 30 Aug. 1996: sec. A.

Ross, Robert. *International Security* 23, no.4, 1999.

Sasae, Kenichiro. "Rethinking Japan-U.S. Relations." *ADELPHI PAPER* 292. 1994: 8-32.

Schwarz, Benjamin. "Managing China's Rise." *The Atlantic Monthly* June 2005.

Shambaugh, David. "China's Military Views the World." *International Security* Winter 1999/2000: 52-79.

Shultz, George. *U.S. Foreign Policy Agenda* December 2002 Vol. 7, no. 4.

Singer, David. J. "The Level-of-Analysis problem in International Relations." *The International System*. Ed. Knorr, and S. Verba. Princeton: Princeton University Press, 1961.

Singer, David. J. "Multipolar Power Systems and International Stability." *World Politics* April 1964 vol 16.

Snyder, Glenn H., "Mearsheimer's World-Offensive Realism and the Struggle for Security: A Review Essay, *International Security*, The MIT Press, Vol. 27, No. 1 (Summer, 2002), pp. 149-173.

Spaeth, Anthony. "Silent Partners." *Time Magazine* (Asia) 27 February 2005: 13.

Swaine, Michael D. "Trouble in Taiwan." *Foreign Affairs March/April 2004*:264, Vol 83, n° 2.

Thayer, Carlyle A. "ASEAN Ten Plus Three: An Evolving East Asian Community?" Comparative Connections January 2001.

Tyler, Patrick M. "China's Military Regards U.S. as Main Enemy in the Future." *The New York Times* 23 June 1999: A 8-9.

Tyler, Patrick M. *The National Interest*. Fall 1997: 52, no.49.

Tylor, Patrick E. "U.S. Strategy Plan Calls for Ensuring No Rivals Develop." *New York Times* 8 Mar. 1992: 17.

Valencia, Mark J. "China and the South China Sea Disputes." *ADELPHY PAPER* no.298. 1997.

Vogel, Ezra. "It Takes Three for This Tango." *Time International* vol.150, no.51, 1998.

Wade, Robert. "The Coming fight over Capital Flows." *Foreign Policy* 13 Winter 1998-99.

Walker, Martin. "The New American hegemony." *World Policy Journal* Summer 1996: 20.

Wallace, William. "American Hegemony: European Dilemmas." *The Political Quarterly* 2002.

Wang, Qingxin Ken. *The Japan-U.S. Alliance: New Challenges For the 21st Century.* Tokyo; New York: Japan Center for International Exchange; Washington, DC: Distributed worldwide outside Japan by Brookings Institution Press, c2000.

Winterford, David. "Chinese Naval Planning Maritime Interests in the South China Sea: Implications for US and Regional Security Policies." *Journal of American East Asian Relations* Winter 1993: 369-98.

Wohlstetter, A. "The Delicate Balance of Terror." *Foreign Affairs* Vol.37, N.1-4, October 1958- July 1959.

Wright, Bruce A., and Mark O. Hague. "The U.S.-Japan Alliance: Sustaining the Transformation" 1st quarter 2007: 60-64, JFQ / issue 44.

Zartman, I.W. "Negotiating from Asymmetry: The North-South Stalemate." *Negotiation Journal* Vol. 1. January 1985: 121-138.

Zartman, I.W. "Prenegotiation: Phases and Functions." *Getting to the Table: Processes of International Prenegotiation.* Ed. Janice Gross Stein. Baltimore: Johns Hopkins University Press, 1985.

Zartman, I.W. and J. Aurik. "Power Strategies in De-Escalation." *Timing the De-escalation of International Conflicts.* Ed. Louis Kriesberg and Stuart J. Thorson. Syracuse: Syracuse University Press, 1991.

Zweig, David, and Jianbai. "China's Hunt for Energy." *Foreign Affairs,* September/October 2005: 28 Vol. 84, no. 5.

Zeng, ka, et al. "Trade Threats, Trade Wars: Bargaining, Retaliation, and American Coercive Diplomacy." Reviewed by Richard N. Cooper. *Foreign Affairs* September/October 2004, Vol 83, N 5.

Conferences & Lectures

Alves, Dora. "New Perspectives for U.S.-Asia Pacific Security Strategy: The 1991 Pacific Symposium." Pacific Symposium: National Defense University Press, Supt. of Docs., U.S.G.P.O, Washington, D.C.1992.

Bottelier, Pieter P. "China's Economic Rise- What Does it Mean for the U.S. and for the World." School of Advanced International Studies: John Hopkins University. 2005.

China Institute of Contemporary Relations: Sigur Center for Asian Studies. "Towards the 21st Century the roles of the United States, China, and Japan in the Asia-Pacific". George Washington University, Washington, D.C. 1997.

Cossa, Ralph. "U.S. Approaches to Multilateral Security and Economic Institutions in Asia." Pacific Forum CSIS: unpublished. 2000.

Clark, Dick. "The Challenge of Indochina: An Examination of the U.S. Role." Aspen Institute, Queenstown, MD. 30 Apr - 2 May 1993.

Iokibe, Makota. "Japan-the US. - China: Toward a True Partnership." Hotel Le Consul, Tunis, Tunisia. 27 March 2007.

Jianmin, Wu. "China and the Future of the World." University of Chicago, 28-29 April 2006.

Gerson, Joseph. "Fresh Look: Re-examining the role and impact of U.S. bases in Asia-Pacific": "U.S. Asia-Pacific Hegemony and Possibilities of Popular Solidarity." Seoul, South Korea. 26-27 June 1999.

Hough, Joseph C., Jr. "President's Newsletter", Union Theological Seminary, March 2003, New York.

Kim, Samuel S. "China's Quest for Security in the Post-Cold War World." The U.S. Army War College Seventh Annual Strategy Conference, the Strategic Studies Institute. 29 July. 1996.

Meconis, Charle. "U.S. Defense and Security Policy In Asia." Briefing Book for Defense Writers Seminar on East Asian Security. Washington, Honolulu, Seoul. 27 Sept –11 Oct. 1998.

Mukai, Gary and Gregory Francis. "Choices in International Conflict with a Focus on Security Issues in Asia." Asia-Pacific Project, SPICE. Institute for International Studies. Stanford University. Stanford, CA. 1998.

Odahara, Takeshi. "National Security and Public Opinion: the Japan-U.S.-China Triangle After 1989." Harvard University, the Program on U.S-Japan Relations: the Center for International Affairs and the Reischauer Institute of Japanese Studies, Cambridge, MA. 1998.

Okazaki, Hisahiko. "China, Japan and the United States and Their Roles and Involvement in Southeast Asia."Pacific Forum, CSIS, Honolulu, HI. 1993.

Olmo, Elizabeth D. "China's Nuclear Agenda and the Implications for United States Foreign Policy." Naval Postgraduate School, Monterey, CA. September 1993.

Owada, Hisashi. "Global Unilateralism." The Lecture at Beijing University, China. 16 May, 2000.

Pan, Esterth. "China, Africa, and Oil." Forum on China-Africa Cooperation-Beijing Action Plan: 2007-2009, Council on Foreign Relations, January 2007.

Power and Prosperity: Linkages Between Security and Economics in U.S.-Japanese Relations Since 1960." Research Fellows Conference, East-West Center, 12-14 Aug. 1998

Przystup, James J. "China and the U.S.-Japan Alliance." Institute of National Strategic Studies, National Defense University, June 2000.

Ralph, Cossa. "The Japan-U.S. Alliance and Security Regimes in East Asia." A Workshop co-sponsored by the Institute for International Policy Studies (IIPS) in Tokyo and the Center for Naval Analyses (CNA) in Alexandria, Virginia, Japan, July 26-29, 1994.

Ralph, Cossa. "Korea: the Achilles' Heel of the U.S. Japan Alliance." Stanford University, Asia/Pacific Research Center. May 1997.

Reynolds, Gary K. "Japan's Military Build-up: Goals and Accomplishments." Congressional Research Service Report for Congress: Library of Congress, Washington, D.C. 27 Jan. 1989.

Rosenberg, David. "The Rise of China in Asia: Security Implications." Ed. Carolyn W. Pumphrey. Strategic Studies Institute, U.S. Army War College. January 2002.

Ross, Robert R. "Managing a Changing Relationship China's Japan Policy in the 1990s", Carlisle Barracks, PA: Strategic Studies Institute, U.S. Army War College, 1998.

Scalapino, Robert A. "The Changing Order in Northeast Asia and the Prospects for U.S.-Japan-China-Korea Relations." La Jolla, CA: Institute on Global Conflict and Cooperation, University of California, San Diego. 1998.

Kim, Samuel, "On China's Concept of Security." Strategic Studies Institute (SSI), 29 July 1996

"The Chinese Perspective of America's Alliances with Japan and Korea." Asia/Pacific Research Center: Stanford University, May 1998.

Tuazon, Bobby. "Current U.S. Hegemony in Asia-Pacific." Conference on "War and Globalisation", School of Economics, University of the Philippines, Quezon City: Philippines. 1 Mar. 2003.

Wilborn, Thomas L. "International Politicism in Northeast Asia: The China-Japan-United States Strategic Triangle." Strategic Studies Institute, U.S. Army War College, Carlisle Barracks, Pa. 1996.

Papers and News Sources

Agence France Presse. "China Accuses U.S. of Seeking World Domination." 1 Feb. 2001.

Agence France Presse. "Japanese FM Again Calls Taiwan a 'Country.'" 9 Mar. 2006.

ABC News Channel. Bush's interview 13 April 2001.

Asahi Evening News. "China, Russia Blast U.S. Shield Plans." 19 July. 2000.

Asia Survey. Nov.1998, Vol.38, no.11.

Business Week May 28, 2001: 126, Issue no. 3734.

The China Quarterly No. 132, December 1992: 999-1028.

Daily Yomiuri 18 Sep. 2002: 8. www.Yomiuri.co.jp /index-e, htm.

The Economist, October 7, 1995, Vol.337, Issue 7935: 35.

International Security 23, no.4, 1999, 81-117.

Japan Times Weekly International Edition, March 30-April 5, 1998, 3.

Korean Central News Agency. "DPRK's Military Warns of 'Annihilating Blow' to U.S.", December 2, 1998.

Korean Central News Agency. "Japan, U.S. Flayed for Tampering with Situation of Korean Peninsula." 26 Sept. 2000.

Korean Central News Agency. "Operation Plan 5027" 14 Dec.1998.

Korean Central News Agency. "'Operation Plan 5027' Carried into Practice." 20 Dec. 1998.

Mainichi Daily News June 1998: 14.

Presidents and Prime Ministers. May-June 1997, Vo.6, No.3: 6.

World Tibet Network News. "China May Join Hands with Russia against U.S. 'hegemony.'" Beijing, China. Tuesday 30Mar. 1999.

Interviews

- Personal interview with **Interviewee 1**. 28 April 2006.

- Personal interview with **Interviewee 2**. 15 May 2006.

- "China and the Future of the World", April 28-29, 2006, Chicago Society, University of Chicago. Among the guest speakers were His Excellency Wang Guangya, Permanent representative of the People's republic of China to the United Nations; Peter W. Rodman, U.S. Assistant secretary of Defense for International Security Affairs, Christopher R. Hill, U.S. Assistant Secretary of State for East Asian and Pacific Affairs; Ambassador Wu Jianmin, Former Chinese Ambassador to France, the United Nations in Geneva, and current President of China Foreign affairs University; **Interviewee 1**, a prominent political science professor, a founder of a new school of thought in political science and currently co-director of a program on international security policy at a major university in Chicago.

- Rehaiem H., Jalel. Question to Secretary Hill: "China and the Future of the World." The University of Chicago April 28–29, 2006. Opening Keynote by Ambassador Christopher R. Hill, United States Assistant Secretary of State for East Asian and Pacific Affairs.

- Rehaiem H., Jalel. Question to Secretary Peter W. Rodman, U.S. Assistant secretary of Defense for International Security Affairs, "China and the Future of the World." The University of Chicago April 28–29, 2006.

Index